David Played a Harp

an autobiography
by
Ralph W. Johnson

Published in the United States of America
by Blackwell Ink, Inc. (Publishers)

ISBN 0-9702713-0-1
Library of Congress Catalog Card Number: 00-106020

Printed by Jostens Graphics
Charlotte, NC

Jacket design by Anita K Blackwell

Inquiries should be addressed to:
Blackwell Ink, Inc.
PO Box 434, 28036
Davidson, North Carolina

Publisher's Acknowledgements

Our thanks to the author, who first shared this work with us over two decades ago, for his ability to put into words emotions, at times so painful and at times so joyous, for his courage, at age 96, to finally decide to release it for publication: and for his insistence throughout the editing process on telling his story his way. It is here now in his words that we see a man's efforts to live an independent life which challenged time-worn roles for blacks and whites.

Appreciation is due Deborah and Bob Cumming, Mary Fetter Stough and Mary Boyer for their help in preparation of the manuscript for printing and to Anita and Greg Blackwell whose graphic art skills helped make this volume possible.

And thanks to the many in Davidson (especially to Irene Blackwell and Erving Johnson who shared author's and publisher's agonies up close) who supported us throughout and thrilled with us at the thought of having this remarkable man and raconteur give us his life's story and with it much about the life of our town during the 20th century.

--Taylor Blackwell

Introduction

Davidson 1900's - this story begins.
Davidson 1973 - it is written as _Horn of Trouble._
Davidson 2000 - year of publication.

The author still holds his views and thoughts of the times
as written but chose the present title for publication. He says
simply, "It's a different world. So much has changed."

--Taylor Blackwell

U. S. Secretary of State Dean Rusk (Davidson College Class of 1931) was one of the thousands of students who patronized Ralph Johnson's barber shop.

Johnson's barber shop in early 20th century Davidson.

CHAPTER ONE

Early Memories

It seems strange now that I have no memory at all of my father's dying, nor of his funeral or burial. And the memories I have of him when he lived are mostly like trying to put together last night's elusive dream.

There is only the fleeting awareness of short episodes of his presence, without a definite image of his physical appearance. There was the bright sunlit day when he let me stand with him and watch a work crew building the new sand clay road past our house. The time he scolded me for throwing pebbles at old man Fess Connor. He didn't speak harshly to me, and it wasn't the words he said that hurt. It was the fact that I had displeased him that made me sad.

Then the time in the buggy when we drove into Grandma Alice's yard. Nothing more. There was just the coming into the yard and knowing that the house before us was where she lived. Grandma Alice was my father's mother. Once we went to Mr. Alex Pickens' house, and Mrs. Pickens gave me a baby duck.

Some time later, after a big rain, it was gone. I was told that it had gotten in the branch in Mr. Holler's cow pasture, a short distance in back of our house, and happily swam away.

One afternoon Father let me go with him to this same pasture to get our cow. On the way back, he was leading Daisy by her chain, and just as he made a wide stride to step over a drainage ditch that crossed the path she suddenly jerked her head to the side. The violent snatch on the chain in Father's hand caused his foot to fall short of the other side of the ditch. He almost fell to the ground. He limped all the way home.

It was some time after this that he went to the hospital. Then he was back home in bed, and they were doing things for him. They put cloths soaked in some kind of medicine that smelled bad on his leg. He must have suffered great pain because he groaned a lot. And he prayed.

One day when he was praying, he asked God what he had done to cause him to suffer so. I wondered why God was doing this to my father. Dr. Wooten came often to see him. I was afraid of the doctor and sometimes hid in the chicken house until he left.

Then all of a sudden, there was more than the usual coming and going of people to our house. There was much whispering and secrecy about what they were discussing, as if it were not for my ears. I sensed that something of great importance was causing the agitation among my elders and tried to understand what it was. Later, I learned that my father's doctor had been shot and killed that day. He had been caught in bed with the wife of one of his friends, and the woman's husband had surprised them and killed him.

After Dr. Wooten's death, Dr. Justice was my father's doctor. It was not until some years later when I knew Dr. Justice personally that I learned of his great professional accomplishments. He was a dentist, a physician and a lawyer, and practiced all three professions from his office over the bank.

Father's suffering became more intense as the days lengthened into months. They said his leg was withering away. Then
it was very quiet in his room, and nobody went there anymore.

His death, funeral and burial must have been so painful to
me that my childish mind blotted them out of consciousness as
completely as if these events had not happened. I have not the
slightest recollection of anything or any circumstance
pertaining to them. There was just the dreadful feeling that he
had suddenly gone away and left us, as if he had vanished and
left a great aching, empty place. Mama said he had gone to
heaven. This wasn't clear to me, and I thought from time to
time that he must surely come back.

In the years to come, this feeling of desolation and abandon -
ment and helplessness would be repeated many times in my
life. It seems as if this episode in my childhood was the
opening chapter in a book of sorrows, of much striving and
disappointment. I was not quite eight years old at the time, but
already an event had occurred that set the stage for my future.

My father was thirty-three years old when he died on the
18th of August, 1912. He was a light-skinned Negro man, a
barber by trade, who operated his shop for white patrons.

At the time of his death, I had already begun the education
he was going to give me, having started to school in the new
Masonic Hall when I was six. The Hall was built on the back
lot of the Negro Methodist church, where my parents were
members. The pastor of the church was the teacher. There was
no public school for Negroes.

I have no memory whatever of anything that I learned during
the time I went to this school, but a circumstance of the
building etched itself into my mind. It was a two-story wooden
structure, unpainted and with a gabled roof covered with sheet
metal. It still stands in back of the now abandoned Methodist
church. The ground floor was a fairly large room, about twenty
by thirty-five feet.

This is where Reverend Johnson kept school. It was also

where the church had socials and "entertainments" on Saturday
nights. Then, once a month the Christian Aid Society had its
meeting there. The furnishings were sparse: homemade
benches without backs, a blackboard and a chair and table for
the teacher. None of these things made much of an impression
on me, and, as I said, I have no memory of anything that I
learned there.

The upper floor was kept locked and used exclusively for
the mysterious rites of the Masons. A few days after I started to
school, some of my schoolmates told me of the things that went
on in the upstairs room. They said that a wild goat was kept
there and that the men who joined the Masons had to ride this
fierce, wild animal, and that it pitched and bucked and threw
them off, but they were put back on it and made to ride the goat
until they could stand it no longer. Then they were put into a
black coffin, the kind you bury dead people in, and they blew
out the lamp and left them there in the dark by themselves. And
the men screamed and hollered all night. They said the coffin
was upstairs "right now," in a dark closet where they kept it all
the time. It was the real thing too, just like the ones they put
dead people in when they buried them. They said the wild goat
was up there, too, but it slept all day and couldn't be heard until
night. I listened from time to time during the day, to see if I
could hear a noise from overhead.

Most of the time at recess we played in the yard between the
back of the church and the front of the school room. It was
some little time before I knew of this other thing that was a
fearful part of our school surroundings.

The school building was on the back of the lot which sloped
off sharply in the direction of a small branch that trickled in
back of it. As a result, the back of the building was high off the
ground, and its underside was a large empty space with an
opening on one side.

One day when some of us were playing nearby, I discovered
that a big, black, strange-looking vehicle occupied this space

under the schoolroom. Schoolmates told me what this thing was. They said it was a hearse and that it belonged to the Christian Aid Society. They said that they put dead people in it and hitched two horses to it and carried the dead people to somewhere and covered them up in the ground.

It was a great big black thing with the driver's seat mounted over the enclosed box-like part where they put the dead people. At one side of the driver's seat was a large, bulb-like glass affair that looked like a light. It had a long tongue made of wood painted black, and singletrees were provided for the two horses that pulled it to the graveyard.

These awesome circumstances of our surroundings helped explain the good order in the schoolroom.

During this first year of school I learned from the others as we went back and forth to the privy at the back of the building that the very worst, most awful thing that could happen to a fellow, even worse than joining the Masons, was to have his "ninny" cut off. I had never thought of any such thing as a possibility, but, now that they mentioned it, the prospect became an awe-inspiring dread. Visions of this occupied my thoughts sometimes at night when I was lying in bed in the dark.

So, with this frightful thing firmly fixed in my mind, the following spring after school was out, I was told that Mama and I were going to Charlotte to spend the night with Aunt Lou, Grandma Alice's sister, and that the next day we would go to see a nice doctor named Dr. Williams. There was also talk among my elders about circum... something or other which, made no sense to me.

The day appointed arrived, and Mama took me on the train to Charlotte. This was a delightful experience. There were red plush seats, and smoke from the engine whirled in the open windows of the Negro passenger car up front next to the baggage car, and the whistle blew every so often.

At the station in Charlotte, a black man carrying a buggy

whip asked Mama something and she said, "Yes." Pretty soon,
a hack drove up and the man got down and helped Mama and
me to get in. The hack was a kind of surrey and had fringe
hanging down all around at the top. It was pulled by a big gray
horse that went clop, clop, clop, as he trotted along the street to
Aunt Lou's house out in Biddleville.

She was expecting us, and made much over me and hugged
and kissed me. Later on we heard a bell ringing. Aunt Lou said
it was the ice cream man and took me out to the street to his
push cart with a top on it and bought me a penny cone, letting
me select the flavor. I should have been warned by all this
carrying on over me.

The next morning Mr. Sonnyboy came with his surrey and
drove Mama and me and Aunt Lou to a house where we got out
and went in. We were met by a heavy-set black man in a white
coat. Aunt Lou called him Dr. Williams and said this was the
nice man I had come to see. He spoke some words to them, and
said he was ready. Then Mama and Aunt Lou took off my pants
and drawers and sat me on the edge of the little white table
with a sheet on it. They said the doctor wanted to look at me.

I had begun to be a little nervous about this strange place
with its white tables and funny-looking cabinets with glass
doors and shiny things inside them. And when the doctor came
over to where I was sitting naked on the edge of the table, took
my ninny in his hand and started looking at it, I suddenly
realized what he was about. He was going to cut my ninny off.
That's what those knives and big scissors were doing on that
other little table.

The thought took me by complete surprise, and what I did
took Mama and Aunt Lou and the doctor by surprise! With one
sudden awful surge of energy, I let out a scream and came
down off the table and headed for the door. They caught me at
the door before I could get it open, but the battle was joined. I
was fighting for my ninny, and I wasn't going to let that big
black doctor cut it off.

Mama and Aunt Lou caught my screaming, kicking, naked figure up in their arms and tried to hold me and talk to me. But I would have none of that. Hadn't they brought me there for that man to do that awful, awful thing to me? The pandemonium became so great and my struggles so violent that they promised they wouldn't let the doctor do anything to me.

This did no good, and they let me out the door, where I escaped to the surrey in the street. They put my drawers and my shirt and pants on in the surrey on the way back to Aunt Lou's house, and they didn't ever mention that circum... whatever it was to me anymore.

After a year or two of going to school in the Masonic Hall, we went to a small new school house. I am not certain that this was the Rosenwald school building or whether that came later but it was small and housed all grades in one room. Miss Zetta Sherrill, a full-bosomed, chocolate-colored lady presided here. Miss Zetta was the essence of kindness, and we all loved her. Too, a Mrs. Reid began to come to our school two or three times a week. She was a buxom white lady with a tender smile, and she led us in singing "Brighten the Corner Where You Are" at least twice every time she came. She also brought a little basket of homemade cookies and passed these out to us. Stories of Jesus and his suffering for our sins were told between the singing and the cookies. I was properly impressed by this and loved Mrs. Reid, too.

My religious training had, however, started sometime prior to her coming to the school. I remember well the Sunday when Mama led her very reluctant son down the aisle of the church all the way up to the Amen Corner where Miss Duscah Harris had her catechism class for small children. I was deposited with some firmness on the hard wooden bench and admonished to remain there. As soon as she let go of me, I got promptly up and followed her back down the aisle to the adult class where she was. This caused some tittering about the room. This time she led me back to the class and turned me over to the personal

charge of Miss Harris, who beamed and smiled and took my
hand in hers and said soothing things to me. I was crying and
her grinning yellow face, with a full mouth of ill-fitting false
teeth under all that hair on her head seemed like the insistent
actions of a witch about to devour me, linen pants and all.

However, with certain inducements, thereafter, I became one
of the regulars in Sunday School, going on to win the small
penknife with green glass handles awarded by Miss Duscah to
the student in her class who recited the Beatitudes without
making a mistake. This early foray into forensic endeavor,
however successful, introduced me to the depths of fear and
chance involved in public speaking. By the time I had gotten
less than half way through the Blessed Are's, my breath was
coming in short gasps, my speech hurried and barely audible to
me, my eyesight blurred, and I was being consumed by a
suffocating heat that was not of this world. When I had
finished, after what seemed like always, I stumbled back to my
seat and resolved never to do anything like that again,
regardless of plaudits or trinkets to be won or lost.

Everyone said I did just fine, and Miss Duscah beamed upon
her star performer as she extended the prize. A shy glance in
Mama's direction, where she sat on the front row, convinced
me that she thought well of her son. But, to me, it was a victory
won at too great a cost.

I was also successful at day school, being considered the
brightest boy in the class. Because of the achievement level of
the class, this was a dubious honor. But it placed me high in the
favor of Miss Zetta. It also put me low in the esteem of the
others in the room. And thereafter I was not shown all the
cordialities common among the other pupils.

I was light in complexion, and my hair was straight, a fact
which made me suspect at the outset among my youthful black
peers. But now, this becoming teacher's favorite pupil called
for concerted action. I was not the only light-skinned student,
however. There were three others, Haden Sloan, Leroy

Torrence and Frank Robinson. But they lived in the area with most of the other students and were accepted up to a point, while I lived a mile and a half away on the north end of town. And I was kin to the Nortons, who were all light-skinned and "thought they were better than anybody else."

Coupled with this, Dr. MacConnel had started me wearing glasses. Also, I was slight in body build, having been what was called a "delicate" child, one of the reasons why my father had a cow. The doctor, when I was very young, said I should have warm milk right from the cow.

(Once, I remember standing drinking sips of milk as it was being extracted from Daisy's teats. I wandered too close to her head and she brought her horns around and hooked me in the side. I learned from that to keep near her rear end but out of reach of her tail, which she flung around with sudden violence and utter carelessness at unpredictable moments. I had already been smacked in the face with that weapon a few times.)

I already had several things going against me at school, plus the fact of a drinking cup which I had to carry to school with my lunch. I lived too far away to walk home at noon. Mama prepared two sandwiches; these were each made of two slices of baker's loaf bread, one with a generous spread of jelly between the slices, and the other made with peanut butter. These delicacies were not the usual fare of my schoolmates. Not only that, but my mother had given me a collapsible metal drink cup so I wouldn't have to drink out of the community dipper in the water bucket that sat on the table in the corner. With all these differentiations setting me apart, I was rapidly building a need for ways to protect myself from bodily harm.

The loaf bread was called "light bread." The jelly and peanut butter sandwiches were classified as fit only for weaklings such as me. Wearing glasses got me called "four-eyed frog." And the way I was getting along with the teacher defied verbalizing. That was expressed by grimacing, licking out tongues, and patting their behinds aimed at me.

My arrival at school on a frosty morning dressed in a Mackinaw coat, wearing glasses, a cap on my head, rib stockings up to my knee pants, carrying a lunch box containing sandwiches made with "light bread" with my own private drinking cup inside, was the signal for the beginning of hostilities for the day.

By first recess time in the mornings things had generally progressed to the point that I knew whether or not that would be a fighting day. And instead of looking forward to the temporary break in school room activities, I regarded it with foreboding, knowing that the time of first combat was at hand. I really had no stomach for fighting.

At recess time we were all lined up in a row inside the building and marched single file outside onto the school ground where the bedraggled column was halted and, after admonitions by the teacher, dismissed to go about our playful pursuits. These consisted for the most part of cat-in-the-hole, wrestling, hopscotch, and shooting marbles. The older students played baseball, a game beyond the capabilities of the junior set.

On days when I was not immediately engaged in fighting, upon our dismissal from the line, I took part in these forms of play. But on many days there would be a black boy either directly in front of me or directly following me in the line who, upon the teacher's words to disperse, would present himself with chest poked out and fists in position. The melee that followed resulted in the two of us being brought back into the school room and made to stay inside during the remainder of recess.

If this did not occur at the beginning, there was always the strong possibility that at any time during the period I would be set upon. I was growing in wisdom, however, and learning something of the art of cooperation. Necessity dictated the formulation of tactics. Most of the time, it was one of a few of the same boys who attacked me. With others I could and did get along without fighting. One day when one of the boys who picked on me and usually gave me a whipping was having a set-to with a boy friendly to me, I joined in the fray. My friend and I gave him a good licking. After I had done this a few times, word got around in our circle that I was really a true friend who could be counted on in a time of need.

Then, on another day, when I found myself in a stressful situation, I noticed with pleasure that one of my friends whom I had helped in a trying time for him pitched in, and we, together, brought a successful conclusion to our combined efforts. The third party ended up with a skinned elbow and a bleeding nose. He was also crying, a dead giveaway of complete defeat.

Our form of mutual assistance was regarded as "dirty" fighting, but it grew in popularity. The hostiles being taken by surprise and finding themselves with two to whip instead of one luckless victim, began themselves to help each other out. This increased the number in the fight to four, then to six, sometimes more, all with flying fists. What had started as something of a concerted attack on me was now enlarged to a situation at recess time in which the number of combatants would grow until many were involved, including some of the girls who began taking part in the action on behalf of relatives and friends needing help or just for the sheer enjoyment of it.

On real good battle days, the school yard assumed the aspect of a free-lance, hand-to-hand testing ground, with arms and legs flying in all directions, cries of pain, and shouts of encouragement or anger from those not yet involved, or who had had enough.

About this time when fighting in mass had become an accepted form of our recreation, playing shinny was introduced to our schoolyard. This was a timely innovation as shinny lent itself perfectly to the development of fighting skills with instruments other than one's own flesh-and-blood endowments.

This game is played with a device resembling a golf club. I never knew whether it was possible to buy ready-made equipment with which to play or not. Our shinny sticks were obtained by finding and cutting a branch of a suitable size growing from the side of a small tree and changing its direction at a sharp angle a few inches from the trunk, thus forming a clubbed end. The extension of the branch was then cut to a length that would answer the need for a handle. This allowed a player to stand upright and hit a ball on the ground with the thicker, heavier club end.

The obvious advantages of this instrument of the playing field in other areas of activity were not lost on us. As a result, shortly after the introduction of shinny to our school, the incidence of skinned shins and cranial lumps increased alarmingly, or satisfactorily, according to one's interests. It was not uncommon to see a scholar with a white cloth bandage on his black shin and nursing a tender place about his head. These injuries were, for the most part, not connected with playing by the rules of the game.

We had by now gone through Miss Zetta and a Miss Portia Miller as teachers And the present occupant of that position was a Reverend McCorkle, a Methodist who lived in Greensboro and made weekly visits home. For some reason, it was thought that a man was needed in the school. He was a fairly large, dark-skinned person who had a broad back. In secret, and always behind his back, he was known to us as "Fatback." Order and discipline were his special province, dealing them to all without favor to any.

We had two recess periods during a normal day. The first about ten in the mornings was called "first recess"; the second at twelve o'clock was called "dinnertime recess." The behavior on the grounds at first recess was such at times that dinnertime recess was dispensed with for that day. This left us to spend the period in our seats, eating our lunches, getting a drink of water, and being excused. Exchanging seat mates at this time was popular, sometimes with old enemies, with the approval of the teacher.

The advent of shinny ushered in a period of violence not known to us before. The shinny stick was a painful weapon, and that, together with the strong-arm efforts of "Fatback," was making inroads into the pugnacious leanings of his students. We were increasingly finding more peaceful pursuits for our energies.

We did not completely adopt peace, however. On one fine spring day, behavior at first recess had reverted somewhat to the old pattern, and the shinny game had become something of a survival-of-the-fittest contest. "Fatback" canceled dinnertime recess and was keeping a watchful eye for spitball throwing, elbow gouging, and other surreptitious acts.

The sun was shining brightly outside, the windows were up to let in the breezes, and Fred Allison, the oldest boy in school, couldn't contain himself. Fred was a friendly boy who managed to keep his place at the foot of the class by a complete lack of interest in anything pertaining to studying or keeping up with his lessons. He spent most of his time in some act of mischief that tended to distract the others. Today was no exception. Fred was in good form. A spitball would pop behind an ear, causing a squeal of surprise. Pieces of folded paper would rise from a mysterious source and plane across the room.

Finally, without saying anything, "Fatback" arose from his seat behind his little desk before the blackboard and selected two switches from his supply standing in the corner. A great quiet descended upon the room. Then he moved leisurely down the aisle to the front door, which he closed and locked. He was at our backs now, and considerable uneasiness had come upon us as to what his intentions might be. Our curiosity was quickly satisfied for he came at our backs with switches swinging indiscriminately. What had momentarily become a place as still and as quiet as a tomb, all of a sudden became filled with cries of anguish and fear. "Fatback" was reaching across the seats and flaying backs drawn down to the tops of the desks in efforts to escape.

Fred was sitting about midway the room. He was looking with wide-stretched eyes and his large mouth had dropped open as "Fatback" came nearer with fury unabated toward where Fred sat. Fred sat as long as he could, then with a sudden bolt he was at a window and scrambled through to the ground and was gone. He never came back. And the next year "Fatback" didn't come back either. They said he was in bad health.

There was another element of personal relations and school vivid in my memory. On the way to and from school, I had to walk the nearly mile-long length of North Main Street. White people lived along this street on both sides, except for Pa and Ma, Mama's parents, who lived at the north end of the street. This was no problem for my cousin Vecue and me. Most days we walked to school together, as we were known to the residents and not bothered, except at one house. This was the old Dupuy place.

The Dupuy residence at the south side of the cemetery had been an elegant home for a fine old family. It had now fallen into a poor state of repair. Its paint was faded and peeled and cracked until it could hardly be discerned. The window shutters hung askew, with the little pieces broken and dangling. The barn out back was a shambles. This house was now occupied by a poor white family named Hager. The Hagers were mother and father and sons, Hamp and John.

These boys began by appearing at the side of the house and making signs and gestures at us, such as thumbs in noses and waving motions with the fingers. This progressed to name calling.

I think it was here that I was first introduced to the word "nigger" and to the awareness that I was a "nigger." This unpleasantness was at first fairly infrequent, but as time went on it became almost a daily expectation. The mother sometimes stood in the front door watching.

Then came the rock throwing and Vecue and I responded in kind. The mother joined in calling us "niggers" and threatened us. This went on long enough for it to be regarded by us as a fact of life, to be expected when we passed the Hager home. We began to prepare as best we could for these encounters by providing ourselves with rocks and other objects to throw. It was not uncommon for us to approach the Hager home with our shirts bulging at the waist with accumulated artillery.

It was a time of apprehension for us because we had been taught not to throw rocks, because there was danger of getting an eye knocked out or of breaking out windows. Experience had taught us, however, that our elders didn't always know what was the best thing to do in some situations. There were things a fellow had to figure out for himself. Vecue liked to fight, anyway. And, since I was in a situation I couldn't very well avoid, there was nothing to do but lend a hand as best I could.

We agreed one day after a set-to with the Hagers that we were both tired of their picking on us. In our boyish fashion, we decided to bring one mighty assault on our tormentors. Accordingly, we laid our plans. We would carry our shinny sticks to school every day, and we would keep our blouses full of rocks when passing the Hagers. We were going into their yard and get them and we were not going to back up no matter what. The Hagers had never come into the street after us, and we had never gone into their yard. So our decision to go after them was a bold one, especially so, since their mama was there and keeping an eye on us. They were white people, too, and this was an added factor.

Since the attacks on us generally occurred in the afternoon when we were on the way home from school, it was at that time that we maintained our state of readiness. Then on a clear, warm day, just as we were almost past the house, they ran out from the back to the side yard and started throwing at us and calling us names. Mrs. Hager came to the front door to watch her boys have some fun.

Instead of just standing our ground on the street, or

continuing to walk and throw rocks back at the boys, we turned and ran towards them, throwing with all our might with one hand and swinging our shinny sticks in the other. This took them by surprise. As we approached them, they ran back around the house with us in hot pursuit. Their mama got to the back door and let them in just before we got there. They were really frightened and had been hollering and calling to her as they ran around the house. In our wild throwing, one of our rocks went through a window and broke out a pane.

With the Hagers vanquished and shut up in their house, we resumed our way home. We felt good about what we had done, but scared because we had done it. What would they do to us for going in their yard? And that broken window really had us worried. We were afraid they would put Policeman Johnston on us for that.

Policeman Johnston was the man who locked people up in the little brick jail with the iron cage in it that stood by the railroad bank just beyond the depot.   And then they put the people on the chain gang where they were turned down over a barrel and beaten with a blacksnake whip until the blood ran off their backs and their behinds were nothing but a raw piece of bloody meat.

The more we thought about this the more frightened we became. We spent some miserable hours thinking what was going to happen to us.

For the next few days, we saw nothing of the Hagers, and, since nothing had been said to us about the affair, we began to think nothing would come of it. Then one day when we came in from school and had stopped at Pa's, Pa called us out to the barn. He was shucking corn. Pa was always kind to us and when he questioned us about what we had done at the Hagers' we told him what had happened, leaving out that we had planned this bit of getting even. After he heard us through, he said that Policeman Johnston had told him about our running and rocking those boys and breaking out a window in the Hager house.

Pa and Mr. Johnston lived next door to each other, and I felt better when Pa said he would talk to him about it and for us not to bother the Hagers again. We never heard anymore about it, and the Hagers never came out to attack us again either. Afterwards, they became friendly, but we never had much to do with them until after we were all young adults. Then we got along all right together.

At some time before the above incident I had absorbed some interesting information about Policeman Johnston. He was, as the grapevine had it, a heavy drinker, and from time to time fell off the cotton platform where he was also official cotton weigher. From what I had learned this was an interesting spectacle to see, providing a gleeful topic of conversation among many of the townspeople who knew about it.

I was curious to witness one of these historic events and looked closely each day when passing the Southern Railway station going to and from school. Just back of the station was a long, wide, wooden platform where bales of cotton were kept, awaiting shipment. At its highest point it was about five feet above ground level, but just back of the depot where the scales were located it was not quite this high off the ground. This was where Policeman Johnston performed his duties as official cotton weigher for Knox & Brown Mercantile Company, a firm that did a lot of business all over the area and bought cotton from the farmers.

My interest in this matter was heightened one night at Pa's when Vecue and I were in the boys' room, which was on the side next to Mr. Johnston's home. We heard a tapping on the window panel and when we tiptoed to the window and eased the shade back, we were startled to find Mr. Johnston standing on the outside, looking in, real queer about the face. He told us to tell Pa to come to the back door, but not to let Ma know. When Pa came back in he told Ma it was Mr. Johnston drinking again, and that he wanted some whiskey. Pa always kept whiskey in the house and he poured some in a glass and gave it to Mr. Johnston.

It was late in the fall and a few months after this that I was walking by the cotton platform and, being watchful as usual, I saw it happen. Mr. Johnston was moving a bale of cotton about with a big cotton hook, and, when he got to the edge, he just kept on walking and walked into thin air. He looked like a huge, awkward bird, with his long overcoat flying up about him as he fell, his wide-brimmed black hat taking off in another direction.

After that I wanted to see it happen again, but I never did, although I did see him being assisted into Mr. Allen's dog cart one day to be taken home after he had fallen from the platform.

As I grew older I was to learn that his falling off the platform was a topic for amusing conversation about the business district and that he did it fairly often. The ones who saw it happen would go about telling others: "He fell off the platform again today."

And everybody knew who was meant and laughed about it.

CHAPTER TWO

A Boy's Life on North Main

Ours was one of five small houses on the east side of the highway one mile north from the business district of the little town of Davidson in North Carolina. From the north side coming south into town, Reverend Brody's house was first, then ours, and, in order, Fess and Lizzie Connor's, the Hamptons' and last the Mayhews'.

One memorable night in my early youth, the Brodys' barn burned down. The barn was not large but the fire was far along when it was discovered and grew rapidly. It lit up the night. Soon there was a crowd around the Brody home and in our yard. I was a little fellow, and they wouldn't let me go out of doors for fear I would get hurt, but I could see the fire from the window, and our house was filled with light from the flames. People were running all around, some were carrying water from our well and from other wells, and they were throwing it on the fire. But it wasn't doing any good.

There was much shouting of directions as how best to fight the fire, but soon the whole structure was in flames and

burning fiercely with crackling and popping and smoke
billowing upward. Someone said that a man had gone into the
barn to get the horse out. Everybody watched excitedly to see
what would happen next. Could the man get to the horse in
time? Would the man himself get out or be burned to death?

Then they said the man was out of the fire, but the horse
was still inside. The horse would not leave the barn. The man
had been unable to drive it out. A hushed silence came over
the crowd as the people just stood and watched while the horse
burned to death. They said the buggy was saved.

Reverend Brody was the preacher at the Negro Presbyterian
church and had for years taught the only school for Negroes in
a small building just back of that church. Mama had gone to
school to him there before she went to Scotia Seminary at
Concord for a year, which was as long as her parents could
afford to send her.

A tall, brown-skinned man, the Reverend almost always had
a big grin on his face. His lips parted widely when he smiled.
Then you could see most of his front teeth. His eyes had a
certain intensity. He was highly regarded by everyone, and
even some white people called him Reverend Brody, but most
of them just called him Brody. I thought he was an overly
pleasant man.

There was a rise in the ground elevation between our house
and the next one that put the Fess Connor home above ours,
though the distance that separated the two houses was
something like two hundred feet.

Old man Fess and his wife Lizzie were real black people
who had no children. They believed in what was called "root
working." They were afraid that someone would poison them
or bring on severe physical affliction by putting down some
substance or other for them to walk over. There was no cure
for these distressing sicknesses except the removal of the evil

influence and power of the potion. This could be accomplished only by another "root worker" possessed of superior powers of magic.

To guard themselves from the lurking threat of evil being done to them, they were careful to search often about their premises to see that nothing was put there that could possibly be construed as an agent of Satanic powers. The steps leading into their house were constructed in such a manner that they were open at all times to visual inspection, so anything at all put under them could be seen at a casual glance.

Their well from which they got water, just like all the others, was walled with terra cotta pipe about twelve inches in diameter that extended into the ground to the water. This pipe also extended above the ground to a height of about three feet. A wooden frame was built around the protruding terra cotta; a windlass was fitted to the back of the pipe and a pulley directly over it. A rope was secured to and then wound around the windlass, threaded through the pulley and tied to the bail of the well-bucket. A box was then built around the terra cotta pipe and a lid made to cover the well which provided a place for the bucket to sit when it was not in use.

But here the similarity to other wells ended. The Connor well was no such open invitation to the tampering of evil-doers; it demonstrated Mr. Conner's supreme lack of confidence in the good intentions of his fellowmen. The closure over his well had a slot in its edge so that the rope could pass through it and allow the bucket to hang in the well when not in use. The lid also had a padlock on it, and Mr. Connor kept his well locked at all times. This was to guard against having his water poisoned.

A wire fence about four feet high enclosed his house and yard with a gate at the front entrance. A lock on the gate kept it securely fastened. Mr. Connor approached his gate cautiously when he came home from work each afternoon looking about on the ground to see that nothing had been put there. Then he unlocked the gate and inspected carefully as he moved along the short, swept-clean dirt walk that led to the steps.

Small shrubs, herbs and flowers filled the yard. He worked there a lot, and it was said that he grew plants from which he brewed magic to ward away the dangers that threatened him. The Connors had no company, nor did they visit in the neighborhood.

Next in the line of houses was the Mose Hamptons'. The Hamptons were a white family. They were friendly people and Mrs. Hampton and Mama were friends. I played with the Hampton children, and we have remained friends through more than sixty years.

The fifth and last house was occupied by the Homer Mayhews. They were also white. Mr. Mayhew was the Singer sewing machine agent. My mother bought three machines from him over the years. He, like all of us, has long since moved to other areas. Mama bought the third machine from him when she was past eighty years of age, going to another town in order to trade with Mr. Mayhew who was then an old man himself.

This accounts for our neighbors who lived along the highway in the row of five houses that comprised what we called our neighborhood.

Looking directly west from the front of our house at a distance of perhaps three hundred feet was Mr. Mack Brown's place. His house faced east; the fronts of our homes were separated by the "big road"(now US Highway 115) and the Southern Railway track that ran parallel about a hundred feet in front of our house. A narrow wagon road ran by Mr. Brown's. Mr. Brown's "place" consisted of a vacant field and four or five acres of land that lay to the back and on each side of his residence. As far as I ever knew, he was a bachelor. He was a man who kept to himself, taking frequent counsel of a whiskey bottle. There was talk in our neighborhood about his comings and goings and the "doings" about his place.

A large white man with a bulging stomach, he was usually mild-mannered and friendly. But when vexations beset him his language sometimes became colorful and loud. This was especially true when he plowed his mule, Jack. Something about his beast's contrary nature inspired Mr. Brown to heights of anger and profane eloquence hitherto unknown to me.

There were two good-sized umbrella trees in our front yard, one to the north side and the other on the south side of the walkway that divided the yard and led to the steps to our front door. In the spring and summer months I would lie on the ground in the shade of the tree on the high side of the lot from where I could see over the railroad and watch and listen to Mr. Brown plowing his mule in the field on the north side of his house. During his abusive tirades he bellowed out his rage at Jack at the top of his lungs. It was here beneath the umbrella tree that I, early in life, acquired a vocabulary that would do credit to any fluent mule skinner and with which I impressed and astonished my schoolmates.

To the north of Mr. Brown's, facing west toward the road that ran by his house, stood the ramshackle, two-story home of Andy Byers. Mr. Byers was a small, elderly black man whose yard and surroundings were filled with a variety of unsightly buildings in the last states of ruin. Among these were his barn and blacksmith shop, which stood to the back of the house.

At times I was allowed to go and watch when he was working in the "shop." He introduced me to the mysteries of the bellows used to blow air under the fire where he heated metal. I was fascinated as he pulled red hot iron from the glowing embers, using a long pair of metal tongs to protect his hands from the heat. He'd place the glowing hot iron on the

anvil, and with a hammer he'd beat it into whatever he wanted
to make out of it. The sparks flew in every direction as he
pounded vigorously on iron and anvil.

In addition to blacksmithing Mr. Byers had another
business. He operated the town's "sugar wagon." The
conveyance used in this enterprise was an ancient, decrepit
four-wheeled one-horse wagon drawn by his mule, also named
Jack, the same as Mr. Brown's mule. Here the resemblance
ended, for while Mr. Brown's Jack was fat, well kept, and
superbly cursed, Mr. Byers' Jack was poor, its ribs showed, and
its coat was shaggy and uncurried. But Mr. Byers prayed as he
plowed with his mule.

The sanitary convenience known as the "sugar wagon"
served as the town's sewer system. According to the need of
the individual household, Mr. Byers called at intervals and
loaded the contents of its privy into a barrel on his wagon,
collected his fee of fifteen cents and departed with much
prayerful muttering at Jack to a destination unknown to me,
where the barrel was emptied but not washed out. This fact,
together with the spillage into the wagon, set up a constant
stench in his back yard where this means of transport stood
when not in use.

Since everyone who was anybody at all had a privy, and Mr.
Byers' service was the only one available, he enjoyed something
of a lucrative monopoly. I thought it a most unattractive and
stinking way to earn fifteen cents, and decided that I wanted to
be a baseball player when I grew up.

When Mr. Byers came to our house to perform in his
profession Mr. Brown's description of his outfit seemed most
fitting to me, even if Mama didn't allow me to use those words.
But then, again, Mama didn't allow me to use a lot of Mr.
Brown's language.

Mr. Byers was in his second marriage, an unhappy one, to a

big, bustling, busy woman named Mattie. She wore a red bandanna around her head. Several people made up their household, and "Miz Mattie's" tongue was in constant motion maintaining the kind of order she imposed.

Husband and wife had frequent fusses, generally staged in their back yard. Her loud-mouthed uninhibited tirades at "Old Man Andy" were a rare form of entertainment for our little neighborhood. She had a full-throated manner of expressing her grievances, and the recited cause of her harangues left no doubt about the many vexatious deficiencies of "Mr. Byers," as she called him, even at the times when he was being most thoroughly denounced. One day when she was particularly wrought up she took up the axe from the woodpile and threatened to throw it at him: "And I won't miss you neither," she screamed. I lay under the umbrella tree and thought this flustered display of temper was very funny. Our forms of diversion were limited.

"Miz Mattie" was a very religious woman and a member of the choir in the colored Methodist church, although Mr. Byers was a Presbyterian and attended that church. The members of my family on both sides were Methodist. That's how I became acquainted with her in-church behavior. She answered the preacher with many loud exclamations, such as "Yes suh! Preach! Preach! Preach! God knows it's so! So it is! I know I been saved! My redeemer lives on High!" all the while clapping her hands in rhythm.

After warming herself up with these vocal exercises, she would rise from her seat and fling her arms over her head and let out with loud screams and cries to the Lord for mercy on the sinners, who were others than herself, of course. Arms flailing up and down and jerking motions of her body caused her hat to bob up and down and assume odd angles on her head as it danced around before falling to the floor. Then she would descend from the choir and move up and down the center aisle, all the time jumping and screaming in frenzied activity. At times she kept at this until some of the other women took her in charge and got her seated again. Then they would fan her and wipe sweat from her shining black face until she calmed down.

None of our folks ever took part in such carrying on, neither the shouting or assisting with the shouters. Mama's attitude towards this was one of cool detachment. Mine was open-mouthed astonishment and some fear.

Out back of Mr. Byers' house, between his barn and the railroad track, was a sizable spot of ground that he used for a vegetable garden in season. And like Mr. Brown, he used his mule to plow in the cultivation of his land. This, too, was instructive to me as I lay under the umbrella tree.

Mr. Byers' approach to the management of his mule was different from Mr. Brown's method, in that he prayed as he plowed, with his voice rising louder and louder as his trials with his mule increased. So what I heard was something like this: "Whoa, hah, whoa hah. Gee, gee. O, Lord have mercy. GEE! GEE! GEE! Lord help me! WHOA, HAH! WHOA, HAH!"

On days when both Mr. Brown and Mr. Byers were working at the same time in their respective gardens, one was in full-throated profound denunciation of his beast, while the other was uttering loud supplication and prayer to God. I enjoyed listening, although I didn't want Mama to know that was what I was doing. On such days I got my *Robinson Crusoe* book and lay under the trees hoping she would think I was reading.

One day when it was real hot and Mr. Brown was sorely vexed with his mule, he stopped at the end of the row and delivered an exceptionally vigorous and profane tongue lashing to his beast. When he had finished Mr. Byers, who was also plowing in his garden, said loudly: "Oh Lord, please help poor Mr. Brown."

There was silence for a minute, then Mr. Brown sang out:

"You go to hell !" There was nothing in my *Robinson Crusoe* book anything like as funny as that.

There was a vacancy of perhaps a hundred feet or more to the north of and between the Byers residence and the first of six small houses strung out along the continuation of the narrow road that ran through that area. These three-room residences for Negroes had been built by old Dr. Shearer, a professor of Bible and later president of Davidson College. This was called Shearer Town.

I wasn't allowed in Shearer Town, although the houses could be seen from our front porch. I had, however, had an earlier experience with one of its residents who, like Mr. Byers, had acquired a far-reaching reputation in our town for reliability and professional skill. This was "Aunt Lizzie" Heiligh.

Aunt Lizzie was a medium to large size yellow woman. She was the midwife who had attended my birth. Since that time, I had had scarce association with her until she was again at our house for the coming of my sister Erving Elizabeth. I was too young and filled with infant lassitude to take interest in Aunt Lizzie's presence in the episode that had to do with me, but my sister was born on the eleventh of June, 1911, and, as I was seven years old on the eleventh of September of the same year, I have some small recollection of that event. I had been warned by my parents that we were going to have a new baby, and I wasn't at all sure that was what we needed.

Aunt Lizzie's services were not available to everyone. She was expensive, and consequently somewhat exclusive. As a result her clientele was limited to the better class white folks and to very few Negroes outside our family. Her fee for everything was three dollars. This included spending a week in the home doing the cooking, washing and whatever housework the new mother was unable to do at this time.

There was another Negro midwife available for less money.

But after all, at thirty-two years of age, my father was a barber serving white trades, had bought and paid for his home at a cost of more than five hundred dollars, had added a room and paid for it, and owned outright a barber shop that required the services of two barbers beside himself. He had a horse and buggy and a cow, and had lately begun to drink rye whiskey, it being of better quality than the corn in more general use. In addition he had recently contracted with Mr. J. Lee Sloan for the purchase of the Mack McCullough house for rental property. Then he had a telephone installed in his home that cost a dollar and a half a month. Haircuts were fifteen cents and shaves a dime. He was a prosperous man so he had Aunt Lizzie as a mid-wife.

Father died the next year. My mother was immediately faced with the support of her family. She was twenty-eight years old and had two children--my sister Erving, a baby of fourteen months, and me. I was not quite eight years old. She could expect some income from my father's business, which was the only barber shop in our little town. It was a prosperous small business, employing three barbers full-time, my father and the two others. One of these, Rob Torrence, had worked for him for some time. The second was Mama's brother Rutledge.

Father had trained Rutledge as a barber. Torrence was an older man, but he was having trouble with his wife, Theodocia, and had taken to drinking. As a youth I heard much about this in our family. They said that Theodocia was a very pretty light-skinned woman and that her trouble had to do with her association with white men. I do not recall ever having seen her.

Mama depended on her brother to manage the shop for her. Soon Torrence's involvement with his wife and the bottle became such that he eventually lost his usefulness as a barber. They said he talked continually about his beloved Theodocia

and her wayward conduct and that his mind became affected.
By this time, Rutledge had taken his younger brother, Hood,
into the shop and had trained him as a barber. This act was the
beginning of more than half a century of strife and bitterness
that in one way or another was to color the relationship of all the
members of our family.

CHAPTER THREE

More School

Our school went only through the seventh grade, and, as time progressed, there were often more than fifty pupils in attendance in the one-room frame building. Under such conditions, it was difficult to acquire much in the way of education.

No particular academic requirements were necessary to qualify the teachers for our school. It was assumed by the white board of education that employed them that they were qualified to teach us if they were preachers, or if they came from a "good" Negro family and had themselves finished a grade school. In contrast, the Davidson public school for white children was a large, two-story brick building with many well-qualified teachers. It offered a high school diploma and was said to have been one of the best public schools in the state. Davidson College, a regional institution and centerpiece of our town, was also for whites only. Its faculty members wanted and, many felt, got the best public education in the state for their children. Since other white children of the community attended that school, they too were the recipients of its superior educational benefits.

But as far as education for Negroes was concerned, hardly any attention was given to it, and it seemed little more than a farce. The teachers in our schools were possessed more of a pretension to knowledge than of any academic achievement. This was in keeping with the prevalent attitude among white people that Negroes needed no education for the roles in life that were assigned to them. As a result, it was impossible for a Negro to get anything even remotely approximate to the quality of education available to white people.

According to the opportunities offered in our school, we did what there was to do in the learning process. Most of the teachers were conscientious and tried to impart to us the little learning they had in their storehouse.

Mama had instilled in me a fondness for reading, and many of my hours at home were taken up with books she got for me. Among these were *Robinson Crusoe* and *Pilgrim's Progress*. I was completely fascinated with Robinson Crusoe's ability there on his tropical island to supply himself with the means to support himself. I think it was from this book that I first absorbed the idea that a person could make his way in life, however difficult, if he used his mind and ingenuity to solve his problems and to better his condition. Later, *The Count of Monte Cristo* was to hold my attention far into the night for the same reason.

Books that told of adventure in the far North and at sea, and of characters that had hard and difficult struggles to attain their worthy objectives were my favorites. Always, I identified with and made my heroes these struggling ones who had been cast in situations which demanded great striving to reach their goals. And when they came out victorious in the end, I had great respect for them.

For home chores, I chopped into pieces suitable for our fireplace the eight-foot lengths of wood Mama bought, carried them in and put them by the fireside. This is the way the house was heated in winter. Stovewood and kindling was cut with the axe, carried in and put in the box behind the kitchen stove. I drew water from the well and tended the fire that heated it in the wash pot on wash days. On cold days, Mama did the wash for our family in a big round wash tub in the kitchen, scrubbing the clothes on a washboard by hand.

After the hand-scrubbing with soap and water, the clothes were rinsed in clean water in another tub, then taken into the back yard and boiled in the wash pot. This done, they were wrung out and hung up on the clothes line in the yard to dry in the sun. Afterwards, they were brought in, and Mama heated "flat irons" on the top of the wood-burning kitchen stove. With hot irons she pressed the clothes smooth on an ironing board made from a broad plank covered with several thicknesses of cloth and supported on one end by the kitchen table and on the other by the top of a ladder-back chair.

Ironing was hot, uncomfortable work in summer when a fire had to be maintained in the stove to heat the irons. One day a man drove up in a buggy and came in; he showed Mama a pretty, nickel-plated iron with a little tank sticking up on the front of it. He said with this modern iron that heated itself the drudgery and heat of ironing was taken away. He demonstrated how it worked by filling the little tank with gasoline and lighting the burner inside the iron. The unusual appliance made a hissing sort of blowing noise, and the fire it made in the iron was blue.

Mama was afraid of it at first, gasoline being considered a very dangerous thing to handle. But the man assured her there was no danger and persuaded her to try it. It worked real well, heating itself as it hissed. Then he showed her how to light and adjust the flame for proper heat, before he left it with her for a trial period. In the end, Mama bought the iron.

Always, she bought gasoline for the iron herself, never trusting this dangerous mission to me. But one day she gave me an empty quart whiskey bottle and five cents and told me to go downtown to Mr. Mooney's hardware store and get the bottle filled with gasoline and to hurry back. I had already been impressed with the dangers of this liquid and was not unmindful of the responsibility.

Mr. Mooney looked at me closely and pursed his lips together before he went out back of his store to the shed and filled the bottle from a steel barrel with a little hand pump on top of it. He replaced the cork stopper tightly in the bottle, took my nickel and admonished me in all seriousness "not to shake that bottle and for God's sake don't drop it." After this successful trip, when I demonstrated that I wouldn't blow myself up, one of my chores was to get gasoline for Mama's iron.

A succession of pets was also a part of my youth. The first one was a white bull puppy given to me by my father when I was a little boy. Jeff grew into a fine specimen and was my earliest playmate.

I don't remember how Billy goat came into my possession, but he was a major joy of my tender years. I first remember him as almost a baby goat, and it was not long before we were fast friends. He was affectionate and playful, and I spent many hours rubbing his brown coat and playing with him. Billy never grew large even when he was full-grown. Sometimes when we played together and ran after each other he would stand on his hind legs and baa-a-a-a his pure delight of living. Then I had a little wagon and harness and Billy pulled me about the yard. He never butted me, except playfully. Often he put his head down and I would take him by the horns and try to wrestle him to the ground. Ours was a fine friendship.

The main highway ran along in front of our house, and just to the other side of it was the Southern Railway track. One day in summer when I was inside the house, I heard the engine of the freight train going south blowing its whistle in short fast blasts. I ran to the door. Billy was running before the engine down the middle of the track. I was frantic with fear for him. The engineer was trying to bring the train to a stop, but it was fast overtaking my little friend and playmate.

As a last act of defiance to the monster that was bearing down on him, Billy reared and tried to attack. I saw the cowcatcher bring him down and grind him under. The engine came to a stop almost in front of our house, and the crew members ran to Billy, and dragged him out of the iron wheels and put him on the ground beside the track. He was dead and mangled. Mama didn't let me to go out there to see him, but one of the men from the train came to the door and said he was sorry.

Then the train went on and left Billy there. Soon some other men came with knives and a tub, and they were laughing while they cut Billy up and put his meat in the tub. They gave me the torn and bloody skin they had taken from his body and went away. I kept the skin in the wellhouse a long time afterwards, and I would go there and look at the skin and think about Billy.

Later on, Pa started operating a corn mill in the old wooden building across from the depot, and I became his helper on weekends. The grinding part of the mill was an old-fashioned affair with two large stones for grinders. The motive power was a big one-cylinder gasoline engine that shook the floor when it ran. It had two tall flywheels, one at each side. One of the wheels had a flat surface pulley wheel made to it, and a long

belt eight inches wide and about twenty feet long ran from the
pulley to the mill and turned the grinding stones.

Getting this rig in motion was an exciting chore for me to
watch. It was dangerous; Pa always attended to it personally,
and left me standing back out of harm's way. Often the engine
had to be primed before it would start. This was done by
removing its one spark plug at the very end of the cylinder and
putting in a small amount of gasoline. With the priming done
and spark plug replaced, Pa would take hold of a spoke in the
big flywheel, and when he had it properly positioned, he would
give it a strong jerk that turned the wheel. This was the way the
engine was cranked. When it was stubborn, as it often was, it
took several jerks to start it running. After each jerk Pa had to
release the spoke quickly and stand back, because if the engine
fired, the big wheel snatched away into high speed at once and
was dangerous.

With the engine running, Pa would pick up the end of the
long, heavy belt that was to connect the engine with the mill.
His aim was to put it onto the spinning pulley at the side of the
flywheel. This was a hazardous undertaking as one wrong step,
a slip of the foot, or an inept movement of the hand could
throw him into the heavy, whirling wheel or entangle his hand
in the cumbersome belt.

Once this conglomerate contraption was going full- tilt and
grinding corn, it set up a din of assorted noises. There was the
heavy, thumping pop, pop, pop from the big engine's
intermittent firings, the sound of the flying, flapping belt, the
rough, grinding clamor of the heavy stones as they mangled
the corn into meal, and the shaking and rattling of the sifter as
it separated and removed the husks. The frame building joined
in this cacophony with its own vibration, and the whole
resulted in a bedlam that made voice communication difficult
inside the trembling building. And after a little while of

operations, the air became white with meal and got all over us so that we resembled ghosts, moving around in a noisy fog.

I was a big boy now, twelve years old and in the seventh grade, the last grade of our school. It was the fall of 1916. My job was to weigh the corn brought in, take the grinding toll from it, sack up the meal and deliver it to the customer. When we were finished with customer grinding, we ground our toll corn and put the meal in peck-size paper bags. These were sold to retail customers for twenty-five cents each. Wholesale to merchants, we got twenty cents a pack, allowing the merchant a five-cent profit on a sale. This is how we got cash money, together with the sale of some toll corn in bulk.

One Saturday a Mr. Winecoff, who was a regular customer, came in to get his corn ground. He had been drinking and walked back from the front to the big engine that was running and popping in full power, the heavy flywheel revolving at top speed. Mr. Winecoff, a short man, stopped just opposite it and was swaying into the flying wheel. Just as he was about to pitch headfirst into it, I got there and pushed him away. In his drunken state, he became indignant because I had jostled him. Pa never said anything, but Mr. Winecoff didn't come back to the mill after that.

Fatback McCorkle's departure as our teacher brought us a new teacher at school. Reverend Moore was a mild-mannered man who was not too good at discipline. I spent my last year in our school under him. That spring I finished the seventh grade which was as far into education as the school went. I was nearly thirteen years old now and needed to earn money to help Mama. At my father's death my mother's brother Rutledge, who had been taught the barber trade by my father, took over the management of my father's barber shop. This arrangement worked out quite well for a while, with my mother deriving some income from the business.

Then Rutledge took in his younger brother, Hood, and trained him as a barber. This was the beginning of long strife and a division in the family that never healed. When Rutledge was drafted in the Army during World War I, Hood assumed management of the shop, and it wasn't long until he and Mama were having trouble. Once I tried to work in the shop as a shoeshine boy, in the hope of later learning the barber trade, but Hood was harsh in the way he treated me and I couldn't stay. He did not make satisfactory reports to Mama of the shop's earnings and was abusive towards her, often cursing and threatening her. When she appealed to Ma and Pa to correct him, Ma took Hood's side and condoned what he was doing. He had always been her pet, and she let him do as he pleased. She influenced Pa to this also.

There was much unpleasantness in the family about this, with father's people taking sides with Mama in the matter. Mama finally went to court to gain possession of the barber shop, which was granted her. But, in the meantime, Hood went to the owner of the building where the shop was situated and rented it from him without Mama's knowing about it. He then set my father's barber shop fixtures in the street. Now Mama had no building and no barbers. She was completely without income, and with two children to raise.

CHAPTER FOUR

Family History

Pa and Ma were Mama's parents. They lived a quarter of a mile south of us on the same road which, at their house, was the beginning of North Main Street in Davidson. Pa was Charles Norton. Some called him Charlie although he always gave his name as Charles. Bessie, my mother and Mamie, their two older daughters, were married. The other siblings in order of their ages were Tinnie, Rutledge, Isabella, Janie and Hood.

Pa had come here from near Stony Point in Alexander County a few years after slavery. He, his parents, two brothers and three sisters were owned by a Norton family in that area. Pa's father was named Harry. His mother was Maria. She was brought over from England as a slave, so the family story goes. I heard it in my youth that Great-grandpa Harry was paid something for his services at his master's gold mine, that he bought his own freedom and was buying his wife when five of their children were sold down South. Pa was kept (owned) as a youngster and obtained his freedom at Emancipation.

He and his brother Rufus never heard again of their brother

and three sisters. This was a source of bitterness with them. Pa's brother, "Uncle Rufe," was gone thirty years without a trace. After the Civil War, he made his way back and found his brother Charles, who was Pa.

As a boy, I went several times with members of the family to visit Uncle Rufe and Aunt Millie, his wife. And I saw them when they visited Ma and Pa. I remember seeing him weaving cotton baskets from white oak strips when he was here once. He was an old man then.

Uncle Rufe was a man of medium size with brown skin. Aunt Millie had a complexion lighter brown in shade; she was on the fairly heavy side. Both of them loved children, although they had none of their own. They did, however, "take in" an unfortunate baby girl in their old age and raise her. She is named Josie and still lives in the area where Uncle Rufe and Aunt Millie lived.

I never knew about Aunt Millie's background. She was a religious woman and regularly went to Torrence Chapel Methodist Church. On Sunday mornings Uncle Rufe hitched his mule to the buggy and drove his wife the nearly four miles to church. In the box back of the buggy seat he put a bundle of fodder for the animal and a pint of corn whiskey for himself. He never went inside the church. During all kinds of weather, hot or cold, wet or dry, he sat in his buggy during the services. Because of this, some made fun of him, and said he was "quare" — meaning queer, eccentric. I have heard it said that he had spoken of why he did not worship God, and that it had to do with something that happened to him in slavery. I do not remember ever having heard him relate any of his experiences as a slave.

Ma could more easily have been taken for a white person than not. Her complexion was real fair, and her brown hair came down to her waist when she unrolled it from the knot at the back of her head. She put a little butter on her hair when she combed it, and it was beautiful as it hung about her shoulders and down her back. She must have been a very pretty young woman when Pa married her.

Ma's mother was named Violet. She was a slender, light-brown-skinned woman of fine, regular features and straight, graying hair in my childhood memories of her. She was known as "Grandma" to her grandchildren and great-grandchildren alike. Grandma Violet had been an attractive young woman. In slavery she was owned by a prominent master with large land holdings. He was a colonel in The Civil War. The colonel was Ma's father.

Ma's name was Isabella. We all called her Ma but she was my grandmother. When I first knew (Great) Grandma Violet, she was living with her husband, (Great) Grandpa Jonas, in a one-room log cabin in the side yard of her son William's house. He, "Uncle Will," owned a farm.

Grandma Violet did the cooking in the open fireplace. The fireplace jamb was neatly whitewashed, and the pots and pans were orderly arranged along the adjacent wall. The floor was scrubbed with sand and homemade lye soap as was her custom, and was almost white in its cleanliness. She swept with a sagebrush broom, and her bed had a colorful quilt made from a patchwork of assorted scraps of cloth that she had cut into small squares and triangles and painstakingly put together with needle and thread. A wooden frame arrangement out back held ashes from which Grandma made soap.

Grandma Violet had six children, five girls. They were all born either during slavery or shortly afterwards.   Grandpa Jonas was a slight black man with woolly gray hair and a perpetual kindness in his demeanor. He died before I was old enough to know much about him.

After his death Grandma lived alone for some years in the

log cabin. As she grew older, she went about among her children staying from one to several months at a time with each of them. During her months-long stays with Ma and Pa, I got to know and love her. There she sat in winter before a lively burning wood fire in the big open fireplace telling stories of the Indians and the deer that roamed at large in the area when she was young. Not once do I recall that she ever mentioned her days as a slave.

Grandma was quite a picture. I can see her now, her small body sitting there in a high-backed rocker, her brown skin glowing in the dancing firelight, her nearly white hair coiled in a tight knot at the back of her head, which had a small round area in the top that was almost bald. She smoked a clay pipe with a cane stem. She loaded it with Brown Mule chewing tobacco, cut from the plug with a pen knife kept for the purpose. She then rolled the tobacco in her palms to loosen it up. The pipe was relit at intervals with a fresh ember from the fireplace. With a hot toddy in one hand, made from a generous portion of corn whiskey, hot water and a little sugar, she was a storyteller that could make your hair stand on end in fright or double you up in laughter. She always joined in the hearty laughter.

When she was very old, her sight became progressively dim until she could hardly see. Then, as if conceding blindness too cruel an imposition for such a spirit, nature returned her sight to her. And until she died at a hundred and three years, she was able to thread a needle by the light of the fire.

One of my early experiences was going down to Ma's. Ma and Pa lived in a one-story, six-room frame house. The "front room" contained some straight-backed chairs, a settee, a high-backed organ and a stool with a round seat that spun around to raise or lower it, and a carpet on the floor. This was the girls' "company room," a place where visitors were entertained. A mulberry tree grew in the front yard by the sidewalk.

Pa was a farmer who owned his home on Main Street but did not own the land he worked. The land was contracted for work on shares. Pa furnished the farm animals, tools and labor; his share of the crop was two thirds. The landowner got the remaining one third. Pa had two mules and a cow which he housed in the barn at the back of the house. The barn had a loft overhead where he kept hay and "roughness" for the animals. Back of the barn was the hog pen, where he raised pork for his family's needs. Off to the side of the back yard at the end of a path that led from the house, was the privy.

My cousin Vecue was a part of this household. He was Mama's sister Tinnie's son and a year younger than me. Tinnie had become involved with a man named Ben Byers and had become pregnant by him. They were married before the baby was born but lived together only a short time afterwards, before she came back with Vecue to live with her parents. Vecue was black, as was his father, and Ma often called Vecue a black mink when she was vexed with him. He was my playmate at the house, and together we went with Pa to the field during farm season and helped with filling the planters and the fertilizer distributor.

We got to go all the way to Mooresville on the wagon along an unpaved road, which is now US Highway 115, when Pa went to the mill to have wheat ground into flour. This was a real excursion; it took the better part of a day to go and come the seven miles each way and get the wheat ground. Pa would stop at a general store and buy small cans of potted meat and cheese cut from the big round "hoop" under the wooden cover with the wide-bladed knife poised over it. We got crackers from a barrel to eat with this, and a strawberry-flavored bottled drink to wash it down.

Then Pa got to taking us to the circus. This was a small show that came to Mooresville each fall. We always went in

time to see the parade. Then we stood by the side of the street
and watched in open-mouthed wonder at the long-necked
giraffes as they strolled by, the striped zebras (did anybody ever
see such funny looking mules?) and great maned lions in the
iron cages made onto heavy red wagons with gold trim painted
on them. We had a delicious fear of what would happen if one
of those fierce things should get out and start eating people.
Even Pa couldn't save a fellow from that. There were wildcats
and an ape, all in cages and guarded by men dressed in uniforms walking along by the wagons. Then came the cute little
monkeys. This procession was led by the calliope, which we
called the steam piano. It made music different and prettier
than anything we had ever heard.

There was a minstrel band of black men in bright red
uniforms with braid on the coats and pants, and high-top caps
with white plumes that waved and moved as the musicians
pranced and played fast music like Dixie. Some had great big
horns that curled around and had big round openings where
the heavy music came out. Others slid part of their horns in
and out in front of them as they marched and blew. When the
parade had circled around and come back by where we could
see it again, Pa would put us in the wagon and start home after
buying us some cotton candy. It was a most wonderful experience, and we told the others in school what we had heard and
seen. Some of them didn't believe there was anything with a
neck higher than the ceiling.

As we grew up, Pa used us more and more as his helpers.
We went with him to the woods, where Vecue and I manned
one handle on the end of the long cross-cut saw while he was
on the other end. This made getting wood faster and quicker,
and Pa would take wood to our house, too.

When they were building the Old Rock Road, Pa hauled
rock and sold it to the highway people. To get the rock, we
went to the Caldwell place and down in the field back of the

old Kimmons house where there were plenty of big rocks
sticking up out of the ground. Pa would take an iron rod with a
star drill on the end and, with a heavy hammer in one hand and
the drill held in the other, he pounded and turned the drill until
he had a hole in the hard granite-like stone.

When the hole was deep and large enough, Pa put in a stick
of dynamite and attached a cap and a long enough fuse to
allow him to get safely away before the blast went off. The
dynamite was always handled very carefully, and while this was
being done Vecue and I had to keep well away from it. With
everything in readiness, we boys were sent down the hill to lie
behind a big rock. We put our fingers in our ears and stayed
there until Pa said for us to get up. Then Pa lit the fuse and ran
to join us behind the rock, where we drew up into a knot and
waited to see what was going to happen.

It generally wasn't long after Pa got on the ground behind
the rock before the earth trembled under us and there was a
big roar up at the rock where he had put the dynamite. Then
we kept real still, and in a little while we could hear rocks that
had been blown into the air begin to hit the ground. This was
the time when we put our hands around the back of our heads
to keep any falling stones from hitting us there.

When we could no longer hear things hitting the ground, we
got up and went to see how much rock had been blown out.
Then we set to work and piled all the loose pieces in a mound.
When this was done Pa would blast again. Most times there
were large pieces that had to be broken with a big hammer
with a long handle. Pa did this while we boys piled. This was
heavy work, and sharp edges of the stone cut into our hands
and made them bleed. After a week or so of this, we would
bring the mules and wagon and load the rocks in the wagon-
bed and haul them out to the highway. We stacked them up so
the man could measure how many cubic yards were there and
pay Pa for them.

During the season when molasses was being made, we went
to the field and cut the sweet cane and loaded it on the wagon
and drove down to Mr. Will Gaston's molasses mill. The mill
was in the side yard of his house which was several miles out
of town toward the river. Pa's brother and his wife lived nearby
also, and we were glad of an opportunity to go see Uncle Rufe
and Aunt Millie.

The molasses mill was in two parts. The first and larger part
was the place where they squeezed the juice from the cane, a
mechanism with a big hopper at the top where the cane was
put in by hand. Under the hopper, it passed between rollers
that mashed out the sweet juice. About the center of the
contrivance a piece of timber perhaps ten feet long extended
horizontally. A mule was hitched to the extended end and was
made to pull it round and round in a circle. This turned the
rollers that extracted the juice from the cane, which drained by
gravity into the container on the ground below. From here the
juice was put into the second part of the mill, the cooker. The
cooker was a trough-like receptacle about six feet long by two
feet wide. It was elevated high enough above the ground to
make room for an enclosed fireplace underneath it.

This was a very important part of the process, and Mr.
Gaston himself presided here, from time to time ordering a
little more wood on the fire or some taken out as the temperature of the cooking molasses demanded. Great spoon in hand,
he dipped periodically into the hot liquid and held it above and
let it drip slowly back into the bubbling mass. This was to test
for thickness and color, both critical to making good molasses.
Mr. Gaston was an expert.

Uncle Rufe took Vecue and me over to where he was standing and he poured some of the hot syrup into a cup for each
of us, saying to be careful and not burn our mouths. Then,
while we sipped the hot, sweet syrup we just sat and watched

the mule walking round and round and round, and the juice
trickling down and down out of the spout into the earthen
crock, and the smoke rising up and up from the low chimney at
the end of the cooking vat.

Sometimes Mama let me spend the night down to Ma's.
There were two double beds in the room where Rutledge and
Hood slept. Vecue and I slept in one bed and our uncles in the
other one, unless they were mad at each other. In that case, I
would sleep with one of them and Vecue with the other. Or
sometimes both of us young boys slept with Rutledge because
we didn't like Hood much and would rather not sleep with him
anyway. He was overbearing and picked on us. At times he and
Rutledge got into fights and that pleased Vecue and me because Rutledge always whipped him. We thought Rutledge
didn't like him much either. Hood was Ma's youngest child and
her pet, so the others said. They said Ma always made them
give in to Hood and let him have his way, and he usually got
the best treatment from her. Anyway, the fights didn't usually
amount to much more than just a few licks, because Hood
wouldn't fight after he had done something to cause Rutledge
to get on him. Sometimes he ran out of the room or called
Ma, who made Rutledge let him alone. They were both young
men, with Rutledge being about four years older.

On winter night visits, in the boys' room, we boiled eggs,
which Vecue and I got from the barnyard nests, in a container
on the open fire, or we roasted peanuts. We baked sweet
potatoes in the ashes too. One night when both of our uncles
were out, we had had a particularly good time stuffing ourselves on goodies and talking, when Hood came in and started
picking at us. He pushed us around and pulled our hair and
slapped at us just to be mean.

When Rutledge came in later we were all in bed, Vecue and

I together and Hood alone in the other bed. We told Rutledge
what had happened and he snatched the covers off Hood and
fell in on him something fierce. He was really mad this time
and gave Hood a good working over, with Hood trying to get
away from him and out of the bed. Then they were standing
up on the floor with Rutledge flailing away with his fists and
Hood trying to dodge the blows.

The bumping and knocking and chairs being knocked over
set up quite a bedlam in the room, and Ma and Pa both had to
come in and pull Rutledge off of Hood that time. After this,
Hood didn't pick at us much, because every time he started to
we would threaten to tell Rutledge on him. But in the mornings
when he got a chance, he would flick cold water from the wash
pan into our faces. The outcome of the fight pleased Vecue
and me mightily, and we talked about it afterwards when we
were having an "eat" by the fire.

In summers we sat on the grass in the front yard and
watched for jaybirds in the mulberry tree. These birds had a
great fondness for the sweet berries and came in numbers to
help themselves. This was an open invitation to our predatory
instincts. We made sling-shots from short lengths of rubber
bands bought for the purpose and attached them to a Y-shaped
prong of a tree limb. A piece of shoe tongue fastened between
the two free ends made the place to put the small stone to be
hurled when the bands were stretched and suddenly let go.
These made fairly accurate weapons in our hands, and we were
a danger to the birds with them.

But the more deadly weapon was the sling made from two
lengths of cord with a piece of soft leather joining them. A
loop was then tied in the free end of one piece of cord and
slipped over the index finger down to the hand where it
wouldn't come off at the throw. The free end of the cord was
held firmly between the thumb and first finger while the stone

was swung in the sling, around and round above the head just as fast as possible until velocity was built up. At precisely the right instant the cord held between the finger and thumb was released. This let the stone fly free with great force. It is impossible to explain how aim is developed in a projectile thrown in this manner, but ours was perfected to the point that, from where we stood in the yard, we could hit a jaybird sitting even in the top of the big mulberry tree.

Hog killing time at Pa's came in the fall after frost at a time when the weather had been cool long enough for the temperature to be established at a level low enough for the meat not to spoil. There was no refrigeration, and natural temperature had to be relied on to keep fresh meat safe to eat. Also, it should not be too cold, for, if it was too cold, the meat would freeze before it cured and this would spoil it. So good hog killing weather was watched for by older people, and when it came, they struck.

On one such appointed frosty morning, the washpot was filled with water and a fire built under it. The big wooden barrel was placed in position by digging a hole and putting the bottom in at an angle so that the hog's body could be pushed down and pulled up back and forth in it for scalding. Knives were sharpened and the sausage grinder washed and made ready. Sage for flavoring the sausages and salt for "salting down" the meat was put in place. Two men besides Pa were there to help.

With everything in order and a roaring fire around the pot of hot water, Pa picked up his axe, and he and his helpers went to the hog pen out by the barn. Someone poured slop in the trough while Pa got over the fence into the pen, axe in hand. His getting into the pen excited the hogs a little at first but that didn't last long, and they put their heads down in the trough

and ate without noticing. With his eyes on the hog he wanted
to get, Pa maneuvered himself into position and stealthily
raised the axe over his shoulder. When the hog's head became
still enough, down came the blunt end of the axe to the top of
the head with all the power Pa could get into it.

Stunned by the heavy blow, the hog staggered back and fell
to its knees. Then one of the helpers handed Pa the long sharp
butcher knife, and he stuck it into the hog's throat as far as he
could get it, all the way up to the handle, and drew the sharp
edge from side to side. This cut a great gaping gash from
which blood came in gushes. The hog was kicking and squeal-
ing for all it was worth by now, and Pa got out of the pen and
one of the men pulled away two bottom planks from the pen
fence and dragged the hog out onto the ground by its hind
legs.

Right away the hog scrambled to its feet and started running
and screaming all around in the hog lot. Blood was gushing
from its cut throat and it was throwing its head from side to
side. And every time it did this, the big gash in its throat
opened up and another great blob of blood gushed out. Pa was
in hot pursuit, axe raised to get in another blow to the head.
But the hog kept running away from him. Then the screaming
hog fell down again, and Pa placed another blow with the axe.
There was a hollow thud when this came, and the hog lay still,
except for twitching of its feet.

Then the men dragged the hog by the hind legs to where the
barrel was in place. They left it lying there on the ground with
its legs jerking and twitching while they carried hot water in
buckets from the wash pot and poured it into the barrel. Then
they slid the still jerking hog's body, hind quarters first, down
into the scalding water and turned it over slowly and pushed it
up and down. They did this until they thought that part was
well scalded, then they pulled it out and put the front end

down into the barrel of hot water and did the same with it.

When they had finished doing this, they laid the hog out on some planks pushed up close together and started scraping the hairs from its body with long knives. It was still now; even the twitching was gone. When the hair was all scraped off, the hog lay there on the planks with its big white body glistening against the black hair that had been scraped off. They cut a slit in each back leg just above the hoof between the tendon and the bones. A hook on the two ends of a singletree was attached to the cuts in the legs, spreading them wide apart. One end of a rope was fastened to the center of the singletree and the other end thrown over a limb of the close-by tree. While the two men lifted, the third one pulled on the rope over the limb until the hog's body was raised off the ground in a head-down position. Then Pa took a long, sharp knife and started to cut high up between the back legs and brought a deep gash all the way down through the hog's belly and to the gaping slash where its throat was cut. This split the hog wide open, making an opening from which the entrails were removed. Then the body was progressively cut up and salted down to preserve it for food.

They gave the bladder to Vecue and me. We took turns putting our mouths to the end of it, blowing air into it until it was a big round ball. Then we played with it in the yard.

Late in the afternoon one day, Mama told me to catch one of our fryers and kill it for supper. The chicken was loose on the yard and I had to run it down, having tried dropping grains of corn at my feet in the hope it would come up and I could catch it while it ate. I had killed chickens for our table before, mostly by stretching their necks on the chopping block at the wood pile and with a quick stroke of the hatchets cutting their heads off, or nearly off. Anyway, I had succeeded in killing them. I used this method of slaughtering them because I discovered while trying to kill a hen by the conventional way of wringing its head off that I didn't have the strength in my arms to hold the bird firmly by the head and swing its body around fast and hard enough to wring its neck off.

Anyway, by the time I had this young Rhode Island Red rooster in my hands I was pretty well out of wind, after much running and dodging and reaching for him only to see him scamper off at full speed just at the instant when I thought I had him caught. Mama stood on our back porch and watched this performance with ill-concealed glee. So when I had him firmly in hand, finally, and came panting up to the chopping block, it was with a feeling that he was going to get just what he deserved, fried for supper.

He was real still after I caught him, and didn't try to get away from me. He just had to be tired too, after all that running and half flying about the yard. Well, as I said, the rooster was real quiet after I caught him and hadn't tried to get away. So I didn't use my regular procedure of holding the hatchet in hand while I adjusted his neck on the block. I trusted the chicken. I put the hatchet on the ground by the block while I fixed the neck in place where I wanted it. All the time, Mama was watching from the back porch. The bird in place, I reached and got the hatchet, but when I turned back to the block, there was nothing there. That chicken had gotten up and was walking away out of reach, shaking himself. I heard suppressed laughter from the back porch. I was so disgusted that all I could do was stand and stare at the fleeing chicken as he got farther and farther away. Mama could contain herself no longer, and let out with a peal of laughter. I found my voice and shook my fist in the direction of the now running chicken and called him an old fool. Until her death Mama recited this incident as an example of my brilliance, and I always feel a little shamefaced about it.

Pa had traded the mules off by now, and had two horses. One was a bay mare and the other a black male named Frank. Frank was a horse with a lot of spirit. He could run real fast and seemed to enjoy it. Vecue and I liked to ride horseback, and, as the horses were gentle, Pa let us ride them. We didn't always use the best judgment in riding, however. And sometimes when Pa let us ride them downtown, we would gallop them through the street. They were both fast horses, and our riding them through town at a hard gallop attracted attention, some of it not good. Once in a while Pa would tell us not to do this as people were talking about our recklessness.

Where we really had fun with the horses was in Mr. Cowan's pasture, where they were grazed. On Sunday afternoons Vecue and I went over to the pasture and rode them bareback and without bridles. We caught the horse by the mane to help us scramble to its back, and once aboard, with switch in hand, we urged the animal to top speed, holding on with our legs tight against the horse's body and leaning low in the wind. It was such adventure to feel the horse springing forward under us with all its might. We tried some stand-up riding, too. We would get to the horse's flank and stand up, but not when it was running. This was strictly slow-motion activity, as we were afraid of falling off if the animal moved too fast with us in this position.

Mama let me go over to Grandma Alice's, too. She was father's mother and lived near the school in the all Negro neighborhood. Often, during school days, I went by to see her. In summer when I went, Frank , the boy she raised from a baby, and I would wander up and down the branch in nearby Jetton's pasture catching minnows. He and I and some other boys made a dam and had a swimming hole there. This was a

favorite place for us to gather on a hot summer day. We all
went in the water as naked as jaybirds.

Once some men from the Baptist church went to our
swimming hole and built the dam up to the top of the ground
and cut a trench around, so some of the water could drain off.
They were preparing for a baptizing to be held on Sunday
afternoon. They had not bothered to ask us anything about
using our swimming hole, either; they just took it over. Sunday
School was held at two o'clock in the afternoon. When it was
out Frank, I, Richard Rivens, Leroy Torrence and some other
boys joined the steady stream of people going to the baptism.
When we arrived, there was already a fairly good crowd around
our swimming hole. In the distance we heard singing, and it
was coming nearer. The Baptist people were coming, marching
in single file and singing hymns like "Take Me Down to the
Water" and "Just Like a Tree That's Planted by the Water." As
they came closer, the singing got louder.

A big black preacher, wearing a long white garment, was
leading them. He had a Bible in his hand, and when he got to
our swimming hole, he stopped and read from it. Then three
or four other people in white robes lined up behind him, and
they all walked into the water. The crowd on the banks were
singing real loud now and clapping their hands in time with the
music. Some began to "shout," they were so happy. Then more
joined in the shouting and singing and handclapping until a lot
of noise was being made. The preacher had the biggest voice
of all, and he was leading the singing. Then he read some more
from the Bible and put his arms about a man standing there in
the water with him and gently let him backwards until he went
under. This set off more shouting and frenzy among the
Baptists gathered at the sides of our swimming hole.

The noise was really loud now with all the singing and
shouting and handclapping when someone went close up and

spoke urgently to the preacher, all the while pointing excitedly to one side of the pond. At once the preacher and the others rushed out of the water looking scared. Some started poking around the edge of the water with sticks, and word went out that a snake had been seen. After some milling around and earnest consultations, the Baptists lined up and marched back to their church. Some said later that Otis White had seen the snake and spread the alarm. This gave rise to much speculation concerning the truth of the matter, as Otis was a young man of devilish and irresponsible character, to say the least.

Otis went about with a banjo strung over his shoulder by a strap, wearing leggings and a wide hat, and leading his yellow hound dog by a string. This was a perfect picture of a worthless, no-account Negro. Folks said he had sold his soul to the devil. He had accomplished this dreadful deed by going to a crossroads at midnight in the dark of the moon carrying black cat bones which he put in a cross mark made in the dirt. After this, he spat over his left shoulder and played a tune on his banjo. There was no retreating once this was done. If a fellow had sold his soul to the devil, then he belonged to the devil, and nothing he could do would change it. He was said to be a gambler, too, and this was very bad.

In the fall of the year after the episode with the Baptists at our swimming hole, and when a revival meeting was going on at the Methodist church, Otis came in and sat down. A shock of dismay ran through the church when he came in. His unexpected coming was a real challenge to the visiting preacher and to the several older ladies in the congregation who made it their business to give personal attention to sinners in need of "saving." Otis more than filled the bill. He was a hellion of the first water.

As usual during revival time, the preacher preached long and

hard on the certainty of a burning hell that awaited the unre-
pentant sinner. God was pictured as angry and vindictive, who
knew and registered in the big Book of Judgment every sin
committed by every person, and on Judgment Day the sheep
would be separated from the goats, with the goats being cast
into Outer Darkness. The sermon was preached in a loud voice
with the preacher waving his arms and reaching his hands over
his head pointing his finger sternly. This was accompanied with
"Amens" and other forms of answering from the pews, together with shouting and walking up and down the aisles,
singing and clapping hands, while the preacher stormed away
against sin and the devil, sweat pouring off his shining black
face. Gambling, stealing, drinking whiskey, lying, playing cards,
and every form of private enjoyment was brought under loud
and severe denunciation. At times he left the pulpit and came
around down front within the railing where the collection table
stood, jumping with both feet off the floor and coming down
hard again.

Pattie Harris and Roxanna Dunlap and several others of
the older women gathered around where Otis was sitting
quietly at the back of the church. They sang over him, and they
clapped their hands over him, and they prayed earnestly over
him. Then they begged him to come to the "mourners' bench"
and be saved. Finally, a group started moving towards the
rostrum with Otis in the center, headed for the "bench."
There was much praising the Lord for bringing this sinner to
the fold. Up front and kneeling, the women and the preacher
prayed and sang over him and clapped their hands for joy. But
he never "came through." At the end of the service, he left the
building still "unsaved." And some of the boys said he had his
pistol in his pocket all the time.

Since I was living a life of sin smoking rabbit tobacco,
fighting at school, playing Rook, doing some lying and drinking

hot toddies that Ma gave me on cold mornings, I became very seriously concerned that the Lord wasn't taking a kindly view of my way of life. I thought of going to the mourners' bench and confessing my sins and getting forgiveness. But I noticed when I missed going a night or two that my conscience quit bothering, and I let things stand as they were.

But I was unable to get this thought out of mind, and I would lie awake at night and think about my sins and pray to the Lord to forgive me and to spare me from going to hell. I didn't tell anyone about this, but I was scared that the Lord would punish me. And I begged Him to show me mercy and I promised to be good. But, somehow, I couldn't change my way of doing. I kept on doing the same things, but I prayed for a long time and was afraid of what would happen to me.

CHAPTER FIVE

More
Family History

Grandma Alice was a heavy-set, chocolate-colored woman. She had four children--Walter (my father), Jenny, Odell and Charlotte, none of whom were fathered by Grandpa Rich Robinson, whom she married after her children were born. My father went in the name of Johnson, which was the name of the white family that owned Grandma Alice's people in slavery, and the name that she assumed until she was married. I was told by a wealthy white man, elderly at the time, that my father's father was the son of a prominent doctor in whose household Grandma Alice worked as a young woman. Grandma Alice never told me this. She evaded the question once when I asked her who my father's father was. My father was of light complexion, and it is almost a certainty that his father was a white man. Who he was, I never learned from her, although I asked her concerning this when I was a young man and before she died.

Her three other children had brown skin and looked like siblings. Aunt Jenny, one of her two daughters, married Ernest

Byers, son of Andy Byers who operated the "sugar wagon."
He became a railway mail clerk and lived in Greensboro, N.C.
for many years. Later he was promoted to the post office in
Washington, D.C., where he died in his eighties.

The other daughter, Charlotte, the youngest, went in the
name of Black. She married Charlie Wilson, who was employed by the Davidson College Athletic Association for many
years and was known widely as "Doc Charlie" because of his
efficiency in treating sprains and injuries of the athletes at the
college.

Odell, her second son, was taken as a small child by
Grandma Alice's sister, Aunt Lou, who was married to John
Alexander (Uncle John) and lived in Charlotte. Uncle Odell
went in the name of Alexander, as do his two children.

Grandma Alice was a very kind person, and Frank, whom
she had taken as a child, became one of my playmates. Frank
was the son of Toon, who was the daughter of Grandpa Rich
Robinson, Grandma Alice's husband. I never knew whether
Grandpa Rich was married to Toon's mother or not, nor who
her mother was, but she was not Grandma Alice's daughter.
Frank's father was a white man of a prominent family.

Toon died in Frank's infancy, and Grandma Alice and
Grandpa Rich Robinson took him as a baby and raised him.
Frank and I were friends and regarded each other as blood
relatives, although there was no kinship between us. As boys
and as young men we were companions and went about
together a great deal. He was a fine-looking person, intelligent,
and could master most jobs he undertook. As we grew older,
our interests were not the same. In later years, we had no
association together although we remained friends. He died the
day after Christmas in 1969 in a fire that destroyed the house in
which he lived with Grandma Alice's married granddaughter,
the daughter of Charlotte.

Grandma Alice had two brothers, Uncle Will and Uncle Otho, called "Tobe" by everyone except Aunt Lou, who always called him Otho. All of them were the children of slaves named Lige and Dilsey. When I was a young man, I was told by a white woman who knew the family that Great-grandpa Lige drove alone in a wagon from near Davidson to Virginia and brought back the body of his master who had been killed in the Civil War. Granny Dilsey survived and lived with Uncle Will and his wife Euphazine and their children until my early youth.

Uncle Will, called "Will Lige" after his father, was one of a small group that founded the association known as The Christian Aid Society. The purpose of this association was to provide medical care for its members. It became an important force among Negroes in the community, most of whom belonged to it. For a monthly fee of fifteen cents, later raised to twenty-five cents, all of a member's doctor bills and medicine costs were paid by the Society. When a member was unable to pay the monthly fee he raised his voice in meeting and called out, "Unfinancial." This excused him from payment that month.

The Society was highly regarded by the town's four white doctors who provided medical attention and by the drug store that filled prescriptions. All bills were promptly paid, and the Society paid one hundred dollars towards the burial of its members. It owned a horse-drawn hearse and bought a plot of ground that became its cemetery. Both of these were free to members. The Society's hearse was the one I saw under the Masonic Hall in back of the Methodist church during my first year of school.

A part of the money to support this undertaking was raised by a picnic held each year on the thirty-first of July. This affair became known widely as the Thirty-First Picnic and was attended by large crowds. Baked chicken, ham and hot fish sandwiches were sold from tables set up especially for the occasion under shade trees on the picnic ground. The fish was fried in a wash pot in grease kept bubbling by a wood fire under it. Homemade ice cream and cake were in abundance, plus lemonade made in a great big metal tub. "Come and get it," they cried. "Ice cold lemonade, made in the shade, stirred with a spade, best ole lemonade ever was made!"

The baseball game held in conjunction with the picnic, with music by the Huntersville band, made this occasion a high spot in Negro entertainment and attracted people from miles around. And throughout the year, the Society carried out its successful medical and burial aid. For thirty-five or forty years it was a great help to its members who were poor and unable to pay for their medical needs. The picnic provided a good time for all.

To earn his living, Uncle Will operated the town's only dray wagon. For years he perched on the plank seat of his one-horse wagon, a familiar sight on the street. Most of his business was hauling for the merchants. Their merchandise was shipped by rail, and Uncle Will carried it on his wagon from the depot to the stores. He was an authority on who had what in the depot, and, without being told, loaded it and promptly delivered it to the owner.

Shortly after his death, his nephew, Uncle Tobe's son, Odell, as he was passing that way, saw his uncle's skull sitting on the windowsill of a student's room at Davidson College. Uncle Will's head was of a distinctive shape that made his skull easily identifiable, and there was no doubt that the skull on the student's windowsill was his. For this act of grave robbing and desecration, a small financial settlement to Uncle Will's family was made. The students involved in this were not prosecuted in the courts, the act being considered one of some white college boys having fun in the nigger graveyard.

Grandma Alice's other brother, Uncle Tobe, ran the only cleaning and pressing establishment in town. Uncle Tobe, like Uncle Will, was quite an institution in the town, as everybody knew him and patronized his place of business. I worked for him after school and on weekends. When I was through with the seventh and last grade in our school, Uncle Tobe gave me a regular job in his pressing club at six dollars a week. This was pretty generous considering that he got only twenty-five cents for sponging and pressing a man's suit.

My job included picking up the clothes at the homes of customers and in the dormitories at Davidson College. Back in the shop we sponged and pressed them. Then I carried them back to their owners. I walked and carried the clothes in my arms, and sometimes I had as many as I could barely get along with. I picked up and delivered as far away as the adjoining town, Cornelius, two miles away. I was real glad to get this job and Uncle Tobe was good to me. He was kindhearted by nature and my favorite uncle. He taught me to clean and press clothes and to do alterations and repairs on them.

Uncle Tobe's pressing club was located in an old one-story wooden building on Main Street. On each side of the narrow double doors at the entrance, there was a single window with ordinary small window panes. Five wooden steps led up from the cement sidewalk to the doors. On the inside a small lobby was formed by a wall about four feet high in the center front of the building. At one side of the lobby wall and in front of a window there was a long, wide table covered with two or three layers of duck cloth. This is where the clothes were sponged and pressed. The alteration and repair department was on the opposite side. Uncle Tobe's sewing machine sat at that window. At the back of the wall clothes that had been finished were put on hangers and hung on long pipes extended across the room.

The equipment used in sponging and pressing consisted of

two metal wash pans about twelve inches in diameter and four inches deep, two hand scrub brushes, a length of duck cloth, a "form" for pressing coats, and a large, heavy , electric smoothing iron made for pressing-club work. The sponging was done by dipping a scrub brush lightly into the wash pan containing gasoline and brushing over the garment. This was the cleaning process and was carried on at the same time as the pressing. Next, the garment was positioned, the duck cloth placed over the part to be pressed, and water from the second wash pan sprinkled on it with the other scrub brush. The heavy hot iron was then moved back and forth over the cloth and the garment pressed amid steam arising from the damp cloth.

Once, when Uncle Tobe's electric iron got something wrong with it and wouldn't heat, he sent me to borrow an iron from W.P. Cumming, a Davidson College student who had it in his room in old Chambers building. When I returned, and Uncle Tobe attached this iron to the current, it burnt out too. We were in a dither then because in addition to our own iron being out of fix, Mr. Cumming's iron was also useless. I had forgotten this incident until more than fifty years later, when I received a letter from the former student recalling this and some other incidents of our earlier years. The former student was Dr. W.P. Cumming, retired professor of English at Davidson College.

The pick-up and delivery service that I did improved Uncle Tobe's business. Partly because of this and partly because he wanted to modernize his business, he installed a new steam pressing machine. This was a self-contained unit with a gasoline-fired boiler attached to provide steam for pressing clothes. This did away with the use of the old iron. Shortly afterwards, he put in a machine to dry clean the clothes. Then he raised my wages two dollars a week. When I asked if he would allow me to put in a shoeshine stand in the lobby, he readily assented, bought all the equipment and gave me all I made from this. I was now earning eight dollars a week at my job and three or four dollars shining shoes at five cents a pair, but many of my customers gave me a dime.

This was all the income we had at home, but with the cow and a pig we got along. I bought a second-hand bicycle, which enabled me to get about faster to pick up and deliver clothes. The bicycle also gave me more time at the shop, where I could get extra money shining shoes.

My schoolmate and friend, Frank, the boy Grandma Alice raised, was working at a confectionery store a few doors from Uncle Tobe's pressing club. In summer there was a good deal of slack time in both businesses. An alleyway led from the sidewalk to the vacant ground in back of the buildings where there were some trees. Since we were just in back and in easy calling range of our jobs, Frank and I spent some of our idle time pitching horseshoes or enjoying the shade of the trees.

Somehow a can of carbide came into our possession. Carbide was used to make gas for the lights on some early automobiles, and we knew of its potential as an explosive. An idea came. We secured an empty gallon-size paint bucket, the kind with the lid forced into the top which can be removed and replaced. Then we drove a nail hole in the bottom about the center. We had some matches. Next we put a few lumps of carbide in the bucket and poured in water. Quickly we jammed the lid in place holding a finger to the nail hole. We allowed a minute for gas to generate, then put the bucket on the ground, removed our finger from the nail hole and applied a lighted match. An ear-smashing boom resulted as the lid was blown from the bucket.

Right away we knew somebody would come to investigate all that noise, so we ran and hid. Sure enough, in moments people came through the little alley into the back yard, craning

their necks to see what had happened. When we walked up a
little later and joined them, they thought we had come to see
what had happened too, not connecting us with it at all. Frank
and I repeated this performance several times and something
of a mystery grew up about the loud explosions out back.
Then one day Mr. Johnston, the policeman, emerged from the
shadows and put an end to our little game. At first, when he
saw what was going on, he just looked at us, cool like. Then he
told us firmly not to do that anymore. And we didn't.

Mr. Johnston was a friend of my father's during his lifetime,
and knew me well from my early childhood. I wasn't afraid of
him, but I didn't want him to have to get after me for doing
things I shouldn't do. I liked him and wanted him to like me.
He had exhibited his confidence and kindly feeling towards me
by lending me six of the ten dollars I paid for my second-hand
bicycle. I repaid him in two-dollar-a-week payments.

Our cow had a calf in early spring. I grazed the calf over the
summer until late fall and sold it at an advantage. It had grown
and put on considerable weight during the summer months
and brought a good price on the market. I decided later to do
this again, only I would have to buy the calf this time. In the
spring, when the weather got warm and grass began to grow, I
inquired about another calf. One day a man drove up in a
wagon with two calves and said he would sell them for three
dollars each. I thought this a fair enough bargain and made the
purchase with money saved from my shoeshine business.

These were real pretty young animals. The man assured me
that they were weaned, but in a day or two I knew they were
not, since they had not yet learned to eat grass. I had to devise
some way to feed them. The only thing I knew to do was to
mix up a gruel, mostly of corn meal and water, and feed this to
them. To get the gruel into the calves, I poured it into a Buf-
falo Ginger Ale bottle and inserted the open end in the calves'

mouths. In a few days, they had become my loving babies and would come running to me for their food. I do believe they thought I was their mother, the way they sucked the gruel from the bottle that I held to their mouths, even hunching it the way calves do when nursing naturally. I had a fondness for animals, especially young ones, and I enjoyed the feeding time. It became a time of play between my full days of duty.

All went well for two or three weeks; then one day one of the calves was sick and wouldn't eat. In a few days it was dead. The other calf got on fine, and I grazed it over the summer. It became such a pet I was reluctant to sell it, and certainly not for slaughter. Luckily, I sold it to a man who wanted a nice heifer to raise for a milk cow.

CHAPTER SIX

Youthful Struggles

Finally Mama was successful in getting a barber to come to Davidson and open her shop. She rented the room that years before had been attached to the side of the building occupied by Uncle Tobe's pressing club. This was made of wood, with wooden steps leading from the sidewalk up to the entrance. It was not much of a building, but it would have to do.

Uncle Tobe, who had stored her barber shop fixtures in the back of his pressing club, helped with getting the things installed. They had been out of use since Hood Norton set them in the street and took over my father's business. Then Cunningham, the barber, started to work. He was moderately successful from the first being a good man at shaving. Barber shop shaving was much in demand at that time. His business got much better until he had a good trade. Some of this was due to the fact that many of my father's friends and customers knew how my mother had been treated about the shop, and they were glad for it to open up in competition to Hood Norton.

Cunningham's business continued to thrive, and Mama was now getting some income from the shop. He was making inroads in the barber business. One day, when he was passing that way, Pa stopped him and ordered him to leave town. Cunningham and Pa were about the same size and age, both being fairly large men. Cunningham let Pa know that he wasn't to be driven out of town. Uncle Odell came up from Charlotte to see about this, and it never happened again.

A few months later, the barber shop was broken into during the night and all of Cunningham's barber tools stolen. No suspicion attached itself to Pa himself concerning this, but there was considerable feeling about it in town as Cunningham was well liked. A week or two after the break- in, the tools were found where they had been thrown in a ditch. Rain and expo-sure to weather had ruined them for use. But finding them thrown away convinced many people that they were taken as an act of meanness to discourage Cunningham and drive him away.

Soon, it was decided that I should go in the barber shop and shine shoes and begin to learn the barber trade. Uncle Tobe got another boy to take my place helping him, and I moved next door to the barber shop. I had built up a good shoe shine business and this followed me to my new location. Cunningham started teaching me to hone razors and to lather faces for shaving when I was not busy with shoes.

When I was working for Uncle Tobe, collecting and deliver-ing clothes kept me on the go part of the time and offered some diversion from staying inside. It was different at the barber shop. I had to stay there all the time. I found this irk-some to my fifteen-year-old energies. To occupy idle time and to indulge a fondness I started reading in the shop. This was an enjoyable pastime, and, aside from keeping me contented, I was gaining some instruction from it. I, long before this, formed the reading habit, but prior to this time I had done practically all of it at home.

Mama was conscious of this inclination, and she was not content with my not going further in school. Accordingly, she made arrangements for me to go to Statesville the following fall and attend Billingsley Academy. This school went all the way through the grades and high school. It was founded and operated by the Northern Presbyterian Church as a means of providing some educational opportunity to Negroes. It was housed in a single two-story building made of wood. Reverend Dockery, who was the principal, lived in part of the upper floor with his family, and classrooms occupied the other portion of the structure. No boarding students were kept.

Mr. Lon Colbert ran a barber shop for white trade on South Center Street. I was to go there in the afternoons after school and on Saturdays, so he could continue my instruction in the barber trade. As I was ambitious to learn and to increase my earning power, these plans were most agreeable to me, and I looked forward to the time in the fall when I was to go and take up my studies again.

As previously noted the public school for white children in Davidson went through high school. And a very excellent school it was, too. But for Negroes, there was only a poor seventh grade schooling available. This difference in provision for learning according to race was well fixed and rigid. Once through the seventh grade, additional learning opportunity for Negroes was very inconvenient and involved expense their parents could ill afford, since it required staying away from home in another town and paying for board and room.

This was the reality of the situation. So in September 1920, with my belongings in a suitcase, Mama and I boarded the train for the twenty-mile ride to Statesville. I think I saw the first aeroplane in flight that day that I had ever seen. It flew along at some distance to the right of the train and in the same direction for several minutes. I watched it out the window with a great deal of curiosity and excitement.

In Statesville, we stopped first at Mr. Colbert's barber shop, as it was only three or four doors from the station. A short, copper-colored man with a little mustache, Mr. Colbert had a pleasant manner along with a certain firmness in the tone of his voice. He showed me about the shop, which had three barber chairs, and introduced me to his son, Walker, who was also a barber. From there, we went a few doors down the street to Mr. Chambers' office. Mr. Chambers was a tall, thin, light-skinned man with a very pleasant personality. He was an acquaintance of Mama's and had made room and board arrangements for me at the home of a widow lady who lived nearby.

The house was old and the room seemed dismal, without provision for heat, but Mrs. Woods was a pleasant person, and, as Mr. Chambers told Mama, her home was a proper place for me to stay, since I would have the benefit of her supervision.

Then we went to the school to see Reverend Dockery. He was the principal, and Mama paid my tuition two weeks in advance. This amounted to thirty cents, it being fifteen cents a week, payable if possible at the beginning of the week when it would come due. He explained that, since the standard of his school was higher than that of the public schools, I would have to repeat the seventh grade in order to bring me up to that level. This was a disappointment to me, as I was already sixteen years old.

At school, I was surprised at the large classrooms and the number of them. There was also a separate place for morning assembly, where one of the teachers read from the Bible. At home we had never had more than one room and one teacher. Here there were several of each; everything seemed better organized and, as I found out later, more conducive to learning.

I liked this school from the start. The students were friendly and helpful. I found none of the meanness I had encountered in our home school. At recess time, we played volleyball, and there was a tennis net and a place for baseball. Volleyball and tennis were new to me. They said nothing about playing shinny, and I assumed they were not acquainted with the game. I did not introduce it to them. We all got along well together, and I enjoyed going there except for one thing. On Friday afternoons each one had to recite a speech.

I got along well with my studies, but the Friday afternoon recitation filled me with fear, after my first frightful experience as a young child, reciting the Beatitudes in Miss Duscah Harris' Sunday School class. I had subsequently committed to memory and recited the Ten Commandments and The Twenty-third Psalm. But they were terrifying experiences, when I sat and waited my time to perform as if I were about to receive some severe punishment. I believe this was a great fear of failure, which I could not bear.

After a few weeks of the torture of reciting a speech each Friday, I devised a plan which was to get me excused from this activity. I told at the school that I wanted to leave there at noon on Fridays in order to get in more work at the barber shop. This was true in every respect, because it was an advantage for me to get there earlier on Fridays, but it was not my real reason for wanting to leave early. It was known that I was working and using my earnings to pay my expenses, so I was thereafter not required to take part in the Friday afternoon program. However, Mr. Colbert didn't require me to come to work until after regular school hours.

On the second day at school, I was surprised to see Fred Allison on the grounds at recess time. Fred is the boy who

jumped from the window of our school in Davidson when
Fatback McCorkle went on a rampage of indiscriminate cor-
rective switching. It developed that he lived in Statesville and
had been visiting an aunt while he attended our school at
home. I was glad to see a familiar face, but no friendship
between us developed because I knew from past experience
that he was not much interested in learning anything and was
going to school only because he was being sent.

At the barber shop, I did better than I had expected. In the
shop with Cunningham at home, I was the shoeshine boy who
was trying to learn the barber trade when I wasn't shining
shoes. Here my status was that of a beginning barber, without
the stigma of being the shine boy to overcome. Customers
more readily got in my chair for work, and Mr. Colbert would
encourage them to give me a chance, saying that if my work
proved faulty he would straighten it out.

In 1920 barber shops were doing a large business in shaving.
The safety razor had hardly come into being and most men
had a shave once or twice a week at the barber shop, the
alternative being a self-scraping with a dull razor while standing
before a small mirror hanging on the kitchen wall. Mr. Colbert
was a good shaver and had many regular customers who would
not let anyone but "Lon" wait on them.

A young barber learning to shave is more afraid than the
customer who entrusts himself to the beginner. I was no
exception to this rule and approached a "hard shave" with
considerable apprehension and trembling of hand. Often when
a difficult customer decided to "give this boy a trial," Mr.
Colbert let me lather his face and put on a hot towel. Then he
came to my chair and did the actual shaving. While he shaved
my customer, I washed the lather from the face of the man he
had just shaved in his chair, combed his hair and let him out.
By this time, Mr. Colbert was finished shaving my customer,

and I could return to my chair and finish with him. Going from chair to chair in this manner was standard procedure in training a young barber. This was before going to barber school was required, and barbers learned their trade by working under an experienced man.

Circumstances sometimes intervened in this switch- about procedure, and I then found myself having to make out as best I could without help. One such distressing incident occurred when a shriveled old man sat down in my chair for a shave. His face was bony and angular, with a tight, thin, tender skin. And he had several days' growth of hard, wiry, gray beard. A difficult combination to manage.

I put him back in the chair and applied the lather, then a hot towel. While I was doing this, I discovered that he had an indentation in his right jawbone that looked as if it might have been made by a bullet. It was all grown over and healed, but there was beard growing on the skin down in this hole. All this was a fairly casual sizing-up of the situation, since I knew from the outset that this was no customer for me to tackle.

But now the hot towel I had put on was getting cold, and Mr. Colbert hadn't yet come over to do the actual shaving, so I put on another one. Then Mr. Colbert motioned me to go ahead with the shaving as he was cutting the hair of a special customer and couldn't leave him. I never knew whether he actually couldn't come to my aid, or whether he was acquainted with the difficulty of shaving the old man and was playing a devilish little joke on both of us. The matter was not mentioned between us afterwards. But my casual approach vanished in the shock of suddenly realizing that I had to shave the face there, with its eyes looking right at me. It set my hands to trembling and my heart to thumping.

Dutifully, I stropped my razor and started in to try to shave the old man. He was lying there in the barber chair with his eyes wide open, and I knew he was watching my every fearful, awkward movement. If he had just closed his eyes, I think I could have stood it better. But he didn't, and through the whole of that awful experience of my trying to get him shaved, he lay there and stared into my face.

I finally got all or most of the beard off, except that down in the hole in his jaw. Try as I did from every angle, I couldn't get the hair shaved out of that hole. Then I gave up, almost completely exhausted and trembling with fright. I washed his face and let him out of the chair. He paid the twenty cents and took a long, steady stare at me, as if he always wanted to remember what I looked like, before he turned and went out the door. I hadn't been there long when this happened, and I don't know whether he had ever been in the shop before or not. But I do know he never came back as long as I was there. If he had, I would have dropped everything and run out the back door. Mr. Colbert never mentioned this matter to me, and I never mentioned it to him. But after nearly fifty years, it is still a vivid memory.

Another time, one of Mr. Colbert's very special customers got in my chair for a shave because he was in a hurry and couldn't wait for his favorite barber. This was a wealthy old gentleman who still rode in his buggy. He had a fine car and a black man in uniform and cap to drive it but preferred the buggy for his personal use in getting around town. The black man in uniform and cap drove this also.

As was usual when he got a shave, he was hardly settled in the chair before he was asleep. I put on the lather and a hot towel; then Mr. Colbert came over and shaved him. This done, I washed his face and let him out. He stood there in the floor and rubbed his face with one hand, then the other. Mr. Colbert asked how I had done.

"Fairly well, Lon," he replied, "but nothing like as smooth as you do it."

After two weeks away, homesickness overcame me and I decided to go home one afternoon and return the next day. I went to the railway station and bought a ticket and took a seat in the Negro passenger section, which was the rear half of the baggage car. Railroading was a glamorous occupation in those days, and I, along with most of the residents of our home community, knew the names of the trainmen. They in turn knew many of the townspeople. Going to the depot at train time was a popular diversion, and at least mutual recognition acquaintances were established. Also, the railroad track ran along on the other side of the highway directly in front of our house. I had since childhood made a practice of waving to the crewmen and they waved to me.

So, when the train was in motion, it was no more than I expected when Captain Morrison, the conductor, came through the coach taking up tickets. Conductors were always called "captain" in those days. He recognized me and asked where I had been, saying he had missed seeing me lately. I explained that I was going to school in Statesville and trying to learn the barber trade in the afternoons and on Saturdays. Also, that I hoped to earn enough to pay my way in school. He was a rather abrupt man with the authoritative manner of a person of importance on the railroad. When he had finished punching my ticket, he left with a grunt and went about his business.

He was through the car several times during the twenty-mile trip, but he paid no attention to me. Then, as we were about to Davidson, he stopped at my seat, and asked when I was going back. I told him "tomorrow morning" on the nine o'clock train, his train. He looked steadily out the window while he told me whenever I got ready to come home or go back to school not to get a ticket but just get on the train, and he would see to it. With that he turned and walked away. Thereafter, when I rode the train he always spoke and asked how I was getting along, but he never said anything about a ticket. This was one of the many acts of kindness shown to me while I went to school in Statesville.

Mrs. Kate Golden ran a cafe two doors up the street from where I roomed. This was a popular gathering place for young people. It was an orderly place of good reputation, and I began going there after work in the evenings. Mrs. Golden's two daughters and I attended the same school, and we began studying together at night in the cafe. Most nights the girls' mother would fix hot chocolate and sandwiches and serve them to us while we got our lessons. This was a welcome thing to me because I had from the beginning supplemented my meals away from my boarding place because the food there was cooked with more grease than I wanted. Indeed, with more grease than I could eat. For some reason I have never been able to eat fats, finding it necessary to trim away even the smallest portion of it from meats. Fat grows big in my mouth and nauseates me.

I liked the way the food was fixed at the cafe and there was a variety to choose from, so I bought a food ticket and began taking all my meals there. This proved a most satisfactory arrangement for all concerned. At meal times when the cafe was full, I voluntarily helped with serving food and cleaning tables. After this went on a while, I noticed that Mrs. Golden didn't punch my ticket for the full price of my meals. When I mentioned this to her one day, she just handed the ticket back to me and said nothing.

Mr. Chambers, the man who ran the moving picture show, and Mr. Colbert, my boss at the barber shop, were good friends and liked to play a card game called "set back." They didn't find much time for playing together because Mr. Colbert was busy at the barber shop in the daytime and Mr. Chambers had to take care of his theater at night. I went to the show occasionally at night, and several times the boy who took up tickets at the door didn't come in. I filled in for him, and Mr. Chambers let me see the show free. One afternoon when I went to work after school, the two men were in the barber shop talking. Mr. Chambers asked me if I could take up tickets some nights at the show and also take the money from the ticket office and put it in the safe in his office next door. This was agreeable with me, so thereafter I did this quite often for him.

Mr. Chambers was a widower whose married daughter and her husband and two children lived in his home. After a few weeks of my working for him at the theater, he invited me to share a double bed with him at his home and take my breakfast there at no cost. He had a nice large room with a heater, and I was glad of this opportunity, especially so since my room at the Woods' had no heat, and the weather had gotten cold. They had provided me with a portable oil stove, but this proved unsatisfactory and dangerous. One cold morning I got up early and lit the stove and went back to bed while the room got a little heat in it. I must have dozed off, because I suddenly became aware that the room was full of smoke and I could hardly breathe. I got the side door open and threw the smoking stove into the yard where it exploded in a ball of fire and smoke.

After I moved in with Mr. Chambers, I considered that my personal circumstances in every respect were quite favorable. My grades were good at school. I had a comfortable room with a good hot breakfast in exchange for my services at the theater, more than half of my other meals in exchange for my help at the cafe, free transportation on the railroad when I went home, and my earnings at the barber shop were sufficient to pay all other expenses, including buying a new overcoat. In addition, I was able to give Mama a little money each week, which she needed.

My major concern now was how things were going at home. My mother, always a small, delicate woman, less than a hundred pounds in weight, had never been in robust health. Now she was under the doctor's care and didn't seem well at all. I had been away from home three months, and I could tell that I was needed there doing chores and being with Mama and Sister. Too, I knew that the income she was getting from the barber shop was not enough to provide for her and my sister, who was now nine years old and going to school.

Christmas vacation at the school began a week early and gave me an opportunity to spend the whole of those days at the barber shop and take advantage of the extra business due to the holiday season. The added earnings were needed at home, and the practice at barbering was useful to advance me in learning the trade. After a week at home between Christmas and New Year's, I returned to Statesville and immediately became involved again in my several activities. But it was not for long. In early March, the barber who was running Mama's barber shop suddenly became ill and left, going to his home in Charlotte. It appeared that he would not come back, as, at his age and in his condition, it seemed likely he would remain with his family.

This closed the shop and there was now no income at all coming to Mama. I persuaded her to let me come home and run the shop until her barber was able to return or she could get another man.

CHAPTER SEVEN

The Young Barber

Everything about the shop was old and run down. The fixtures were the ones that my father had, and they were fast becoming out-dated at his death in 1912. This was 1921, and styles of barber equipment had changed. The building that housed the shop was old and falling apart. The roof leaked, and the floor in the back room had fallen in where a sill had rotted out. Mama had no money to improve the fixtures, and the building's owner would not repair it.

The situation looked near hopeless even to me, an incurable optimist, sixteen years of age. But there it was, as it was. It was all I had, and it had to do. Somehow, I had to take this and earn a living for the three of us, Mama, Sister, and me. So I opened for business in these surroundings on the twenty-fourth of March, 1921.

The barber who had been there was not to come back, and I was on my own. I was by no means a finished barber, and there were many things that needed doing. When the first rain came, I discovered the leaky roof. It had not been leaking when I left in the fall. In the attic the cans and other containers that had been placed under leaks ran over and through the ceiling into the shop. Mr. Sloan said, if I wanted to repair it, I could do so at my own expense. This I did by buying some rolls of tarpaper roofing and having it put on. This stopped the leaks. Uncle Tobe's pressing club was still in the other side of the old building, and he gave me encouragement about going on with the shop, which I intended to do anyway. There was nothing else I could do.

Many of Cunningham's customers would not entrust themselves to my abilities as a barber. I had to do the best I could about getting patrons. There were some who let me wait on them, but many others still thought of me as the shoeshine boy and would not patronize me as a barber. I was very painstaking with the ones who would try me, though, and this gradually brought more customers for shaves, a major part of the business at that time. I was also gaining something of a reputation among the young fellows as a good haircutter. This soon brought boys and young men who wanted stylish haircuts to me for their work.

Shaving, however, was difficult for me to master. This was especially true concerning older men who had tough beards; as the custom was, they shaved only once or twice each week. With the young men who had few whiskers, I got along well and got more and more of that trade.

One hot day in summer, a great big man with a week's growth of heavy black beard on his face filled the door, and seeing me sitting idle by the shoeshine stand thought I was the shoeshine boy. All of those whiskers sent a chill of fear through me. When he asked where the barber was, I told him he was gone and wouldn't be back that day.

In the fall of that year I was successful in getting a young barber from Charlotte to come and help me. Preston was older than I was by seven or eight years. He had been working in a good shop in Charlotte and was real good at cutting hair. This was a great help to me as I could learn from him and have his assistance in the shop at the same time. He proved popular with the students at Davidson College and with the people in the community. Business in the shop picked up rapidly, and it soon became known as a place where good barber work could be had.

Preston was also something of a comic, and, while he did his very artistic haircuts, he kept the customers entertained with his wit and good humor. The good work of the shop and the lively humor did much to offset the poor equipment and the old building. By the end of the year, we were having fair success in our earnings. Haircuts were twenty-five cents and shaves fifteen cents. This made it necessary for us to do a considerable volume of business in order to have a little left for ourselves after expenses. We had become good friends, and Preston was rooming and boarding at our house, sharing my room with me. This gave my mother additional income and wasn't burdensome to her. At night, we entertained ourselves by playing Rook and listening to the phonograph.

I induced Mama to trade in the old out-of-style barber chairs for two second-hand ones of a later model, with hydraulic lifts which allowed them to be raised and lowered by pumping a lever at the side. This brought us more in line with current style and helped our image a little. Then we put linoleum on the plank floor and gave a fresh coat of paint to the wooden walls.

One morning a man with a heavy beard rushed in and got in Preston's chair for a shave, saying he was in a big hurry to catch the train to Charlotte. Preston was not too good at shaving heavy whiskers either, and having to do it real fast in a stressful situation was not being fair to him. He started in, however, with the man urging him to greater speed at the slightest pause. Quickly he had the stubble all off, except under the nose on the thick part of the lip. Poising his razor carefully, he made a quick stroke to remove this last cluster of hair and sent the blade into the flesh.

In one fast movement Preston put his razor on the work stand without closing it and caught up the styptic powder to try to stop the flow of blood. The customer raised himself up in the chair trying to see in the mirror how badly he had been cut. But blood was flowing in his mouth by now and he couldn't tell.

Blood flowed freely from the cut and washed away the powder as fast as it was applied. Preston was wiping it up with a towel and trying to stem the flow enough for the styptic to do its work. He was excited by now and a little frantic in his movements. Then his presence of mind returned and he caught up the lip between his first finger and thumb and by holding it firmly, cut off the blood from the wound. With a towel in the other hand, he got the blood from the customer's mouth and the surrounding area.

A plenteous amount of the yellow powder brought the final seepage under control, and Preston picked up the piece of flesh the size of a pea and pressed it firmly back into the place where it had been cut out of the lip. This was an unusual thing to do, but in the excitement it seemed the only thing to do with the hunk of meat lying there in the way on the bloody towel. Anyway, Preston certainly didn't want it. He was sweating as he raised his dazed customer to sitting position and discharged him from the chair. Some days later, we were told that the man was on the train halfway to Charlotte when the little chunk of his lip fell off into his hands. We lost that customer for good.

One of Preston's customers was Davidson College's star

track man of the season. He and Preston carried on a lot of fun together and one day after a meet, when the track star had easily defeated his opponent, Preston, as a joke, told him that anytime he wanted to race he'd show him that he could outrun him. On the face of it, this was a ridiculous statement, and the student should have taken it as he knew it was intended and let the matter stop right there. Instead, he kept urging Preston for a race and made a frolicsome issue of it among his fellow students, so that many of them knew about it and joined in the fun.

Preston was anything but an athlete. His belly was too big, his legs were too short, and he was somewhat splayfooted. Running at all seemed almost out of the question for him. One bright spring day he was standing on the sidewalk watching a group of students at play on the campus when the track star approached with a stick in his hand. In fun he made a lunge at Preston. Unexpectedly, Preston started running across the campus. The track man took up the chase and the race was on across the grass. The boys at play stopped to look, as did people walking along the sidewalk. In full view of perhaps twenty-five spectators, Preston outran the track star as neatly as anything you ever saw. This caused much laughter and good-natured teasing of the track man who was never quite able to understand how it was that a person as awkward as Preston could outrun him.

The railroad station in the 1920's was the focal point where much of the male population gathered at train time. Policeman J. A. Johnston took a dim view of this practice and in the long drawl characteristic of his speech, delivered himself of many caustic remarks on the subject, to the amusement of his hearers on Main Street. He often commented on a group of Negro youths who got together off to the side and made a lot of noise with loud talk and what Johnston called "squabbling."

One day this group remained on the yard after the train and the other spectators had gone and engaged in a minor melee, mostly noise and a few fist blows. Policeman Johnston was a regular attendant at the station at train time for no better reason than the others had. He was simply there to see the train go by. But he heard about this incident and seized on this chance to bring the law to bear on this group.

He had only one witness to the affair, one of the persons who was there but not engaged in the affray. Basing his case entirely on the proposed testimony of Sidney, the trial was held in the large ramshackle room that extended across the back of the building that housed my barber shop and Uncle Tobe's pressing club. There was no town hall.

Mayor Hamilton presided at this court. As was his custom, he was wearing his frock coat and hard collar with the little points turned down under his throat. A sparse man, clean-shaven and of long neck, he made an odd contrast in his formal attire to the tumble-down, rough-floored, unpainted, and windowless space where he sat in a worn, ladder-backed chair behind a wooden packing box which served as his desk. A goodly crowd, black and white, had assembled to hear the proceedings and for much the same reason that they went to the station at train time — they had nothing else to do, and there was a promise of some entertainment.

Policeman Johnston presented the case to His Honor by explaining what had gone on between the boys, as he had heard it, and begged to call his witness. Poor Sidney, the witness, a thin black boy with a clean-shaven head, was in a tough spot. He was told by the court to tell what he had seen that day. Now, on the one hand, he was afraid of what would happen to him if he failed to testify as Policeman Johnston expected and wanted. Then, if he did, there was the wrath of his friends to be confronted, And they had spoken to him on this subject.

He stood by the box when called and turned a confused facial expression in the direction of the stern and forbidding visage of the tall white policeman with the handlebar mustache. Then he brought his gaze to rest on the expressionless faces of the little knot of black defendants. He shuffled his feet and turned his face to the floor and announced under oath in a hardly audible voice that he hadn't seen anything at all that day in the station yard.

Policeman Johnston, eyes glaring in anger, confronted him and demanded that he tell the truth. But Sidney's eyes had consulted the faces of the black boys again, and he stuck to his story. The policeman then angrily told the court that the witness was the noisiest one of the group and should be punished for not telling the truth. After silent judicial consideration of the matter, His Honor levied a fine of six dollars on Sidney, the witness, and turned the others loose. The hapless witness had no money to pay his fine, so it was arranged as an act of kindness for him to pay it at two dollars a week until settled. Thus the scales of justice were balanced.

As if ordered to disturb the small but growing success of our barber business, it was announced that the old building that housed the barber shop and Uncle Tobe's pressing club would be torn down and new structures built on the site. The only vacant place available for us to move into was the last building on the south end of Main Street. The meat market that had occupied it had recently gone out of business. Mr. Withers, the owner, was willing enough for Uncle Tobe and me to move our shops there.

This brick building, containing a single open space, was a

great improvement over the old wooden shack that we were presently occupying, but it was out of the area on Main Street where most business was conducted. In the immediate vicinity of the old building were such businesses as the drug store, the cafe, shoe shop, a popular knick-knack and confectionery store and the post office. The Davidson College campus was just across the street. This generated a lot of foot traffic in the area from which our shop benefited. We were afraid moving into a location removed from the beaten path would be detrimental to our trade, but we had to go.

Before we moved, another incident having to do with the frustrations of Policeman Johnston happened. Commencement week at Davidson College at that time was full of many activities on the campus and attracted a large number of people. That year among the many visitors and fine cars were three automobiles so exactly alike in make and appearance that it was impossible to tell them apart. These were Hudson Speedsters, a popular make and style of the day. Each car was black, with a tan cloth top, a motor-meter at the radiator and red wire wheels.

About four o'clock on Friday afternoon when there were many college boys and their visiting girl friends stirring about the town showing off their pretty cars and fancy clothes, there was heard at the north end of Main Street a sudden roar in a cloud of dust bearing down hard on the business district along the street. It was a Hudson Speedster with the driver hunched low over the steering wheel. The car tore down the unpaved Main Street with mufflers blasting noise and a dense, swirling fog of dust following in the machine's wake.

The roaring noise and dust attracted people to the street side from the business places, and it wasn't long until the street was filled with curious people. This entire act was a direct insult to Officer Johnston, and he commandeered the town's taxi and gave chase to the culprit. Amid the dust and confusion and speed of the other car, he didn't have a chance to catch up. He had seen the car, though, and was sure he could identify it. So he came back and waited.

Thirty minutes later, one after the other, three identical Hudson Speedsters drove up in front of the drug store and parked, and none of the drivers nor passengers — none — could tell Officer Johnston anything at all about a car that had raced through the street.

Soon after this we moved to the new location. We erected a wall about four or five feet high to set a portion of the front of the room as the barber shop. The pressing club was in the rear. Our barber business wasn't as good at this location, but we had a good reputation for quality work, and soon business got better. Since I had been in the barber shop, I had, so far, been able to provide at home and do some needed repairs to the house.

Then Mr. Knox, a wealthy farmer, began making preparations for a new building farther up the street, and promised to rent me a space for the barber shop when it was completed. I had high hopes that our trade would improve in a better location. Uncle Tobe was also promised space in the new building; we would then be side-by-side neighbors as we had been in the old place. I had by now made a complete commitment to the barber shop, as there was no other employment I could get that would pay me a decent wage.

The work at the shop was exacting and tedious, and the hours were long, but it was not heavy or hard labor. We opened at eight in the mornings and kept open until eight at night, except on Saturdays when we worked until eleven o'clock at night. There was no afternoon or day off except Sunday. After the long hours of standing on Saturdays, I felt like spending most of the day in bed on Sunday.

A barber has always to work with great care and exactness with the sharp instruments of his trade in order not to mar his work or injure his patron. Because there is little room for error in his work, a certain tenseness is present as a result of being ever on guard against the slightest mistake in the deftness of his movements. This, together with standing in one place, can cause a bone-weary fatigue after a busy day around a barber chair. On Saturdays when most of the rural trade came to town we had the long hard grind of uninterrupted work. Other days were fairly light. But when business was light, my earnings were off in proportion, so I looked forward to the end of the week when business was good.

My mother's health was a constant concern now. She was under continuous treatment by the doctor, but unable to get relief from an illness that kept her weak and nervous. There was a feeling of great distress, without much pain, and she was unable to eat properly. Everything she ate seemed to disagree with her and to increase the tension and nervousness. Bills for the doctor and medicine were a constant drain on my small earnings.

I had not much time nor hardly any money for activities other than work. I had a girl friend who was attending Livingstone College at Salisbury which was thirty-five miles away. I went there occasionally to see her, and in summer, when she was at her home, was unable to see her much more often because she lived in another town and I had no means of transportation.

Our friendship was carried on largely through letters. But we were sweethearts, and I was devoted to her. During that summer, she visited in Davidson for a week in the home of an older married relative of mine, and we spent many pleasant hours together. I was greatly disappointed a few weeks later to hear that she had eloped and was married.

I was eighteen years old at the time and had no intention of getting married, but I did enjoy the sentiment of being in love with this pretty, witty girl. Her marriage left me with the feeling that she had not been honest with me, since she had not mentioned such an intention. Being a soft-hearted sentimentalist, I had kept all the letters she had written to me. Some of these I reread, then burned all of them. I hadn't realized fully that she was the one bright, joyful thing in my life. Everything else was a chore or a duty, or a hard reality of struggle against difficult odds.

Her marriage lasted about two years, and she was divorced and back in school. I had some letters from her, but my romantic interest in her was gone. Some years later, she married again. This marriage ended in divorce also. She went back home, and I saw her from time to time. We exchanged some friendly letters. Years later, she married again, and this time it lasted until her death. I sent flowers for her grave. Our friendship lasted through nearly fifty years. I always enjoyed her carefree, happy approach to life.

I had had an earlier experience in what I had come to regard as the treachery of the female. The year before I went to Statesville I had a crush on a pretty brown-skinned girl who was a year older than I. We went for walks together, and I was in love with her, too. One weekend, when I was home from school, I learned that she had run off to South Carolina and married. I was sorely disappointed in her for this because I thought her much too good for the fellow she married.

Two years later, she had one small child, and her belly was punched way out to here in a second pregnancy. She had a silly grin on her face, too.

During the spring of that year, a man who had spent some years in the Army and had attained the rank of sergeant decided at the end of his enlistment to come out of the service

and settle down, as he put it. He had recently married a young
lady in Davidson, so he decided to make his home here. Now
"Sergeant," as he was called, had earned for himself a
reputation as a hard-boiled soldier type, yet a good fellow and
very likable. He rented the building next door to the barber
shop and announced that he was going to open an ice cream
parlor, a type of business wholly out of character with the
sergeant's personality. He bought a Charlotte drug store's used
ice-cream-making equipment and busied himself with getting it
installed, having high hopes for the success of his venture. He
knew nothing of the business and arranged with a Negro man
who was a cook in a nearby boarding house to mix the
ingredients for his ice cream. He then employed a young white
man as his assistant in this enterprise. None of these people
knew anything about making ice cream or running a business,
but the idea seemed a good one to the sergeant.

The sergeant's progress was slow getting started. He
encountered many unexpected expenses and his capital
dwindled away. By midsummer, business was much improved.
He loaded his family in his new Maxwell and took off for
Virginia Beach, leaving his white assistant in charge. Provisions
had been made before his leaving for all needed supplies in his
absence, milk, ice, cookies and whatever else the business
should require. All of this was to be bought and charged to his
account. At the end of two weeks, Sergeant was back, tanned
and in high spirits. The vacation was just what he needed. He
was pleased to see that the usual amount of milk and other
supplies had been purchased, indicating that business had been
good while he was gone. There was some silver in the cash
drawer, amounting to a few dollars. This was as it should have
been; the paper money was not kept there. That night when he
asked his assistant for an accounting, the answer he got to
increasingly insistent questioning was always the same. The
money was in the drawer.

This went on for several days, with the answer always the same. Sergeant had gotten shrill by now, and the vocabulary he had acquired as a top sergeant was being put freely to use in his description of the affairs at hand. But the answer he got never changed.

Then his assistant got peeved at what he considered insinuations about his good name and quit. The ice cream parlor was closed that fall. For some years afterwards, any mention of this brought a far-off look to the sergeant's countenance.

In anticipation of moving into the new building Mr. Knox was going to build, although construction had not begun, I proposed to Mama that we enter into a partnership with the barber shop and buy new fixtures and have a modern up-to-date place of business. She was afraid the debt would prove too heavy a burden on me, if indeed we could arrange to buy the equipment on credit.

I had been buying the supplies needed in the shop from Connor & Walters Barber Supply house in Charlotte, and had made the acquaintance of Mr. Walters, a partner in the firm. He was a jovial, good-natured person, and I had talked with him from time to time when I was in the place. He always seemed interested in me and would inquire about my progress. The next time I was there, I went into the office to see Mr. Walters and told him about the proposed new building in a better location and asked him about buying new barber chairs, work stands with mirrors and other items I needed for a complete new outfitting of the business.

After we talked about this, he showed me through the catalog he had and helped select the type things I wanted. I was eighteen years old at the time and couldn't sign a legal contract. But he said he would let me have the things we had selected if Mama signed with me.

Mama came around to my way of thinking and agreed to the plan. Although the new building had not been started, we decided to buy the equipment and begin making payments so as to have as much of it paid as possible by the time the building was ready,

In the contract dated December 12, 1922, the following articles of equipment were purchased and the terms of payment noted:

1 only #413 - 3 Chair Mirror Case .... $ 240.00
2 only #372 Chairs #131
   Leather 510 Arms .... $ 304.00
1 only Boot Black Stand .... $ 24.00

Sub-Total .... $ 568.00
Allowance for 3 section Mirror
   Case and two Chairs .... $-125.00
                        Total Due .... $ 443.00

On which I or we have this day paid $160.00 and in addition I or we promise to pay to Connor & Walters Company, on order, balance of $283.00 in installments as follows:

Jan. 15, 1923	$23.50
Feb. 15, 1923	$23.50
Mar. 15, 1923	$23.50
April 15, 1923	$23.50
May 15, 1923	$23.50
June 15, 1923	$23.50
July 15, 1923	$23.50
Aug. 15, 1923	$23.50
Sept. 15, 1923	$23.50
Oct. 15, 1923	$23.50
Nov. 15, 1923	$23.50

Dec. 15, 1923 .... $24.50
A note or series of notes, bearing six per cent
interest per annum and conforming to above
agreement is hereby acknowledged.

Nowadays this seems a small matter, but then, in the year
1923, with haircuts at twenty-five cents and shaves fifteen
cents, it represented an obligation that was to put a severe
financial strain on me. The debt, together with normal home
expenses, Mama's ever mounting medical costs and things for
my sister, now twelve years old, called for very stringent money
management on my part. The payment represented ninety-four
haircuts or 150 shaves each month.

During the summer, construction work began on the new
building. Hope for better times in the future was about the
only thing I had to keep my spirits up during this period, and I
looked forward to the completion of the building when I could
move into it and hopefully improve my earnings. The new
equipment for the barber shop had been delivered and was
stored in the shipping crates in the part of our building where
Uncle Tobe had his pressing club. I had been making payments
on it every month since the first of the year.

Preston's mother was murdered that year, and that brought
much sadness to us. His sister, married but separated from her
husband, was living with her parents when the husband fired a
shotgun through the window one night and killed their mother.
This was a terrible tragedy in a nice family and Preston was
understandably very upset over it for a long time afterwards.
There was a trial during which the whole thing had to be
relived and recounted, making a very difficult time for the
family.

CHAPTER EIGHT

A Man's World

Late in the afternoon, towards the last of summer, Pa and Ma's house burned to the ground.

I have said nothing of them since Hood treated Mama so shabbily about my father's barber shop, and they had taken sides with him in his shameful conduct. Hood was married now, and a part of the Norton family went to live with him until they could get located again.

Rutledge and Janie came to stay with us. When he was discharged from the Army after World War I, Rutledge went into the shop Hood had established after he threw my mother's things into the street. There had been a strained relationship in the family since that episode, but Rutledge had not been here and taken an active part in it. While he had gone in with Hood, he had not maintained an arrogant, hostile attitude as Hood had consistently done. My father had taken Rutledge into his shop as a farm boy and taught him the barber trade. He in turn taught Hood before going into the Army during World War I.

Janie, Mama's younger sister, had always stayed some with

us, particularly at nights after my father's death. This arrangement continued until the early months of 1924 when Ma and Pa re-established their home on a farm they bought. This was nearer to us than the burned home had been. Mama's sister Tinnie had married and their family now lived next door to us. Members of Mama's family now occupied two of the houses near us. This contributed to a resumption of some of the original family relationships. Mama was sick and wanted her family about her, but I never cared much for any of them after the way they treated her about my father's barber shop.

Too, both Rutledge and Hood were now my bitter competitors in the barber business. When I came home from Statesville and went into Mama's shop, they had taken the attitude that I could never get much trade and were somewhat contemptuous of my efforts. But as time went on and my trade improved, they took a different view of the situation and began to resort to acts which were detrimental to all of us. One particularly harmful thing was their consistent refusal to join with me in raising the price of barber work. This made it difficult for me to get or keep a barber working for me, since prices in other towns were higher. Too, Davidson was a college town and this caused the business to fluctuate seasonally, with less business in summer than during the months when college was in session.

They were willing to hurt themselves in order to place me at a disadvantage. I knew this and redoubled my efforts to increase my trade. By doing much more work, I hoped to offset the disadvantage of low prices. In furtherance of their objective to make things hard for me, they had instituted a new low price for shaving. We depended heavily on our shave trade and when they sold tickets that allowed a customer ten shaves for a dollar instead of the regular price of fifteen cents each, they did a hurtful thing to our earnings.

They knew I was planning to move into a new location which was nearer to them and that I had bought new furnishings which would make our shop the more modern of the two. They thought I was in debt for my new equipment and figured that the reduction in the price of shaves would make it impossible for me to make payments and keep the business going.

As a matter of fact, at the end of that year all payments had been made on the barber shop equipment, which was still stored in the shipping crates in Uncle Tobe's pressing club. I had finished paying off my debt and was ready to move into the new building without any debt hanging over me.

On the other hand, I knew that both of them were in debt themselves. I reasoned that if they were both in debt and I wasn't, then I was in better position to make it hard for them than they for me. And since they wanted to play the game that way, then I would do what I could to counter their moves and at the same time improve my trade. My reaction to their reduction in the price of shaves was to issue tickets to Davidson College students giving them five haircuts for a dollar. This was an immediate success since it saved them five cents on the haircut. It was also an inducement for more of them to come to my out-of-the-way place of business. I was able, by this move, to keep my earnings at about their previous level by the increased business from the college boys, although I had to do more work.

The new building was not yet finished, but Mr. Knox had indicated to me the space where my barber shop was to be located. My hopes were high about this because work was progressing on the building and it would be only a matter of a short while now until I could move in. Free of the payments I had been making for the past twelve months, I could breathe a little easier except for one ominous circumstance, Mama's health.

The doctor said unless her condition improved in the near future, he was going to send her to the hospital for surgery. Going to surgery in 1924 was a frightful thing for anyone to contemplate. But for Negroes it was much worse, since provisions for our care were very poor. We were not allowed in the "white" hospitals as patients, and the places called hospitals that were available for our treatment were poor excuses for the needs of the sick.

The room where the barber shop was to be located was the first one to be completed in the new building. The people from the barber supply house came and installed the fixtures, and I moved in on the 24th of March, 1924.

With the purchase of a few additional items we had an up-to-date but not an elaborate barber shop. Everything except a few customer's waiting chairs was new, including the building. This was quite a step-up for me. The shop was attractive and excited much favorable comment as a fine addition to Main Street.

Too, I was now a full-fledged partner in the business, owning one-half interest.

Running water and sewerage were not yet available and a row of privies was built at the back of the building along the bank of a drainage ditch that carried away rain water from the street. These were the toilet facilities for the occupants of the brand-new building. Dr. George Withers, whose office was soon established upstairs at the back of the building, had windows that exposed his view to the row of open privies under them. Indeed, one of the privies was for his use. All of us got water from a pump in a vacant lot across the street among some trees.

Business increased at the new location. The Nortons, now hurting from my sale of haircut tickets, were soon anxious to abandon their reduced shave prices, if I would stop selling haircut tickets to the college boys. I had started this practice with the hope of attaining this result because the prices were too low before they instituted the cut-rate price for shaves. But since I knew they had started the low prices in the hope of starving me out of business, I pretended a lack of interest in their proposal that we both stop selling the cut-rate tickets, hoping this would be a lesson to them not to try such tactics again.

The doctor said my mother must have an operation. There was no hospital in Davidson. Her doctor sent his surgical patients to Long's Hospital in Statesville, which had a wide reputation for its good surgeons. They did surgery on Negro patients, but did not permit us to occupy rooms there. For this purpose they had a house in the Negro section of town where Negro patients were transferred immediately after they came out of the operating room.

The doctor said Mama had to stay there three weeks after surgery for treatment before she would be released to go home. The cost for this, including post-operative care was $124. There was no charge to Negro patients for surgery. This concession was said to have been made because the doctor who owned the hospital had been saved from drowning in his youth by a Negro man. I had saved $125 and felt fortunate indeed that I was able to pay the cost of her treatment.

No ambulance service was available. A friend consented to take my mother to the hospital in his car. On the appointed day, we made her as comfortable as possible in the rear seat and drove her there. While she was in the operating room, we sat outside and waited for whatever news we were to get. Finally she was brought out and put in the hospital's ambulance. We followed it to the house where Negro patients were hospitalized.

The only attendants there were the Negro man and his wife who lived in the house. There was no nurse to care for the Negro patients. The room where she was taken was furnished with an old white iron bed, a table and a chair. The bed clothes were not clean, and, when they put my still unconscious mother down, I felt a deep resentment for the treatment she was given and for what she could expect in this place. I thought she was not being treated as a human being, but as a despised thing. There were no better accommodations to be had and nothing could be done to improve the situation.

It was a helpless and a frustrating feeling. After three weeks there, she was able to come home again where we could give her better care than she got in that shameful, makeshift hospital.

My mother's health continued to improve, and the next year was an uneventful one. Business in the barber shop was quite good in the new location. I went on a three-day vacation, the first I had ever had and one of the few I was to take in fifty years.

Then Preston left me and went back to his home in Charlotte. He had never been the same after his mother was slain, and he wanted to be with his father and sisters. His going left me at a disadvantage in the shop. I was soon able to get another man, however, and carried on with him.

Uncle Tobe was prospering in his pressing club in the new location and had built a new house and bought a car, a Ford sedan. Then his health began to fail. Because he was only in his late thirties, his illness was thought to be a temporary condition. But he remained weak and said he felt sick all the time.

Then one Saturday someone hurried into the barber shop and said he had fallen to the floor in his pressing club. When I got next door to him, he was dead. Dr. Justice was there and had taken off his hat in respect to the dead. This was a polite consideration not usually shown Negroes.

Uncle Tobe was my favorite kinsman, next to Mama and my sister. We had been really close and his passing was a major loss to me. Always, I could rely on him for good counsel and encouragement. Besides he was a sincere friend and the one family member who had taken a supportive interest in all my striving to establish myself in the barber shop or in my personal welfare. I was sorry indeed when his son, four years my junior and until his father's death a very reliable person, showed no interest in the business. And despite my urging and offers to help him take hold and carry on, he came under other influences and, in a matter of three or four years, lost everything his father had accumulated during his very useful life.

In the summer months when college was not in session, business in the barber shop was reduced to a considerable extent. This worked a hardship on me because I had to depend for barbers on men I could get to come here from other towns where the seasonal change in business activity did not exist. Ordinarily, their earnings were about on a par with what they would be anywhere else when the college boys were here. But during the three-month period in summer when they were gone, the barbers became restless and dissatisfied with their lower earnings. Also our price structure was lower than other places and I couldn't get it raised because of my competitors, who were under the domination of influences at the college. I thought this situation could be remedied if my barbers were local people accustomed to the seasonal nature of business in the shop. I began to look about for prospects with this in mind.

My cousin, Ed Wilson, was pleased at the opportunity to come in with me if I would teach him the trade. Soon I took in

another young man and began training him too. Both of the
boys soon became popular with the shop's customers. And
while it was a tedious job training them, I thought it well
worthwhile for my own advantage. This also gave them a
chance to learn a trade with prospects of a steady job at better
than average pay for Negro men in other work available to
them. I was well pleased with Ed and Bernard and their
progress in learning the barber trade. They were enthusiastic
about their work as well as good friends.

One Sunday they, in company with three companions, drove
over to Hickory to spend the afternoon. About eleven o'clock
that night Ed and the other boys came to me and said that they
had stopped in Statesville on the way back from Hickory and
had some drinks and that Bernard had somehow gotten
separated from the group. They had looked for him, but were
unable to find him. As he had been drinking, they were
disturbed that he had just vanished from sight.

I went back to Statesville with them to see if we could find
him. Thinking perhaps he had been picked up by the police, we
went to headquarters and made inquiries. The police knew
nothing of him, and I asked them to be on the lookout for him
and to phone me at my home if they were able to locate him.
Then we looked around the town some more and came home.

By now, all of us felt that something really bad had
happened. At nearly three o'clock the next morning when we
returned to Davidson, we told his family of his disappearance.
They thought we had done everything that could be done for
the present, and that we must now just wait for developments.

The next day an engine crew sighted his body down a steep
embankment along the railroad fifteen miles east of Statesville.
It was never known how he got there. It was theorized that,
when he became separated from the others, he went finally to
the railroad station and boarded a train, thinking it was going

to Davidson, which is south of Statesville, and that, when he realized the train was going in the wrong direction, he somehow got the door open and fell out down the embankment.

Some people in Statesville with whom he was said to have been riding in a car that night were arrested, but they were never brought to trial. One circumstance was that there was no road near the spot where the body was found. This gave credence to the thought that he was on a train and fell from it.

I had retained my fondness for reading and was reading whatever books I could get. However, I had no access to any place where numbers of books were on display and there was an opportunity of browsing and making selections of reading material.

A small public library had recently been opened in Davidson. It was a large room upstairs in the building where the barber shop was located. I had wanted to go there and ask for books, but I knew that Negroes were not permitted the use of library facilities and had not gone for fear of being considered out of place and refused.

As if sensing my dilemma, which I had not mentioned to anyone, two young white friends of mine in the town came one day to the barber shop. During our conversation about other things, one of them mentioned casually that he was going upstairs to the library and get a book. I knew he had not much interest in bookish things but thought nothing of his remark until the other one said he, too, was going to get a book. Then they invited me to go with them and get something to read for myself. Both of them knew I liked to read.

I thought this a good time to go in company with them and see if I would be refused. None of us mentioned the known fact that it was against the rules to permit Negroes to use

library books. The front door of the barber shop was
immediately adjacent to the steps that led to the upstairs offices
and the library. The librarian, a friendly and courteous lady,
knew me and always spoke pleasantly in passing.

We entered the room and told her we had come to borrow
books. She very courteously explained to my white friends that
they could have books. Then she turned to me and in the same
courteous tone told me that she could not lend me a book,
because she was not permitted to lend books to colored
people.

This was a very humiliating moment for me. I had expected
to be refused. But when I was faced with the actuality of it, I
had a choking sensation in my throat and was unable to speak.
Then the thought came that, if I had come alone, at least I
would have been spared the agony of being refused in the
presence of my friends. I turned blindly to leave. The young
men with me mumbled something about coming back later,
and we left and came silently down the steps to the street.

Some days later, the lady librarian came into the barber shop
and explained that, while she could not allow me to come to
the library, she would bring books to me and let me read them,
if I would let her know the ones I wanted. I thanked her for
her very gracious kindness but never accepted the offer.
Something inside me took fire at the thought of my having to
be served in this manner. I had been made to feel that I was
less than human. I appreciated the fact that she was conscious
of the injustice and had taken the only means available to her
to correct it in my individual case. She, too, was caught up in
and dominated by a cruel and arbitrary rule that was rigidly
enforced against Negroes.

There had, a year or so past, developed in the town a
circumstance that on not infrequent occasion relieved the dull

tedium of Main Street. A new hard-surfaced highway had been completed between Statesville and Charlotte, a distance of some forty miles. Davidson was at the halfway distance between, and the highway was our Main Street down the middle of town.

This road now provided a convenient artery of traffic for the white whiskey-hauling bootleggers in high-powered cars who transported their wares from Wilkes County, the point of origin, to Charlotte, the point of ultimate consumption.

A police officer in Mooresville, also on the highway and seven miles to the north of us, had begun giving chase to some of these often heavily laden vehicles and their dare-devil drivers who depended on their own skill as drivers and the speed of their cars either to elude or outrun the pursuing officers of the law. This was an exciting and dangerous adventure for all participants.

Our little town then became a place of high drama when we were treated to the thrilling spectacle of a high-speed, open race down Main Street, with the policeman leaning out the side of the big Hudson firing a rifle at the tires of the fleeing bootlegger. Our own officer, Mr. Johnston, had much praise for the bravery and enterprise of Mr. Woodside, the Mooresville officer, for making an effort to put a stop to the liquor traffic on the highway. When one of these episodes occurred, Mr. Johnston always went after the speeding cars in a taxi to see if he could be of any assistance to his friend, Mr. Woodside.

(Neither town had police cars at the time. Mr. Woodside as well as Mr. Johnston depended on a taxi for transportation. Mr. Woodside's driver was a man named Kimmons who operated a big seven-passenger Hudson touring car in the taxi service at Mooresville.)

One lazy summer afternoon the quiet lethargy of Main

Street suddenly awakened to the raucous, straining noise of hard-driven engines. The sound was familiar, but this time the cars were closer together and there was a hard insistence in the driving that indicated the determined effort of the drivers, one to get away, the other to overtake.

They roared through the business district, the big Hudson, its cloth top billowing out in the wind, closely tracking the four-cylinder Essex as it rounded the bend in the street. Officer Johnston hastened to a taxi and was in quick pursuit. This time it seemed there would be a catch, and excitement ran high on the street. Soon word came back that the liquor-laden car had been caught, but there was no immediate word about the driver. A little later, it was said that the driver had been apprehended also, an unusual thing. Then there were quiet whisperings and talking in undertones. When the word reached me, I could hardly believe my ears. The low-voiced talk became louder, and the name of the driver was said so it could be heard.

Soon afterwards, Officer Johnston was back on the street, and he looked real grim and crestfallen. One of his friends approached and asked him the identity of the driver of the liquor car. Mr. Johnston looked him coldly in the eye and his voice trembled as he replied: "It was my son, Lewis Johnston. That's who it was."

The student at Davidson College whose electric iron Uncle Tobe had borrowed and burned out a few years ago was back again. He was now Dr. W. P. Cumming, professor of English. Friendship was re-established between us during his trips to the barber shop, and he began bringing me books to read. This was a great advantage to me because he made good selections of literature that I was not acquainted with, and he discussed the reading with me, giving me much background information about the authors and the books.

He also invited me to accompany him and another young professor on a trip to Europe one summer. I wanted very much to do this, but my circumstances would not permit me.

During one of our conversations, Dr. Cumming told me that the reading I was doing was a great help to me, but I should try to get some organized course of study to further my education.

I had become very conscious of my lack of knowledge and had been trying to make up in part for it by reading widely. The idea of an organized course of study appealed to me strongly. But where was I to get such instruction? This was about 1926. I was twenty-two years old and hadn't finished the seventh grade when I left school. Going back to school now was out of the question. I had to work and make a living.

However, I began searching in my mind for some way by which I could accomplish this. The thought came one day that I had seen somewhere an advertisement about getting courses of study through the mail. I began looking through magazines to find such an advertisement. I found one in the *American Magazine*. It was a new day of hope for me.

In about two weeks, I had an answer to my inquiry from the American School, Drexel Ave. at 58th Street, Chicago. I promptly enrolled for their high school course. This was the beginning of a period during which I studied intensively over the next ten years, always by correspondence courses.

I was soon to discover that this method of study was far different from going to school. The questions at the end of each lesson assignment had to be written up and sent to the school for correction and evaluation. This was a very good course, whose purpose was to provide a means of education to people like myself who wanted to remedy their educational deficiencies through home study. The study material and the questions were so organized that they required a high degree of concentration and attention to every detail of the subject. This necessitated a new form of discipline on my part. But I found the information I was gaining so fascinating that I enjoyed it thoroughly and didn't mind the application required.

My interest in learning was such that I found myself spending the time on my books when I was not actively working on customers in the barber shop. We worked in the shop until eight o'clock each evening except on Saturdays when we worked until eleven. After work hours, I studied at home and wrote up the assignments for mailing.

More and more of my spare time went into this, and soon practically all of my Sundays were spent that way, to the exclusion of going to church. I didn't care much for going to church anyway, and I thought studying a more profitable way to spend my time. This brought heavy censure from the church people and the preacher. I gradually discontinued my association with friends with whom I had been spending some of my time at nights and on Sundays. They regarded my behavior as being related to the success I was having in the barber shop, thinking the reason I didn't have time for them anymore was because I was getting "above" them, as they put it.

The truth was that our interests were not the same, and they could not understand why I preferred to stay home and study instead of enjoying myself with them. They had no understanding of the value I placed on learning. I, on the other hand, put no value on the things we had been doing together for pleasure or amusement. So we grew farther and farther apart, and, as time went on, our interests became more widely separated to the extent that, although we remained friends, we had not much in common.

They were content to drift with the tide, so to speak, and were not interested in putting effort into advancing themselves economically or educationally. I had ambitions in both directions. So, for the most part, I reduced all social activity to a minimum and gave practically every moment of my time to work or study.

I had always tried to save a part of my earnings, and, when a Building & Loan Association was organized, this seemed a good thing to join. Also, we needed to make repairs and build a room to our house, and I thought this a good way to finance the project. Mr. Hamilton, the man who had held court and fined witness Sidney a few years back, was in charge of the B&L. He was my customer in the barber shop and had talked to me in a general way about his high regard for the B&L.

My mind made up about this, I went to the office over the barber shop and said to Mr. Hamilton that I wanted to take some shares in the B&L. After what seemed like an embarrassed silence, he told me that the B&L had no provision in its charter for colored people, and that he couldn't issue shares to me. This was a stunning revelation. I had thought the B&L something like a bank and had not anticipated a refusal from this source on account of my race. He seemed very thoughtful, and I believe the man actually had never thought of this before. He said he would talk to the board of directors about it and let me know what they decided.

Later, Dr. J. Moore McConnell, a professor at Davidson College, who was a director in the B&L and one of my customers also, talked to me about the matter. I explained to him just what I had in mind about borrowing to do the needed work on our house. Then one day Mr. Hamilton informed me that, if I would come Saturday when the B&L office was open, whatever shares I wanted would be issued to me.

This was a pleasant surprise for I had decided that this, too, was closed to me. On Saturday I explained to Mr. Hamilton what I had in mind about the repairs and an addition to our

house. He said the purpose of the B&L was to encourage
people to own or to improve their homes, and they would help
me with my plan. I then subscribed to ten shares at twenty-five
cents a share per week, thus becoming the first Negro to join
the B&L in Davidson.

A contractor agreed to build a new room, plaster three
others, underpin with brick, paint and put a new shingle roof
on our house for one thousand dollars. This was in 1928. The
B&L loaned me the money and the work was done. My
payments were $3.66 a week for approximately six and one-
half years.

Our house was comfortable now, although we had no
running water or sewerage facilities. Business was quite good
at the barber shop, and I thought I could take on this added
expense. There was nothing to indicate that the Great
Depression was close at hand.

CHAPTER NINE

Friends and Neighbors

Small town barber shops traditionally are focal points for all sorts of information, with personalities and the doings of individuals being the subject of much conversation. I had a wide circle of friends and acquaintances, and we enjoyed discussing the peculiarities and peccadilloes of our mutual acquaintances. It seems, also, that Davidson had more than its share of odd-balls and eccentrics. Too, there were the incidents that occur between perfectly normal people, but are of interest because of the bizarre turn of events. These things were a vital part of my existence in Davidson and from time to time I shall try to let you live with me in some of them.

I had noticed that Ritch Heath, an aged Negro man, had for the past few weeks been going up the steps next to the front of the barber shop. These steps led to the second floor of the building, and I suspected that he was going up to see Dr. George Withers. Ritch had in years past worked on the farm owned by the Withers family, and he and "Dr. George," as he was called, were old friends. This time, Ritch had a health problem, and he was calling on the doctor for medical attention.

He was old now, was much overweight and puffed for breath upon exertion. Going up the stairs taxed his strength, and the doctor, when he knew Ritch was on the way up, would come out of his office and assist him up the stairs. The visit over, he helped Ritch back to the street level. This required considerable effort on the doctor's part, too, because he was overweight himself. As far as both of them were concerned, there was no thought of payment for medical services.

It was found that Ritch had dropsy and a heart condition. Dr. George prescribed medication and put him on a rigid diet. In the matter of the diet, Dr. George took great pains to explain just what to eat and what not to eat, how much and at what time, so that Ritch would be sure to understand that he was to lose weight. All of this attended to, the doctor helped Ritch down the stairs and told him to follow directions carefully and come back in two weeks.

At the end of two weeks, Ritch was back again. On the scales, it was found that he weighed three pounds more than when he was put on the diet. Dr. George didn't understand this and questioned Ritch closely about it.

"Now, Ritch, did you follow your diet like I told you?"

"Yessir, Doctor."

"How you been feelin'?"

"I been feelin' better."

"Did you take your medicine like I told you to?"

"Yessir. Just like you told me to."

"Then how in the hell is it that you weigh more now than when I put you on that diet?"

"I don't know that, Doctor, but I been eatin' my regular meals and then eatin' my diet just like you told me to do."

Late one night in winter, an insistent knocking at his door awakened Dr. George. He was told that an old woman who lived six miles away out near the river was sick and would he come? Complaining bitterly about night work, he dressed himself and set out in his Model T over the muddy road.

Once there, he sat at the fire and warmed himself. Then he examined and prescribed for his patient. She was quite old, and he didn't recall ever having treated her before. He was curious about this, and before leaving asked her many questions about her health. To every question, she gave a direct answer. Finally, he asked: "Have you ever been bed-ridden before?"

The old lady gave some thought to this and then quietly replied, "Oh, yes, Doctor, I been bed rid' before, and several times in a buggy."

Once in the spring, when the election for mayor and the board of aldermen was held, politics reared its ugly head in our midst. Mr. J. Lee Sloan, a prominent citizen, had been mayor of the town for several years. Dr. Zachariah King Justice, who practiced medicine, dentistry, and law in his office over the bank, had this year announced his candidacy for the office of mayor, "at the urging of friends." Dr. Justice, considered by many a little queer in his ways, didn't have a large practice in any of his professions, so he was for the first time extending his talents into politics.

He and policeman Johnston had some things in common. Each had a distinct manner of speech that set their voices apart from each other and from every one else. Dr. Justice had something of a left-over North Carolina mountaineer twang in his voice, while Mr. Johnston, whose manner of speech was widely mocked behind his back, had a long, soft drawl that was decidedly his own. It is impossible to describe, but once heard the memory was likely to remain because it was so unlike any other voice. They shared a fondness for corn whiskey, but never drank together; the doctor considered himself a cut above the policeman socially.

As soon as Dr. Justice announced his candidacy for the office of mayor, Mr. Johnston began actively politicking for the incumbent Mr. Sloan. He made quite an issue of it, and was really the only one who had anything much to say on the matter, since it was relatively unimportant to most which one was elected. But Mr. Johnston became increasingly vocal on the subject as time for voting drew near. Dr. Justice had become aware of this activity and had made some statements concerning getting a new policeman for the town when he was elected. Davidson had only one policeman.

Enmity grew up between the men, although on the surface they spoke politely when they encountered each other. On these occasions, each was strictly on his dignity. But as time went by and the election became imminent, tension grew between them. There was more conversation on the street about the relationship between these two men than about the election, as they had openly begun to say things about each other. Speculation was rife as to what would happen if Dr. Justice were to win. Mr. Johnston had been policeman for years, and was considered by many to have exclusive rights to the job by reason of long possession. But if Dr. Justice were to become mayor, Mr. Johnston might just find himself unbadged, so to speak.

The election was held in May. Policeman Johnston's elation over what he termed his success in defeating Dr. Justice was such that at every opportunity he managed to introduce the subject into his conversation, always pointing out that it was due to his efforts that Mr. Sloan was victorious and that Dr. Justice had lost. The doctor regarded this with dignified contempt, but it was evident that he had developed an active tempt, but it was evident that he had developed an active dislike for the policeman. This state of affairs continued all summer, and the ever-growing enmity between the two men was now a subject of amused conversation up and down the length of Main Street in the business places. It was known that both of these men were strong-willed characters, and there was something of a grinning expectation of what would arise out of this relationship.

One day late in summer, Mr. Johnston came into the barber shop with a more than usual glum and thoughtful look on his face. From past experience I had learned that in such circumstances it was best to wait until he was ready to talk about whatever it was on his mind and not to ask questions. Every day for several days he came in and sat and stared into space with an air of injured innocence. This was habitual behavior when he was mad or displeased about something. I knew the signs and let him initiate all conversation, knowing that before long he would let go and tell what was troubling him.

Then he told me what it was. He had a toothache. Due to the amusing possibilities inherent in his trouble, I almost laughed in his face, but caught myself in time not to incur his ire. I knew as well as he did that Dr. Justice was the only dentist in town. Both of us knew of the grim and uninviting prospect of his seeking dental care from that direction.

I was not the only one Mr. Johnston told about his toothache that day, and pretty soon it was the main topic of gleeful comment on the street. All at once, everybody seemed to know about it, and their minds ran to the eventual outcome of this new development. It offered possibilities.

Each day, Mr. Johnston was now answering all questions about his tooth with a lengthy and profane discourse on the torments he was undergoing with the aching in his jaw. If no

questions were asked, he gave the account anyway. These
revelations evoked no sympathy from his hearers, although all
pretended a great distress at his sufferings. Nobody was glad
because of his affliction and the hurting he was enduring,
because most people had a fondness for him. But the comedy
of the situation in which he found himself was overwhelming
as reports went from mouth to mouth in the daily talk on the
progress of this toothache. Comment on the weather ceased,
as all attention was focused on the progress of Mr. Johnston's
toothache.

A knot arose on the side of Mr. Johnston's face, and his eyes
were red and bleary after a matter of ten days had gone by. He
had on one or two occasions during that time been noticeably
under the influence of corn whiskey. All of this contributed to
the mounting glee on everybody's part except Mr. Johnston's.
He was now a very somber person. There was no longer joy in
winning the election. Gloom and despair were evident in his
countenance. When he sat, his hand shielded carefully the knot
on his face, as if he were fearful it might explode if touched or
shaken.

Then one morning, in a voice as if from the tomb, he
announced that he had been up to Mooresville the day before
to have his tooth pulled, but found that Dr. Voils was out of
town and wouldn't be back for two weeks. "I can't stand this
aching anymore," he said. "I haven't had a wink of sleep in a
week." Then he added what I knew he had been thinking
about. "Ole Justice," he said, "has been mad at me since the
election, and he'd try to kill me if I went to him." I felt sorry
for him this time because he was in agony and afraid, even if
he wouldn't admit the fear.

I didn't see him again until the next afternoon when he
came in and sat down very carefully, so as not to jostle his
head. The knot was still on the side of his face, his eyes were

red and there was a strong odor of what he had been drinking on his breath. In as sympathetic a tone as I could muster, I asked about his toothache.

He sat silent a minute before a strange-sounding, hollowed-out voice replied, "It's out."

"Out?" I asked in surprise.

"Yes, it's out. I couldn't stand it any longer, and even if old Justice was mad at me, I had to go to him." I kept quiet and waited for more details. "When I went upstairs to his office yesterday afternoon, he looked at me like I was a bear and wanted to know what I wanted there. I spoke as nice as I could to him, because, like I said, he's been mad at me ever since Mr. Sloan beat him in the election. I told him I had an old tooth that was about to kill me, which he could tell by the way my jaw was swelled up. He growled something under his breath and told me in his meanest, hatefulest way to 'set down in the chair there and let me look at it.'

"I set down in the chair and opened my mouth. My jaw was so sore it hurt when I opened my mouth. He looked in and put his old dirty finger around my gum and grunted. I knew he was going to get even with me for working against him in the election.

"He probed around with his finger some, and then reached for the biggest pair of forceps he had, without putting any medicine at all in my jaw to kill the pain. I shut my eyes, and he started pulling and snatching and twisting on that sore tooth until I thought I was gong to die. But I sat there like a man and didn't make a sound. After he had gouged and tore at me for what seemed like an hour, he stood back with that hateful sneer on his face and told me it was out.

"I was hurting so bad I was sick, but I couldn't let him know how bad he had hurt me. I sat there a minute or more till I got my breath and felt a little better, then I told him to pull that

other one right there next to the one he had just pulled. And I
sat there and let him snatch it out too. Hell, I wasn't going to
let him get away with me."

Our family had a very real reason to appreciate Dr. Justice's
knowledge and ability in spite of his very unique ways. On an
occasion Pa was diagnosed by another doctor as the victim of
a stroke. Afterward he was confined to his bed unable to walk.
One day at the barber shop Dr. Justice told me to tell Pa that
he'd been thinking about his case and he felt he knew what was
the matter with him. "Tell him I'm coming to see him this
evening."

When he arrived, Dr. Justice pulled my Pa's leg from under
the covers and to the side of the bed. He examined it carefully
for quite a while, then he gave it a sudden hard yank and
special twist. Pa yelled out from the pain, but got up and
walked for the rest of his life with no further such trouble. Dr.
Justice said he figured the problem was a pinched nerve in the
hip joint. His fee for the night's work? No charge!

The national election was coming up in the fall of 1928. I
decided it was time for me to start voting. By November 2nd,
the date of the election, I would be a little past twenty-four
years old. I was old enough, according to the age requirement,
and the decision to vote may seem commonplace enough. But
there was not one single Negro registered to vote in the town
of Davidson, and not more than a bare few in the entire
county.

At that time, Negroes were kept away from the polls in the
South by one expedient or another. A common practice was to
deny registration after subjecting the applicant to "tests" as to
whether he could read and correctly interpret a section of the
Constitution. This "test" was not required of white applicants

to register, it being presumed that if a person were white, then he was sufficiently educated and intelligent to exercise the ballot.

The presumption, as far as Negroes were concerned, was just the opposite. They were each regularly forced to satisfy the registration officer of their "competence." This could and did have the effect of Negro college graduates being disqualified by registration officials who, themselves, were unable to read the Constitution, let alone interpret it. The official simply passed a copy of the document to the Negro who was brash enough to present himself for registration and pointed to any part of the writing and demanded that it be read and its meaning explained. "Explained" meant to the satisfaction of the person conducting the "test."

After the test was failed, and this was practically always true, it was made known in the community of the Negro's residence that so-and-so had tried to register to vote. This exposed him to reprisals by elements in the white community. If the Negro happened to be one who was well liked or useful, he was "spoken to" by one or several white persons who "had his best interests at heart." Since most Negroes worked for white people, a word from his boss was generally all that was necessary to stifle any ambitions to participate in political activity.

When these measures were insufficient to dissuade him, stronger medicine was often prescribed. If he were a tenant farmer, he could be driven off the farm where he was, at best, barely grubbing a subsistence-level maintenance for his family. Credit could be denied him at the store where he bought provisions to last from one crop year to the next. He could be fired from his job and put on an unofficial black list that would effectively keep him from getting or keeping a job. Or there was an actual threat to his personal safety. It was not uncommon in some circumstances for Negroes to be beaten and even killed by mobs of whites.

I was aware of this climate of thought about Negroes voting. However, I discounted the severity of its application in Davidson. I had been told also, by some of the older white people, that my father had voted regularly, and I had never heard them speak of his voting in a disapproving manner. But my father had been dead since 1912, sixteen years before this time, and new elements had arisen and come into control and were now exerting their influence. My mind kept returning to the stark fact that no Negroes were registered to vote in the town. The matter was so well settled that it was not even discussed as a possibility. There didn't seem to be the remotest likelihood that one would so far forget himself as to try to invade this sacred and exclusive province of the white man.

I turned all of this over in my mind, and I was disturbed by the ominous chance inherent in my trying to exercise what seemed to me the right of a free man to vote in a presidential election. It did not seem right that here in America a person should be afraid to cast a ballot in the choice of a public official. Yet, all the evidence pointed to the hazard of my attempting to do that. Running a barber shop for white patrons, as I did, placed me in a vulnerable situation economically. Aside from that, it was not good to be known as a "smart nigger."

I wanted the friendship and goodwill of everybody in the community. Still, I thought it unfair for them to demand of me that I not exercise the rights of a citizen in order to receive their approval. The more I thought of all these things, the greater was the fear and conflict that arose in me. I knew that if worst came to worst, I would be abandoned by everyone, white and Negro alike.

The whites would forsake me in answer to the universally accepted credence that a Negro must be kept in his place. Part of their action would be dictated by hidebound conformity to the mores and behavior patterns enshrined in their lives above the consideration of human rights and dignity. Part would be in answer to their identification with the white race as the master race, which could suffer no incursion or menace, however irrationally conceived, from one assigned unalterably to a position of inferiority, servility, disgrace, and dishonor.

There was the part that fear would play in their actions. While they must instill fear to bend me to their wills, they were imposing this fear on me because of the great and consuming terror that lay slumbering in their hearts and was continually gnawing at their innards.

I was acutely conscious of the fact that, if for whatever reason, sentiment turned against me for trying to vote — and it was very likely to do so — I was in a very precarious position. First, I thought of the consequences to my little business, which depended wholly on the patronage of white people. It could just fade away without explanation, leaving me without a means of earning a living. Once the mark of censure and disapproval was on me, it would be difficult for my business to survive. Or, it could result in some other hostile act towards me.

The more I thought on all of these things, the greater the tension grew in my chest. Somehow I couldn't dismiss the whole thing from my mind and go along with the pattern other Negroes followed of humble acquiescence and keeping the relationship unruffled. It might be remarked here, in passing, that wherever in the South it was said that a community had "good race relations," it was based firmly on the docile submission of Negroes to the authority and acknowledged mastery of the white people.

The idea of voting wouldn't go away. It was as if I were in the grasp of some unrelenting force that compelled me to go

in this direction. So, I went one day the few steps down the
street into Mr. Walter Henderson's jewelry store to present
myself for registration. This was the registration place and he
was the registrar. So great was my tension that my heart was
pounding, and it seemed that my chest was full almost to the
bursting point. I knew the worst he could do was to embarrass,
refuse, and rebuke me. The other would come later, and I was
extremely aware of the dire consequences that could result to
me from this course of action.

Mr. Henderson, a kindly disposed man, knew me well. He
looked up from the watch he was repairing and spoke pleasantly as I entered. Then he asked what he could do for me. I,
with the little breath I had left, said that I had come to register
to vote. He continued with what he was doing for a minute or
more in silence. Then, abruptly, he put down the watch and
walked the length of the store and reached under the counter
which separated us and brought into view a large ledger and
opened it on the smooth surface of the counter.

"Can you read the Constitution?" he asked.

"Yessir," I was able to mumble.

"What party do you want to affiliate with?"

"I would like to register as an Independent."

For the next minute or so, he was busy writing in the ledger.

Then he said, "All right," and closed the book and put it
back where he had gotten it from under the counter. He was
courteous throughout the procedure. I thanked him and went
back to the barber shop, which was only two doors away, with a
great uneasiness in my mind. Yet there was, too, some feeling
of elation. I had milked a bear! But what would the result of
my action mean to me later? Several days went by, and I heard
nothing. The days lengthened into weeks and everything was
just as it had been before.

Then, Policeman Johnston came into the barber shop to sit

and talk a while one day. There was nothing unusual about this. It was his custom to come in and discuss events and happenings of the day. On this particular day, he seemed in a more than usual good humor. Finally, he came around to saying he had noticed that I had registered to vote. It was no surprise to me that he knew it. One reason was his interest in politics. It was regular procedure for interested persons to keep up with new registrants, so as to contact them and ask their support of certain candidates for office.

But I had a feeling he had other interests in me and my registration to vote. He had always been friendly towards me, and I wondered what his approach would be. Then he began to talk on the matter. He advised me in the kindest manner and most confidential way that he had thought about this and was sure I would be making a mistake to vote in the election. He went on to point out that many people might not like it, and that this could be hurtful to my business. His mood and disposition seemed entirely that of an older man giving what he considered good advice to a younger friend. I listened attentively and politely to his very true words. And resented bitterly every one of them.

It was not his telling me that I resented. I had the feeling he was sincere in his advice and wasn't trying to intimidate me. What he said was true in every respect. But giving him the benefit of every doubt, he had thought it not in my best interest to cast a ballot in the election. I was unwilling and ashamed to accept the idea that I was so far removed in worth from other men that I had no right to have a part in choosing an elected official.

On election day, I went and voted for Herbert Hoover. It was a most uneventful occasion, other than that I was in mental turmoil. Nothing was said to me about it, except that in conversation, politics were more freely discussed with me. Two

years later, in the election for state officials, Policeman
Johnston came to me and asked for my vote in support of a
candidate in whose election he was interested. Thereafter, my
vote was regularly solicited by candidates and poll workers at
election time.

For many years, I was the only Negro voter in Davidson, as
my father had been a regular voter during his lifetime. If there
was opposition to this, I was not made aware of it.

The high school course I was studying by correspondence
was occupying practically all of my spare time, both at work
and after hours. And although it taxed me at times to
understand some of the subject matter, I felt that I was making
some progress in dispelling the shroud of ignorance that
engulfed me. I looked upon this as an avenue to learning, not a
distasteful chore. It was an opportunity to find out about the
things in the world about me, about people and language. This,
to me, was the means to knowledge, communication and
understanding. I was certain that the most desirable things in
life were attained through the proper use of these things. Now
that I had found a way to acquire at least a smidgen of the
things that exist in the fairyland of the mind, I had no
intention of being distracted from it.

There were many influences to lure me away from my quest
for education, not the least of which was the sheer physical
weariness from long hours of work in the barber shop. I was a
young man, too, and I hungered for association with people of
my own age. The gregarious impulse had to be satisfied with
my customers while I cut their hair. This I enjoyed, but it was
not the same thing as social intermingling with people of both
sexes out of the atmosphere of the workaday world. Being a
Negro, I was not a part of the world in which my white
patrons lived. Theirs were lives set apart from mine, however

kind and considerate they were on many occasions.

But I was tired now, and needed a break from a life that consisted of almost nothing but work and study. So I was receptive to the idea of a vacation.

CHAPTER TEN

A Journey
North

One Sunday night in the early part of the summer of 1930, I was sitting on a stool at the counter of a restaurant on Second Street in Charlotte eating a sandwich. I paid no attention when someone occupied the vacant seat beside me. But when I turned my head, I looked right into the smiling face of Rex Wellman. We expressed mutual pleasure and a little surprise at coming upon each other at that place and at that hour. It was past ten o'clock. I lived twenty miles to the north, and Rex lived nearly forty miles to the west of Charlotte, so it was a little bit of an odd coincidence that we should meet there.

Rex lived at the foot of Crowder Mountain with his parents when I first met him. They lived just off the campus of Lincoln Academy, a small boarding school maintained for Negroes by the northern Congregational Church. I had met him on visits to the school and through the family of the wife of my uncle Rutledge.

During the course of our conversation, he told me that he

was planning a trip up to Massachusetts to bring his wife and
their young son home, and asked if I would go with him. His
wife was a native of Massachusetts. She was visiting her
mother there.

I had never been to New England and the idea of going
with him was very appealing to me. This was a chance for a
nice vacation. So, after further discussion of the proposed trip,
I accepted his invitation.

Back home, I made preparations for the day when we were
to start on the trip in his car. We were to leave on Sunday
morning two weeks later. Everything about this proposed
holiday seemed just what I wanted to do. And I was very
grateful for the opportunity of having someone like Rex to go
with and to have the advantage of being with a family in the
area when we arrived.

I was in very great need of some pleasant diversion in an
unaccustomed setting. For the past three years I had been
committed to a rigid discipline which allowed me hardly
anything except work and study, winter and summer, twelve
months in the year. I was tired and in low spirits. It seemed
that however hard I tried, and whatever personal sacrifices I
made to advance myself, measurable progress moved at a
snail's pace, continually demanding more achievement than I
was able to produce, a frustrating existence and one conducive
to restless anxiety.

About mid-morning on the Sunday appointed for our
departure, a decrepit vehicle came to a shuddering halt in our
driveway. It was Rex and he was ready to go, after explaining
that he was late because the Ford wouldn't start that morning,
and he had had to replace the battery. We hadn't discussed the
condition of his transportation when I agreed to go with him.
I had assumed that it was in good running order and safe. But,
without close examination, what I saw standing in the yard as a

means of getting us all the way from North Carolina to
Massachusetts and back left me with misgivings and doubts. I
thought of backing out and not going. But, then, I was all
ready and I wanted to go.

We loaded my bags in the rear seat along with his and got
set to go. This was one of the first models of the Ford after
the "T." It was also the first model with the gearshift lever in
the floor. Rex started the engine and shifted into reverse to
back out of the yard into the highway. When he engaged the
clutch, there ensued a palsied shaking of everything, including
us, accompanied with grabbing and groaning noises emitting
from the bowels of this thing we were sitting in. Then, with a
thump and a bump from down there somewhere, it took hold
with a snatch, and we were moving backwards into the road.

The same procedure got us moving forward and we were on
our way. Rex made no comment on the mechanical tone of his
car and I, being his guest, offered none. (Even so, it was better
than I had. I didn't even have a bicycle.) His only observation
was, as we talked animatedly of pleasant prospects, that we
could take our time since we were in no hurry. I thought this
seemed a wise precaution. Then he settled her into a steady-
forty-mile-an-hour gait.

Among other things that I noticed as I took a more careful
and painstaking view of the craft in which we were riding was
that the gas gauge was standing near the "E." This was of
fairly immediate concern because we had already passed
through Mooresville, and the next town of any size where we
could get gas on Sunday was Salisbury, twenty-two miles across
country. He re-assured me there was no cause for worry on
that score, saying there was plenty of gas to last. He added as
an afterthought that the gas gauge wasn't working properly.

Near Salisbury, a roadside gas pump was in operation and
Rex pulled in. We had agreed to go 50-50 on gas and oil for

the trip, so I thought I would get the first fill-up here, then we could alternate the buying as we went along. Rex, in his good-natured way, would have none of that. He insisted on making the first purchase, getting out of the car to superintend the operation. The gas pump was the old-fashioned kind with a five-gallon glass container at the top into which gasoline was pumped by hand, then drained into the car through the hose with a nozzle on the end.

The gas tank on this model Ford was just in front of the windshield, and from where I sat the amount of gas pumped up was in plain view. It went up to the two-gallon mark; then the attendant let it run into the car and replaced the tank cap. Rex paid him and got back in and wrote the amount and cost in his notebook. I said nothing, but made a mental note that this was certainly not too much gas to buy on a trip that, there and back, could run close to two thousand miles. I wondered if the gas tank leaked above maybe the three-gallon level.

This transaction completed, we again took to the road, with much pleasant conversation on this hot July day. I had resolved, however, that at the next stop, I would fill the gas tank full and stop the necessity of constant gas gauge watching. That is, if Rex said it was safe to do so.

We had both packed a lunch box abundantly full of fried chicken, sandwiches, boiled eggs, peanut butter, pickles, etc., along with a one-gallon glass jug of water. There were two reasons for all of this. One was economy, the other necessity. But primarily our reason was that we had not much alternative. In 1930, it was most inconvenient, and sometimes almost impossible, for a Negro to buy prepared food from restaurants in the South. In some places, it was possible to go to the back door of a cafe and buy a sandwich. or even to go into the kitchen and eat a meal. But we were going into strange territory and didn't know where the places were that permitted this.

Too, we didn't care for this humiliation if it could be avoided. And there was the money angle. Neither of us had any to spare.

So we jogged along quite merrily, with stops for gas and oil. We ate from our lunch boxes as we rode along, sharing one with the other whatever we had. Throughout the day, Rex insisted on buying only two gallons of gasoline at a time, regardless of who was paying.

Over in the day, I relieved him at the wheel and immediately discovered some other hazards associated with riding in that car. In addition to the shuddering and thumping on starting off, the steering was so loose that the wheel turned a quarter of the way around before it took hold. I had noticed some peculiarities in Rex's manner of controlling the car, and I had observed that the steering seemed loose or unresponsive, but I was not prepared for what I found. The condition had probably developed gradually, and he had adjusted to it as it became progressively worse. He knew just the right touch to keep it in the road.

But with me, I felt that I had no control over the car. If I turned the wheel enough to make it take hold, the car veered in that direction. When I tried to correct it, the thing went too far in the other direction. I was certain we had been traveling much too fast at forty miles an hour.

Rex cautioned me to take it easy, and I would soon get the hang of keeping it in the road. He admitted that the steering was "a little loose" and advised me to "be careful of the brakes and to shift into low gear" when I wanted to stop.

As for the brakes, it was just about useless to push in on the pedal, except to hear the jangling sound of metal scraping against metal and to keep in practice. All of a sudden, I understood why Rex had that tired, haggard look on his face. Driving that car kept your guts in a knot.

But it was just as he said. With practice, you developed a feel for the thing and could keep the car in the road, and by shifting down into "low" you used the engine for brakes. Bringing the car to a stop and making even a slight change in direction at the same time required both a considerable knowledge of mechanics and a certain dexterity of movement.

As darkness came on and it seemed that we were to drive far into the night to reach Washington, D.C., Rex relented on his two-gallon rule, and we filled the tank. So far, I was having a wonderful time on my vacation, except for being a little tired and somewhat scared.

It was past two o'clock in the morning when we arrived at a taxi stand near the Capitol. We bought a half-pint of bootleg whiskey from a taxi driver and engaged him to lead us to Uncle Ernest's house. We did some driving around to get there. Then, while the taxi-man banged on the door, Rex and I drank the whiskey and gave him back the empty bottle.

Aunt Jenny and Uncle Ernest had been expecting us to spend the night with them. They thought we would have been there much earlier, and she was worried that something had happened on the road. If she had known what we were riding in, she would have been in shock. We got our things inside and left the car standing in the street. There was no concern about anybody stealing it.

And another thing, I knew Aunt Jenny was bitterly opposed to drinking under any circumstances. She must have been able to detect the fresh, strong aroma of what we had so recently consumed. But then again, there were conditions surrounding our mode of travel that Aunt Jenny was not acquainted with. And I was not about to explain these matters to her. She might have considered that we were riding in a death trap and insisted on curtailing my vacation.

We got a late start from Washington the next day, without

sending any postcards back home bearing the familiar legend, "Having a wonderful time, wish you were here." The next night was upon us by Philadelphia. In fact, it was near midnight when we got to Philadelphia. From a pay station telephone, I put in a long-distance call home and gave an animated account of our very pleasant vacation trip to that time. When I left the telephone booth, I saw a sight I had never seen before. I had heard of this, but I had never actually seen it. What I saw was a Negro policeman, all dressed in a blue uniform and swinging a billy-stick. For a fact, I was in Yankee territory. Back home, this was unthinkable.

Traffic was heavier in this area and we had to be extremely cautious with our car. Rex had a relative living in Newark, New Jersey. This was our next destination.

The road between Philadelphia and Newark was crowded with heavy trucks and cars moving at high speed in the night. Both of us were strangers to such traffic conditions. And considering the mechanical condition of the car, we were in real danger now. One large apparently heavily laden truck was traveling at a speed we thought we could maintain, so we fell in behind it and followed closely. A fog had come up now, and we were depending heavily on our sight of the rear of the truck for guidance.

During the night, we became aware of a car that passed and re-passed us repeatedly, always moving at high speed. It would pass going in the direction we were traveling. Then, in a few minutes, it would meet us going the other way. We became curious about its movements and watched for it.

We noticed, too, that since we had been trailing the big truck, the car seemed to meet and pass us more often. By now, the fog had gotten real bad and we were looking for a place to get off the road.

Presently, we got off into the yard of a large roadside eating establishment. We bought food and explained our problem to the friendly man behind the counter. He told us to drive the car up close to the side of the building, close the windows, lock the doors and go to sleep. He promised to wake us up when the fog lifted. We followed his kindly directive and later were awakened by his insistent tapping on the glass. The fog was all gone. He said that many of the trucks traveling the road at night were hauling illegal whiskey and that the car we saw repeatedly was probably operated by someone keeping an eye on some of them to prevent hijacking. It was probable, he said, that we were being watched when we trailed the big truck. We needed no such involvement as this to further complicate our travels.

Before daylight the next morning, we stopped in front of the apartment where Rex's relative lived in Newark and went to sleep in the car. It was near mid-morning when we woke up and went inside.

We got late starts from our stopovers. This was responsible in part for our having to drive at night, which increased our hazard. The driving condition of the car was growing steadily worse. The horn had stopped blowing, and I noticed before we left Washington that two of the tires were almost without tread.

In all fairness, it must be said that the Model A Ford was a wonderful little car. It just happened that this particular one had received extremely severe service on the narrow, steep, rock-strewn paths that served for roads around Crowder's Mountain. This, together with rough handling and lack of lubrication was sufficient to bring it to its present state of mechanical degeneration though it was only two years old. It was a 1928 model, but it had had a lot of rough usage.

We had hoped to reach Worcester, Massachusetts, early in the evening of that day. But, at twelve o'clock that night, we were stopped at a roadside service station and lodging place seven or eight miles from New Haven, Connecticut. A bulb had burned out in one of the headlights an hour or so earlier, and we had not been able to replace it at any of the stops we made. Headlights of that vintage had small bulbs that fitted into them. They didn't have one at this place either.

We must have been a dejected and worn-out looking pair as we bought more gas for the continuation of our one-light journey through the night. Some young white men, noticing the North Carolina license plate, had come up to engage us in conversation. Two of these who said they were Yale students talked to me about football teams in the South. Davidson College, which had North Carolina's championship team in 1926, was in my hometown, and I had some familiarity with this subject from hearing the teams and games discussed in the barber shop.

While we were talking, a lady seated at a screened window nearby called to me and said we looked tired and that we had better come inside and spend the balance of the night and go on the next day. She was apparently a person in some authority at the place, because she said they had a furnished room upstairs and that we were welcome to use it. A heavy-set person of about fifty, she was genuinely concerned about us and went on to say that we were several miles from New Haven and that beyond there the road to Worcester was extremely dangerous, with a particularly bad hairpin turn where several persons had been killed in motor mishaps. She added that we had no business on that road at night under the best of conditions, and certainly not with one headlight.

What the kindly lady didn't know was that, in addition to one light being out, we had hardly any steering left. The wheel was turning loose for nearly half a turn before it engaged at all. The brakes were gone. And, if it mattered, the horn had started to blow again.

Rex and I had a low-voiced consultation and decided to go on. We were already overdue in Worcester, and we felt we could make it.

The lady then insisted that we come inside and drink a cup of coffee to keep us awake if we just would go on. When we came outside to leave, the two Yale students were standing by in a smart and shiny Ford roadster of the same model as ours, only theirs was in nearly new condition. They said they were going to drive in front and lead us into New Haven and to a place where they thought we could get the light fixed. This was unexpected good news, and we gladly fell in behind them on the road.

We were deeply appreciative of the kindness shown us by these white people who were strangers to us. But, being Negroes, we were so unaccustomed to being treated with such courtesy and kind consideration by white people that we were somewhat bewildered by it. The idea of being offered a bed in a white place of business was something that would not enter into our imagination at home in the South, regardless of the circumstances. But here, the offer had been made in the kindliest spirit by a white woman who was interested only in our comfort and safety. She had addressed us as "you boys," but in her tone and manner of speaking there was a quality of interest in other human beings. It was entirely different from the "you boys" with the contemptuous overtone in wide use in the South.

Then there were the two young men in the car ahead. They had volunteered to drive these many miles in the middle of the night just to be of help to us. It was customary in the South for white people to treat strange Negroes with indifference or hostility, certainly not with this kind of civility and human consideration.

Before long, the lights of New Haven were visible. In the

city, the young men ahead found the all-night service station
they had told us about and explained our problem to the
attendant. He disappeared inside and presently returned with
two "high power" bulbs which they all suggested that we use in
the headlights. These installed, we were ready for the road
again.

Our young benefactors were still with us, and, when we
were ready to go, they told us to follow them and they would
show us the way out of town. We followed them across New
Haven to a crossroad where they stopped. There they pointed
out the road to Worcester and wished us good luck. We got
out of our car and thanked them for their help and told them
how much we appreciated it. Then they were gone in the
darkness and we were on the lonely road to Worcester.

We made it through the last leg of our journey and arrived
in the morning hours at the address where Rex's wife was
staying with her mother and Aunt Ella.

Rex and I were pretty tired and stayed close in for the next
few days, he playing with his year-old son, and I getting
acquainted all around. We were in complete agreement that
something had to be done about the car before we were ready
to go back home. Rex considered selling it, and we would all
go back on the train. But when he went a day or so later to a
used-car place to see about this, he found that he could buy
salvaged parts there for his car and decided to do so and repair
it. He never said what they offered to pay him for his car, if
anything.

We spent the next several days in the back yard of the
apartment installing a complete steering assembly, including
steering wheel. We wanted nothing left of the old guiding
mechanism. A gear or so in the transmission stopped the
thump and growl there. Brake drums and new linings took
care of the problem of bringing it to a stop.

The car was now in good condition for the return trip except for the two tires that were almost bald. The engine had given no trouble. By now, we were tired and worn-out from all that hard work on the car. But, at least, we thought we had a safe conveyance for the trip home. Rex's wife and the baby would be with us on the return trip, and we certainly could not take chances with their safety as we had done with our own.

So far, my vacation outing had brought me a substitution of one kind of tension-producing activity and hard work for another. There had been no relaxation, and the strain was much greater than that produced by work and study at home. It was different, with different people, in different surroundings, and now I was a long way from home. Aside from the people I had seen and come in contact with, there was little to be said for it.

During this time, I had formed the acquaintance of a barber whose shop was in a business district several blocks from the apartment. In the afternoon, I passed his place of business and stopped in to chat. This resulted in his taking me a few doors away to a speakeasy where we had a drink together. When we were ready to leave, I bought a bottle of gin and carried it back to the apartment with me.

On my return, I signaled Rex to my room and showed him my recent acquisition. He was overjoyed, saying that this was just what we needed. He sneaked some ginger ale from the icebox and, behind closed doors, we mixed and had some drinks. I don't know why we did this surreptitiously, since I had always been used to having whiskey about. Anyway, this dispelled the gloom, and we decided to have a pleasant vacation for the rest of our stay.

During these several days of our acquaintance, Aunt Ella, an old-maid schoolteacher and Rex's wife's aunt, had, for reasons not discernible to me, come to the conclusion that I was a fit and personable companion for a young lady of her church. This information was imparted to me on the eve of our going to a party at the home of one of her friends.

She gave me glowing accounts of this young woman's work in the church, including the fact that she was a Sunday school teacher. She was to be at the party and Aunt Ella had already phoned her about me. The more she talked on this matter, the greater was my conviction that Betty was indeed a fine person who probably had two left feet and snaggled teeth.

Anyway, I felt a distaste for what I considered the matchmaking proclivities of an old-maid schoolteacher. I had painfully decided a year or so earlier, after the termination of a particularly fine relationship with a young woman, that I would not become so sentimentally involved again. At least, not until my present life situation was changed.

The party was at a large, two-story house on the outskirts of the city. A lot of people were there when we arrived, and when I had been introduced to the host and his wife and several others, I detached myself from our little group and wandered around on my own, finally taking a seat on the glassed-in front porch with a number of other young people. Aunt Ella went in search of her protégée. I think I was trying to avoid her.

I fell into easy conversation with a pretty young woman who sat in the swing with me. She was quiet, dignified, and had an intriguing New England accent. I thought I would stay out here and maybe Aunt Ella wouldn't find me. Then, the bulk of her filled the doorway and she searched the area until her eyes came to rest on me. Her face was beaming as she approached and announced that she had been looking all over for us, "and here you are out here together." This was the girl she had wanted me to meet. All of a sudden, Aunt Ella's stock went away up with me.

One night all of us were invited to a dinner of roast duck
and Boston baked beans at a clubhouse near a lake. This place
made a beautiful setting in the moonlight. The room was a
large rectangle with a huge fireplace at one end. The food was
served on long tables and was delicious. I had never eaten
roast duck before and, of course, the baked beans were a
regional specialty. There was some liquor about, and the mood
was relaxed and congenial.

After dinner, some girls assembled themselves in the vacant
area before the fireplace and, with the lights out and a spotlight
on them, proceeded to do Oriental dances. This was very
pretty and added much to the pleasure of the evening. When
they had finished, Rex volunteered to do an exhibition of the
Charleston, a popular dance of the period.

I was not aware that he could do this dance, which required
considerable physical activity and great dexterity in the fast
movement of the feet. His was a superb demonstration,
however, with his feet flying and never missing the fast rhythm
of the dance. His performance was so good that he was asked
to repeat it, which he did. Everyone thought he had
contributed much to the evening's entertainment.

That is, almost everyone. His wife was furious at what she
considered an undignified exhibition of himself. She said
nothing at the time. But when she got home, she put poor Rex
in the doghouse. Much was said of her embarrassment and
humiliation in the presence of her friends who witnessed his
conduct.

Poor Rex was guilty of nothing more than giving away to a
spontaneous impulse of somewhat joyous participation during
an evening's pleasure. The episode seemed to have been
regarded in this light by the others present, and Rex gained
popularity from his innocent clowning. I thought he deserved
this measure of carefree enjoyment after what we had gone

through to get there, not to mention the work we had done on the car after we arrived.

But "Wifey" was adamant in her denunciation and insisted that she had been shamed by his conducting himself in such a manner in public. Also that if he had not had so much to drink, he would not have behaved as he did. Rex tried to defend himself with soothing words, but they availed him little. The talk went on.

The next day, Rex was in a very downcast frame of mind because of what he had come to regard as his supreme folly of the night before. To me, the whole thing was a huge joke. Of course, he had had some drinks the night before. So had most of the others. Sure, he had done a flying, winging dance in the glare of the spotlight. But what of it? It was all in fun and enjoyable fun. I thought his wife was being much too severe and made up my mind to say to her that Rex had done nothing disgraceful. The opportunity for this came sooner than I expected. Later in the day, we fell jokingly into conversation concerning the way she was treating Rex about taking a drink. Afterwards, she became cheerful towards him and the incident was forgotten. We were "having a wonderful time on our vacation. Wish you were here."

I had tried during this time to take my mind away from the responsibilities of home and the barbershop. So far, I had been able to keep this promise to myself. From letters regularly received, it appeared that everything was in order. But as time to return drew near, I became somewhat restive and impatient to get back. Established routine is not easily broken, not even by a pleasant interlude.

On the day of our departure, we loaded our things into the Ford with the expectation of a much faster and less exasperating trip than we had encountered coming here. Rex's wife and baby were to be with us on the return trip, and when we got the things she was bringing into the car, along with our baggage, we were pretty well crowded for space as we set out for home. The weather was hot, and the baby became fretful in the cramped space of the rear seat with his mother. We tried to make a lark of our discomfort. But, lark or not, the discomfort remained and the heat was oppressive. The car was performing beautifully, however, and we decided to make Baltimore our first stop. I would go by train to Washington to visit with Aunt Jenny and Uncle Ernest until they came by for me.

As the day wore on, I decided I should go on by train from Washington home. With me and my baggage out of the car, there would be more room for Rex and his family to travel in comfort. I told them of my plan at the railway station in Baltimore, but they insisted on my being at uncle Ernest's place when they got there.

As luck would have it, when I got off the train in Washington, a red cap asked if I happened to be from down around Charlotte, North Carolina. He went on to say that a passenger had given him a return ticket there, and, if I could use it, he would sell it to me for three dollars. At that time, the Southern Railway was selling a round-trip limited-time ticket from Charlotte to Washington and back for ten dollars. As I recall, this was less than one-way fare, and its object was to promote vacation travel by rail. I had not expected such good fortune to come my way, and I was glad to buy the ticket after checking with the agent in the station to see that its time limit had not expired. Then I went to the home of Aunt Jenny and Uncle Ernest.

Aunt Jenny was my father's sister. I never knew who the fathers of my grandma Alice's four children were. But Aunt Jenny and my father both had freckled faces, which none of the others had, and I assumed from this that they could have been full sister and brother. She had married Uncle Ernest years ago before they left Davidson.

He was the son of old man Andy Byers, the one who prayed as he plowed his mule, Jack, in his vegetable garden and drove the "sugar wagon" and cleaned out open privies for fifteen cents. Uncle Ernest was an educated man by his own inference.

"I attended Biddle University," he was fond of saying.

At the time he went to school there seventy years ago, Biddle started in the grades and went through college and seminary training. His attendance there could have meant anything from finishing the fifth grade to becoming a graduated preacher. He was not a preacher, and I am reasonably certain that he did not go to college. But he was smart, and would have made a deserving student. He entered the railway mail service as a young man and worked on mail cars between Greensboro, North Carolina, and Atlanta, Georgia, having established his residence in Greensboro. After many years of this work, he was transferred to the Washington, D.C. post office. A fast-talking, fast-walking black man with a good mind and a pleasant disposition, he was well informed and very alert.

Aunt Jenny and Uncle Ernest had been interested in the welfare of my father's family since his death. They had several years ago, before they moved from Greensboro, kept my mother and sister the better part of one winter when Mama's health was bad. Too, they were well aware of the difficulties Mama had experienced with her people, the Nortons, concerning the barber shop my father owned when he died. They were acquainted with my efforts to support the family and gave this their approval.

The three of us had a long talk the morning after my arrival, culminated by Uncle Ernest taking me into the basement "to show me some keepsakes." These were lodged in an old trunk

which he said had been brought over from Bremen, Germany.
There were many old letters and photographs there, as well as
articles he had cut from printed pages over the years. These
were treasures to him, and he handled them carefully and
lovingly as he displayed them one by one.

Finally, he came to an item stuck away in a corner at the very
bottom. It was wrapped in tissue paper, browned with age.
He put careful hands on the bottle of old Scotch with the
solemn assertion that this was kept for very, very special occasions. We then had a "little smile" together. I left on the noon
train for Charlotte and home.

CHAPTER ELEVEN

The Depression

At home, affairs seemed to have gone on quite well in my absence. Ed had been left in charge of the barber shop and, on the surface, everything there appeared to be in good order. But somehow, something seemed amiss there, as if there were something that I was not being told about. Anyway, I was glad to take up with my work and studies where I had left off three weeks earlier. I had been studying the high school course by correspondence for three years now, and I had noted with satisfaction on my vacation that there was a decided improvement in my manner of speech and my basic understanding of things. I wanted to get on with it, because the farther along I got in my studies, the more enjoyable they became. I had the feeling that I was making real progress. But it did seem slow, very slow.

One thing that vexed me upon my return was the resentment that some shop customers had towards my going "up North" on a vacation. At the time, there was among Southern white people a distinct aversion towards Negroes going North.

The feeling was that when a Negro left the South, he somehow freed himself of restraints drummed ceaselessly into his mind and that new and unaccustomed freedoms of actions and associations unfitted him for the role of the subservient and obsequious life pattern into which he had been molded by fear and oppression.

Some years earlier, many Negroes had been attracted to the industrial North by the availability of good-paying jobs. Living and working conditions were much better there than in the South and migrants numbered into the thousands. This affected the work force in the fields to such an extent that many legislatures in the South passed laws against solicitation of Negro labor for work in the North. During this period, much sentiment was aroused against whites who came South in search of Negro labor. A generalized hostility towards Negroes going North was the result of this situation. Negroes who had gone away and returned for a visit were looked upon with suspicion of enlisting others to leave. A residue of these antipathies, plus the hangover of Civil War indignation, reduced going North to an unacceptable practice for Negroes.

In addition, I was studying in the shop during spare time. This did not meet with the approval of some who thought that learning "ruined a good nigger." The prevalence of this attitude was in part responsible for the almost total lack of public support for Negro education above the most elementary level.

Negroes had been taught that they needed no education. Many devices were employed to induce them to hold in contempt any of their fellows who aspired to learning. It was said of them that they were too lazy to work. Or, a favorite one, that they thought themselves better than the other colored people. Negro parents were told that their children needed to be at home helping them, meaning in the fields, rather than going to school.

In this atmosphere and state of opportunity, it was extremely difficult for a young Negro to maintain any consistent educational direction. If we accept the theory of equal per capita distribution of state educational funds, Negroes received approximately thirty-seven per cent of the amount due in 1930. There were some, however, who managed to succeed in gaining knowledge and education. More often than not, this required an almost superhuman effort and great sacrifices on the part of parents and student.

So thoroughly had most of the Negroes in Davidson been imbued with the idea that they needed no education, that none of the boys thought of going beyond the seventh grade level of the local system. A few girls went away to small boarding schools. But their parents were generally unable to keep them there for any length of time, and they were soon at home again and in the traditional role of servant in a white home. The pay was always low, and the cycle of ignorance and poverty repeated itself over and over again.

My failure to accommodate myself to these attitudes placed me in the position of one who was willfully refusing to bow to customs of the region. There was no clearly discernible or open hostility towards me. But a remark here and there and a change of attitude towards me by some of the whites were sufficient to convey the lack of their approval.

The fact that I was in business on Main Street and had two barbers helping me was cause of resentment towards me among some whites and Negroes alike. Our home, situated on a main road on the outskirts of town, and thus in plain view of everyone, had been recently remodeled and was much better than the average Negro home of the area. These circumstances, plus the fact that I was now "trying to become educated," as some said, did not endear me to a certain faction of the population, white and Negro.

The development and emergence of these attitudes seemed
strange and incompatible when applied to me. Only a few
years back, when the barber shop was in the ramshackle old
building up the street, the fixtures out-of-date, and our home
in need of repairs, I had been the object of some disdainful
appraisals for my efforts to improve these conditions. They
considered me a young fool, doomed to failure as a reward for
my impertinent fling in the face of chance.

Now, after some years of hard work and sacrifice which had
resulted in a betterment of my situation, many of these people
were scornful of me because of the small measure of success
that I had earned. They behaved as if I had in the process
broken a cardinal rule, or had taken something from them that
might have been theirs under other circumstances.

Among Negroes in particular, the view was held that "good
luck" was the factor that brought one into possession and
enjoyment of the desirable things in life. It was this that
accounted for some of their resentment towards me. They
believed, in effect, that good luck wandered about and every so
often touched a person and conferred on him such favors and
possessions as he was able to acquire. And if that other person
had not been standing in the way, he, himself, might have been
the recipient of good luck's bounty. It followed then that he
considered himself as having been cheated by someone else
standing in his way. The little success that had come to me was
explained away by many with this thinking in the background.

Since we lived on the road that formed an extension of
North Main Street, I had to traverse the length of that street
going to and from work. I had formed the practice of carrying
books back and forth between work and home. This was so I
could study at the shop during times when I was without a
customer and at home after work. The Davidson College
professors who lived on the street also carried books back and
forth from the college.

At the time, most of the white families whose homes lined each side of the street had Negro maids or cooks. It so happened that at about the time when I went to work in the mornings, the maids were sweeping the walks that led into the homes where they were employed. A few of them, and one in particular, seeing me carrying books, took delight in scornfully calling to each other and loudly commenting that "the professor is on the way to his work, carrying a book. Ha, ha! Wonder where he's teaching at today?"

It was worrisome to me to endure this ridicule in the mornings, and I wondered why they would take this attitude towards me. I knew them all and had always spoken pleasantly to them. Their actions were a measure of their own absorption of the prevalent idea that Negroes should remain static in a condition of ignorance and poverty. They were never able to better their own situation, if indeed, they ever tried. They didn't think I should try to better mine. In time, in fact, they resented my trying to do so. They equated my efforts with trying to be better than they were.

There were many white people, however, who were sympathetic to my efforts at self-improvement. These people were of the better class, most of them, of some means and education. They knew of the disadvantages with which I was confronted as a Negro and respected my trying to soften them as best I could. Many of them offered me encouragement in my studies and were helpful in advising me with problems I was unable to work out for myself. There were those who made a practice of showing their kind feelings towards me.

Another thing that became increasingly noticeable was the gradual shifting or changing of the type of people who were regular patrons of my barber shop. This was a subtle and slow moving process, but I had observed that for some time past more of the substantial or better class residents in the area came to my place.

This is not to say that my business had before been made up
of lower class trade. It was not. But I noticed that more
landowning farmers and merchants and their families and
friends were giving me their patronage, together with other
important people of the community. There were also poor and
honest people of good character and friendly disposition who
came. Too, it had became the place where the better class of
young people of the small towns and rural areas came for their
barber work. I made many fine friendships among all these
people which I cherish to this day.

Numbered among my friends of that day were many young
men who were attending Davidson College. A large number
of these good people are now in positions of honor and trust.
I benefited greatly from having known them during their
college days. Some exceptionally fine friendships have extended over the years until the present time.

Taken as a whole, I was in a much more favored position in
every respect than I had previously been, but I was also the
subject of heavy criticism from some quarters. One of these
sources of censure and rebuke was the membership of the
Negro churches and their pastors. I, along with all of my
relatives, was a member of the A.M.E. Zion Methodist
Church. However, I had early in life come to view it with
disfavor because of its financial structure and the generally low
preparation level of the pastors. It seemed to me that too great
an emphasis was placed on draining funds from poor local
congregations for the central organization. There seemed also
a corresponding lack of interest by the conference in the
welfare of the ministers, many of whom were sincere men,
even though they were limited in their ability to perform
services for the membership. These circumstances set up a
condition within the local churches where the ministers found
it necessary to spend a considerable portion of their efforts in
getting money from the membership of their churches to

satisfy the demands of the central organization. This was the cause of a great deal of dissatisfaction and caused strife between the ministers and their congregations.

I became increasingly dissatisfied with the almost constant pressure from this direction. And especially so at conference time, when the ministers often cleaned out every available small treasury in the churches to meet the quotas at the annual conference. This procedure often required measures of individual persuasion and deception that left the ministers without the proper respect of their congregations. It seemed to me that a church was not the place to engender so much strife and ill feeling.

Never an ardent churchgoer, my attendance at services declined to the point that I was hardly ever there. Many other young Negroes of the 1930's were falling away from the authoritarian concept of compulsory church attendance that had grown up. But there was still that residue of older members who exerted pressures on the young to attend. This was strongly buttressed by the ministers who used their influence on the old to bring the young in line with their desires. As is usual in such a situation, this brought resentment and further rebellion by the young.

The admonitions and persuasions of the older people were not confined to the young of their own churches. A person who was derelict in his church affiliation was subject to the censure of everyone, regardless of denominational persuasion.

My disaffection was regarded as being "without thankfulness to the Lord," because it appeared that I had been the recipient of special favors by reason of my comparatively better economic situation. There was no understanding other than that I was behaving in a very ungrateful manner. This was a part of the "good luck" philosophy and had no insight into personal convictions, motives or strivings.

Another reason for lack of attendance, aside from that set
out above, was my constant application to studying and a
general disinterest in activities which had no appeal to me. But
whatever my reasons, I was looked upon with contempt as a
sinful person who had forsaken God. No distinction was made
between God and a church organization. One was synony-
mous with the other. The fact that I seemed to have prospered
intensified their feelings against me.

Many times I felt a great loneliness and despair at my almost
total withdrawal from social intermingling. I had lost interest in
the things that occupied the minds of my former associates.
They regarded me as being no longer one of them, although
our relationships were cordial enough when we chanced to
meet. But I had a commitment to keep with myself. In 1930, I
was twenty-six years old and had not yet finished the high
school course I was studying by correspondence. There was
no time for distractions and diversions that would take my
attention away from this goal. I had chosen the direction I
intended to follow. There was no intention to deviate from it,
regardless of whatever censure or condemnation it brought
from others. I had settled this with myself. I would bear with
the frustrations, the deprivations, the mockery and the
aloneness if I could attain my objectives, which I thought were
worthwhile. I could see no other way to do the things I wanted
to do.

I was, indeed, a loner. My eyes were set upon a future that
was too rapidly unfolding. My progress was painfully slow, my
impatience agonizing. With this appraisal of my situation, I set
myself to the task of getting on with whatever was required of
me to accomplish whatever I could of my aims.

By late summer of 1930, the ever-deepening effects of the
Great Depression were becoming increasingly apparent. Shad-

ows of impending doom were gathering everywhere. Money
had grown scarce. Unemployment was a continually rising
apparition of further and more wretched times ahead. Business in the barber shop was in a decline. Adjustments to new
conditions had to be made. I hoped they were temporary. But
all around me, evidence was accumulating that was not reassuring. A forlorn atmosphere of defeat had crept into the thinking of many people as the situation worsened. The price of
cotton, a major cash crop, had tumbled. More and more workers were being let out of work.

Up to the start of this upheaval my earnings in the barber
shop, while by no means large, had provided me a considerably
better income than that of other Negroes in the community.
Too, I had from necessity learned early in life not to be waste-
ful of anything and, if possible, to save a part of my earnings.
Habits of frugality had earned for me the nickname of "Jew-
boy" among some of my Negro associates and friends. It had
also enabled me to have a bank account, which none of them
had. I was not stingy, nor did I deny my mother and sister
comforts and things that enabled us to have a fairly good
standard of living. As a matter of fact, we enjoyed in our home
a much better standard of living than that of other Negro
families. But I was selective in my spending, strictly so. And
thought went into a proposed purchase before money was
spent. We did not contract debt for luxuries. Nor was my
money spent for "fancy" living.

These practices had brought me practically debt free into
the beginning years of the Depression. My only outstanding
obligation was to the B & L for the balance due on the one
thousand dollars that had been borrowed to remodel our
house. This was payable at $3.66 per week and had about four
years to go before full repayment.

The Depression wouldn't go away. Its tentacles grew longer and longer and wound themselves tighter and tighter around the throat of the economy. The beginning of 1931 offered only a prospect of more of its devastating effects. Business in the barber shop continued to grow worse as my customers had less money to spend. A haircut could be put off a while longer, even if the hair were already growing over the collar. It seems odd now, 1973, that there were many men then who a year or so earlier had been in a condition of some affluence but now found themselves hardly able to pay for a twenty-five cent haircut. My $3.66 a week payment to the B & L was becoming burdensome to pay.

To meet my own needs and those of the drastically changed times, I instituted a system of barter in the barber shop, exchanging haircuts for farm produce and other goods my customers had to trade. This gained me many friends among my hard-pressed customers and provided me with things needed at home. So, as the Depression deepened, it was not unusual to see one or more of my customers walking along a country road carrying a parcel and headed for Johnson's Barber Shop. They brought me eggs, chickens, chunks of fatback, hams, meal, black walnuts, hickory nuts, peanuts, molasses, blackberries and whatever else they had to trade of farm produce. Some of just about everything produced on the farms and in the gardens hereabouts was brought in and exchanged for haircuts. There were times when the goods brought in were in excess of what was needed to pay for present haircuts. In those cases, they were left as deposits for future use by the persons bringing them, or for their friends who were glad to be able to borrow the means of a haircut from a neighbor. Many times a long-haired individual came in to say that "So-and-So" said it was all right for him to get a haircut on things already brought in, or to get it against something to be brought in the future. Some came and got one without any promise at all. Anyway, a fellow could always get a haircut at my barber shop, money or no money.

In season, I was well supplied with garden-fresh produce such as tomatoes, beans, cabbages and other vegetables, not to mention cantaloupes and watermelons, which were in abundance. During the hunting season, rabbits, mostly trapped ones, because hunters didn't have money to buy shotgun shells, were brought in such large quantities that at one time this meat was a staple food item on our table in winter. Possums could have been had too. But we had never eaten any of that meat at home, and the line was drawn against them and squirrels.

We were using a wood-burning cook stove, and I had been buying wood ready cut for that purpose. Now, I was trading haircuts for this, too. The going rate was two dollars a wagon load. This figured out to exactly eight haircuts. As time went on, some competition set up in the rotation of customers who were to bring me wood. After all, we needed only so much for our cooking stove.

One day a young man who was one of my suppliers announced that he just had to bring me some wood now, because "me and Pa and my brother and the Sherrill boys have got to have haircuts." I felt guilty about this, because I hadn't realized that they were not getting haircuts when they had not brought wood to pay for them. My system of bookkeeping on all these transactions was a very loose one which relied on the memory of the individual customer to keep our accounts reasonably straight. I explained to Robert that I expected them to get their hair cut whether they had brought wood or not. This was good news to him, and he got his done at once and sent the others in later for theirs. Forty years later, this man was still my customer and friend. A short time ago, his wife sent me a jar of the best pear preserves I have ever eaten.

A man who dealt in bootleg whiskey stealthily proposed that he furnish me with my needs of his commodity in exchange for haircuts. His offer was readily accepted, and thereafter, when I was in need of something to brighten my spirits and drive away the gloom from my weary existence, the means was in constant supply.

These adjustments to an increasingly money-less existence was a great help to me, both from the standpoint of furnishing me with things which I needed and in keeping customers coming to the barbershop. But, with all of this, my circumstances were steadily deteriorating. Financially, I was becoming poorer by the day, along with everybody else. What I was doing did not take the place of having an adequate sum of money to buy my needs. Nor did it supply me with a surplus for savings. The little money coming in was urgently needed to defray expenses that had to be paid in cash. There were such items as rent on the building that housed the barbershop, $12.50 per month, light and water bill, laundry and supplies. My barbers had to be paid, and some money was necessary at home.

My only area of progress was in my studies. I had by now finished the high school course I was studying, and I had a real feeling of accomplishment in this. It proved a great benefit to me from an educational standpoint, and as a builder of morale in the sense that it gave me a feeling of personal worth. I could understand the difference it had made in me, and I was extremely grateful for the opportunity it provided for instruction. But I was also very tired from four years of uninterrupted work and study, except for the three weeks in Massachusetts.

One of the many benefits I had derived from my studies was having my horizon enlarged in many directions. While this was advantageous, it also had the effect of making me less

satisfied with my progress in every area of my existence. It
made me even more demanding of myself as I became to a
greater extent conscious of the heights to which it had been
possible for some men to reach. This contrasted unfavorably
with my station in life. And I thought that I, too, might dare to
dream of a time when my own life situation could be enhanced
to the extent that poverty and ignorance would be driven from
it. My intention was to go on studying and constantly add to
the small beginning I had been able to achieve.

Except for this, my trend had been reversed. The outlook
for financial gain became increasingly dim. The trading and
swapping was not the road to independence. It was a means of
survival. And as time went on and the Depression spread
deeper, life became more difficult as the need became greater
and more people were in need. This was a particularly bad
time for me, because I felt at the end of my wits to bring
myself into a more abundant life situation. All around, the
condition was the same. There was failure, loss, and despair.

Then, late one night the telephone rang, and I was told that
the barber shop was on fire. Arriving shortly thereafter, I
discovered the building filled with smoke. A fire had been set
in the stairway that led from the upper story to an exit adjacent
to the back door of the barbershop. A supply closet built
under the stairway inside the barbershop was burned out. As
there was the smell of oil about, it seemed clear that the fire
had been deliberately set and that its object was to destroy my
place of business. This was the thought of the volunteer fire
department which had extinguished the blaze.

Added to my other problems, I certainly did not need a fire
to burn me out, especially one that was set by someone as yet
unknown. Had it started from some known cause within the
shop, such as from an appliance or a faulty electrical circuit,
this could have been remedied and its recurrence forestalled.

But, under the present circumstances where it seemed certain that it was ignited by a person or persons hostile to me, there was nothing I could do in the way of preventing a second and successful attempt at a later time. I thought of moving my bed into the back room and sleeping there. Mama would have none of this. She thought my being in the place would serve only to expose me personally to a danger that was at present being directed only at the barbershop.

By this time, the town of Davidson was employing a night policeman. He had smelled the smoke and upon investigation sounded the alarm. This was the largest building in town and housed three other business establishments on the ground floor besides the barber shop. In addition, there was the office for the Town of Davidson, the library, a medical doctor, and a dentist upstairs. If the building were destroyed, all of these would be burned out too. So, the promise of the policeman to be especially watchful in that area was buttressed by the importance of protecting the other occupants as well as the building's owner from loss. I was satisfied that a reasonable watch would be kept.

But a new and different problem was posed. What attitude would the owners of the other businesses and offices take towards me as a fellow tenant whose presence in the building exposed them to the possibility of having their property and businesses destroyed? Would Mr. Knox, the owner of the building and my good friend, ask me to leave? I could understand if he did.

All of these people had good and reasonable cause to want and to insist upon the removal of any element that posed such a threat to them. I was the only Negro tenant; the others were white. I was ashamed that my presence could endanger their property. Yet, on the next day, I had from them only expressions of their indignation towards the act that had been committed against me. None gave expressions to thoughts of the danger to their own property, yet I knew they must have been greatly concerned about this. They were my neighbors, my customers and friends. They behaved as such.

Widespread suspicion pointed its finger in the direction of one individual as the person responsible for this outrage. But it had been done in secrecy and no evidence was found to connect anyone with it.

Three nights later, another fire was set in the stairway. It was discovered and put out before any damage was done. This was conclusive proof that the first one was intentionally set. Any lingering doubts, or the probability of accident, were now set at rest. These blows struck at me in the darkness were taking their toll. Sleep was coming fitfully during the night.

Then it happened again. This time I was not called when it was discovered. I learned about it the next morning when I arrived for work and found a fire truck parked in front of the barber shop. This time, the fire had gained some headway in the same area as the others and had burned out flooring and a door in the supply closet.

A good deal of anger was about now as public indignation became more pronounced. Word had gotten around that someone was trying to destroy the barber shop. People came in and looked and shook their heads and spoke in undertones, or departed in grim silence.

This time the fire truck was left standing on the street in front of the barber shop for several days and the watch intensified.

I was certain now that I must go, that the barber shop would have to be closed. No one would allow me in a building after all this had happened. My mental agitation was great. I knew no other way to try to make a living. And if I had, the times were such that it would be next to impossible for me to keep my head above water.

This was a sickening experience. A fire truck had to be kept in waiting at my place of business, and a watch had to be kept on the premises to protect the interests of other people who were near me. Yet I had done nothing to invite such attacks from any source. I had contributed nothing to cause this enmity other than the fact of my existence in the world.

In desperation, I decided to wait it out and let them ask or tell me to get the barber shop out of the building. Any alternative to this that I could think of would serve only to reduce me to public charity. There was no other way at all for me to earn a living.

The attitude of my fellow tenants and the building's owner never wavered. They continued steadfast in their sympathies towards me, and not once was a suggestion made that I should do other than continue with the barber shop.

Beyond this was the ever-gnawing fear now that in some manner, somehow, these attacks would be continued. I had to walk home at night after we closed the shop at eight o'clock along a dark section of road for about a quarter of a mile beyond where the lights of Main Street stopped. On Saturday nights, the shop was often open until after eleven o'clock. This meant that on weekends I had to walk this way alone at nearly midnight. Cars passed along this road, and my mother was afraid I would be shot from one of them as I walked home. I had thought of this, too, but had not mentioned that possibility in the hope she would not think of it and increase her worries.

There was also the thought that our home might be set afire and burn us all to death some night. There were four other houses strung out along the highway with ours in our little neighborhood. But in the light of recent developments, we could not feel too secure about the occupants of two of these. It was dark at night where we lived, as there were no streetlights. A person bent on mischief could move without heed of possibility of discovery.

Fear for the safety of our lives had been thrust into our thinking. It was a constant companion to walk with, and to try to sleep with.

As the Depression became more severe and widespread in its effect on all segments of the population, hope seemed to drain away and despair to take its place on all sides. Many were without food or adequate clothing, their houses cold for want of fuel. Commerce of all kinds was near the vanishing point. Cars were made into "Hoover carts" and drawn by horses. Men raked leaves for fifty cents a day on W.P.A. projects and smoked Golden Grain cloth-bagged tobacco. The script issued in payment was good only for food items at grocery stores. Cigarettes and tobacco along with some other non-approved goods were often secured by connivance with the grocery man. A food item would be bought and then traded back for whatever else was wanted.

The woods and fields were scoured for rabbits and other wild game. Berries and persimmons were much sought after. Jokes were told about men falling out of persimmon trees where they had climbed for food. Some said they had eaten so many rabbits they could no longer look a hound dog in the face without feeling the urge to run.

Farms and homes were lost for want of money to pay mortgage loans and taxes. Some formerly wealthy farmers piled up bales of cotton in their yards rather than sell it for five cents a pound. Many of these men still owned cotton they had refused to sell for forty cents a pound just before the beginning of the Depression. They thought it would go to forty-five cents. Now it was rotting and they were in dire need of money.

Pa, Mama's father, had bought a farm back in 1924 after his home had been destroyed by fire one summer afternoon. He

borrowed money to pay most of the cost of this with the hope
of paying it off by raising high-priced cotton. Things had not
gone with him as he expected. His production of cotton was
not great enough in later years to bring in enough money to
meet land payments and support his family and a tenant on the
farm. Promises made by his sons to help with these payments
were not kept.

The Norton family behaved as if they owned the land
outright without any debt. They assumed the attitude that their
possession made them masters of the place, and that there was
no particular responsibility to pay off the mortgage. As a
result of this thinking, they were careless about keeping up the
payments.

They had built a small building on the highway and operated
a store and gasoline station. Payments of the land could have
been met had they tried to do so. Instead, there was some
extravagant living on the part of his daughters who kept the
store. There was money given to a nephew who was kept in
style without much work on his part.

Pa was an old man when the Depression came on. Never a
good manager and not a productive farmer, his affairs had
begun to deteriorate after the first two or three years on the
land. Ma had developed diabetes and was in poor health. This
was before the doctors had an effective method of controlling
her disease. In good health, she had been the driving force in
the family, and the one with better managerial ability. She had
a mean streak, however, and was conceited to the extent of
considering anything she wanted to do as right.

The family, just prior to the beginning of the Depression,
had begun to talk about how to save the farm from being sold
for debt. A variety of schemes and stratagems were proposed
by which this could be accomplished with Pa and his family
retaining possession. None of these plans were effective in

staying the inevitable time of reckoning with their creditor, because none of them produced the money to pay the debt. They were delaying tactics and would come to an end.

Buried deep in the latest design was a secret aim of the Nortons to induce me to assume payments of this loan in exchange for a promise of a part of the land. They had dealt warily with me for a long time, because they knew I had cared nothing for them from the time when they connived together against my mother and took over my father's barber business when he died.

I was a boy at the time this happened, and my only reason for any association with them whatever from that time was that they were my mother's family and she retained her family ties and depended on them for help in time of sickness. It was extremely difficult for her, a widow with two children, and in poor health, to break away from her family regardless of their mean treatment. As for me, I was detached from them and regarded them without affection.

As I grew out of boyhood into young manhood, it became apparent to me that whenever possible I was the object of their criticism. They found fault with whatever I did. And if in a given situation I did nothing, fault was found in that. This was especially true after I went into the barber shop. If they couldn't get something from me or use me in some manner to further their own ends or designs, then I was distinctly in disfavor. It was as if I ought not to be, that I was in their way.

So it was dreadful necessity that prompted their proposal to me that I become "a part owner of the land," as they put it. The idea was advanced as a great favor to me. I was to be "given" some acreage at a time in the future, unspecified as to extent or time. Word had already reached me that they intended to cut me off a few worthless acres at the back side of the place. All I had to do for this was to make the payments on the whole thing. I listened to their spiel in rising anger. Then I told them all that I would have nothing to do with their slick little scheme.

After this, I was regarded with hurt looks and with no little contempt as the mean one who could help them in their time of need but wouldn't. It was their last chance to save the farm, and they were not to be easily dissuaded from trying to bring me into this quagmire of their deception. They tried crafty means of persuasion. And when this failed, they tried to bring pressure on Mama to influence me. I had to stop this with some frank talk, as I had no intention of becoming involved with them in any way.

Aside from having no desire to become entangled in their problems, the fact was that money continued to be harder to obtain. The $3.66 I was paying to the B & L each Saturday towards the loan on our house repairs was no longer the easy matter to manage that it had been when I started with it.

About this time, I was awarded a scholarship in a correspondence course in commercial art. This didn't seem a very promising way for me to advance myself, but it did provide something for me to do in spare time after work hours. I was in low spirits about my prospects for advancement and, indeed, about my safety. So, I went into this as a sort of last straw activity that just might free me from my problems by opening a new avenue of earnings. Mainly, it was something in which to invest my hopes. This was badly needed at the time as I had arrived at a gloomy outlook on my situation.

I had very little, if any, talent for drawing, but I was willing to try. The next two years were spent in close application to working at this. I followed much the same regimen that I had established for working on the high school course, which was to devote practically all my spare time at work, plus my nights at home and Sundays, to some phase of this course of study.

It was rewarding too, as I was able to create some designs that were satisfactory. There was also the fantastic realm of color to which I was introduced, and I spent many Sundays at this. It is difficult to work effectively in color under artificial light, and it was only on Sundays that I had an opportunity to exercise my art during the daylight hours.

Aside from working at the course, I developed an interest in fine art and, independently, did a great deal of reading on that subject and about the great artists of the past. In this manner, I was able to develop a delightful sense of appreciation for a variety of the forms of art. I also became acquainted with the works of various famous artists, the times in which they lived, and the circumstances under which they worked to produce such wonders of beauty and thought.

Beyond the cultural benefits derived, there was no reward in this for the two years expended on this course. There was no way I could turn this into additional income except for sign painting, which I didn't care for, although I did some of it.

CHAPTER TWELVE

A Favored Place

Since the barber shop was a favored place for the discussion of happenings of the day, and a clearing house for information of all kinds, I was in a position to get firsthand news of stories concerning my fellow townspeople. My association with these same people as a barber enhanced my awareness of their individual characteristics. So, let's back up a bit and relate some of the activities that had to do with interesting personalities.

I would be remiss if I failed to speak here of my old friend and customer, Dr. Caleb Richmond Harding, professor of Latin at Davidson College. Many stories about this odd little man have been circulated over the years. While he was held in highest esteem by all who knew him, he had gained a reputation for doing ridiculously impractical and out-of-the-ordinary things. It was my great good fortune to know him over a period of many years and our conversations were often quite animated. Dr. Harding was a man of rare good sense, but, at the other end of the scale, he was capable of doing such seemingly silly little things.

He was possibly five feet six inches tall, and slight of build, and the hair he had around the edges of his small, nearly bald head was already gray when I first knew him. He wore pince-nez spectacles with an air of distinction, the upper portion of the lenses being cut away, leaving only the lower, bifocal half. These he was wont to wear fairly low on his nose so he could look over them entirely. The stiff collar around his scrawny neck was the straight-standing variety with points that turned down and outward under his receding chin, on which grew a small goatee of frizzy white hair. There was a black four-in-hand neck-tie, or a string bow at times.

A swallow-tailed black coat topped off the upper portion of his body. His pants, often of the hickory-striped variety, were held securely about his person by suspenders and a belt, reflecting his conservative and carefully decorous way of life. The shoes on his small feet were properly black, as was the derby hat upon his head. Dr. Harding was a true gentleman of the old school, both in manner of dress and in thought. He was regarded as being stingy. He referred to his nearness with money as "good stewardship."

He was known by sight and reputation to most people in the community, since he probably lived here sixty years or more. More often than not, he was present for both the Sunday school and church service at a Negro church. At one time, he was particularly fond of the preaching of Presiding Elder Hunter of the A.M.E. Zion church, and made it a point not to miss service when Elder Hunter was there every three months to hold the Quarter Meeting. Dr. Harding sat and listened attentively as the large-bellied black man preached his powerful sermons. Often he was seen to wipe away a tear from his eyes when Hunter bore down on the Scriptures and the sins of man. At times, when he wasn't certain as to the time of Elder Hunter's next visit, Dr. Harding would come by the barber shop and inquire of me, "When will that man Hunter be here again?"

I never heard him call a Negro minister "Reverend" or "Mister." Always, he just called him by his last or surname, or "you" when he spoke directly to him. Neither his custom nor religion extended to granting such dignity to Negroes, although it is certain that he expected all Negroes to address him formally and would have been insulted had they not done so. He was accustomed to sit apart from the Negroes in their churches, usually on a front seat in the Amen Corner, where he sat properly alone.

To the many students who passed through Davidson College during Dr. Harding's long tenure, he was known affectionately as "Dicky." The only time I ever heard him refer to his nickname was one day when he and a Mr. Bob Knox were in the barbershop at the same time and they fell into easy conversation at the barber chair. Both of them were old men at the time and Mr. Knox, a wizened old man with a handlebar mustache, asked Dr. Harding what that little bit of hair he had growing on his chin was for. Dr. Harding explained with a twinkle in his eyes that it was a goatee and that it meant that he was "maybe a little goat." This explanation pleased Mr. Knox and both of them joined in some cackling laughter over this bit of merriment. The laughter over, Mr. Knox came close and asked another question: "Don't they call you Dicky here at the college?" "Yes, they do," the little professor answered. "I'm the one they call Dicky."

Dr. Harding's wife, "Millie", as he called her, was a large and imposing woman who dressed in the feminine finery of the day. Her size contrasted with the small stature of her husband, and was another incongruity with Dr. Harding's small, even delicate build. It was said about that she was quite short in patience with some of her husband's shortcomings and very vocal in her forthright denunciation of them.

One such incident had to do with his practice of engaging his visiting friends in long discourses on the Christian religion. A favorite partner in these philosophical examinations of fundamental religious concepts was Dr. Hood, he of the imposing beard and impeccable dress and manner. One such exchange between them had carried far over into the night and Mrs. Harding had listened from an adjoining room to as much as she could stand on the subject of the hereafter and what it was like, including the accouterments of wings and golden slippers with which the good doctor expected to be equipped as a reward for his righteous living. Finally, it was told, this long-suffering lady framed her ample self in the doorway that separated the rooms and addressed herself first to the distinguished and profoundly scholarly Dr. Hood.

"Dr. Hood," she said in a firm voice, "you get yourself up out of that chair and go home where you belong at this time of night." This said, she turned a withering blast upon her equally distinguished husband: "And you, Dr. Harding, you come to bed and stop all this talk about heaven because you are not going there anyway. You ole devil, you are going to hell when you die."

On another evening when Mrs. Harding had in other wives of professors for a very proper "hen" gathering, Dr. Harding donned his long white nightgown and went to bed early to read and to think. It was in summer, the weather was hot and he did not bother to pull any other cover over his body. As the evening wore on, Mrs. Harding had occasion to take the ladies into the kitchen. The nearest passage was through Dr. Harding's bedroom, and his wife went there first to see that her husband was decent. She found that he had dozed off and woke him gently and told him to pull the sheet over himself as the ladies were coming through presently. When she had gone out, the good man conformed sleepily with her request and went back to sleep. The ladies were horror-stricken a few minutes later when they trooped through to find the doctor peacefully asleep with his nightgown pulled snugly up about his neck and his scrawny nakedness exposed to view.

He was possessed at one time of a large and elegant Locomobile automobile, a make long since discontinued. It would not have been consistent with his ideas of frugality, as he called it, or penny-pinching nearness as others called it, to purchase such a fine and expensive car. It was said a wealthy daughter had presented it to him as a gift. He was never noted for his ability to drive and there was talk of a loose automobile in the streets when he ventured forth as a motorist.

Well, one fine day he drove the twenty miles to Charlotte, the nearest city, with a population of perhaps forty thousand at the time and very conscious of the importance of "the Square", as its main cross street was called.

A traffic officer was in place at this "cross roads of the Carolinas" as Dr. Harding approached in unhurried dignity in his impressive car and began a left turn. The traffic officer blew on his whistle and hastened up to put a stop to this desecration of the spot over which he had zealous dominion. Dr. Harding eyed him haughtily as he approached to interfere with his plan. The officer, noting the fine car and the evident dignity of the goateed gentleman at the wheel, was quite deferential as he told Dr. Harding that he couldn't make a left turn there. With a wave of his hand the old gentleman told the policeman that he could make it if he, the officer, "would just stand back out of the way and let me by." He then proceeded to make his left turn and went on his way, leaving a very per-turbed officer standing in the middle of the street waving his arms.

Dr. Harding went one day to the post office and bought a one-cent postal card—that's what they cost then—and wrote

out an order on it to an out-of-town firm for some seed oats to
plant on the large lot at back of his house. The writing completed, he encountered a farmer of his acquaintance and told
him of the order he had just written and was about to mail.
The man told Dr. Harding that he had seed oats and could
spare him all he needed at a reduced price. Their negotiations
completed, the little professor went back to the desk and wrote
the following message on the order: "Please cancel this order
as I have been able to get oats locally and cheaper than you sell
them." Then he dropped the card in the mail.

There were times when Dr. Harding didn't dress as formally
as when he wore his long claw-hammer coat, although it was
common practice for him to wear it about town at any time.

In the mid 1930s a man made a practice of coming, maybe
twice a year, to Davidson College for the purpose of selling
yard goods of "real imported cloth" to those members of the
faculty who "wanted something more elegant than could be
bought in the area stores" in the way of suit material. The
material was relatively expensive, and its Scottish origin in
serious doubt, according to A. Gerskov, the tailor.

Anyway, Dr. Hood, a fine dressing professor and friend of
Dr. Harding, was a patron of this man who sold cloth, and had
had Gerskov the tailor to make him some suits from it. Dr.
Harding was a great admirer of Dr. Hood's taste in elegant
clothing and asked his aid in selecting cloth for a suit for
himself.

Selection of the material completed, a weighty and time-
consuming undertaking, Dr. Harding hied himself straightway
to the old Jew, Gerskov, to have his suit "tailor-made." Much
time was taken in measuring the doctor's scrawny frame to
insure a proper fit, with him giving directions about this and
that and cautioning the busy Gerskov to be sure of his measurements. Gerskov, tape in hand, measured here then there,

then stood back and measured with his eyes as he looked over his wire-framed bifocals, a wrinkle of perplexity on his brow.

I knew this was an act on the part of Gerskov because he had told me with much laughter about his "hand-tailoring" activities. And on this occasion he had alerted me to be present while he measured Dr. Harding for his "tailor-made" suit. I was standing respectfully to the side and out of the way but close up enough to see and hear what was going on in this important transaction. The preliminary episode out of the way, and Gerskov having set down many figures on a blank form, he informed Dr. Harding that he would want to see him again in a few days to check the measurements when he cut the arm holes.

When Dr. Harding left the store, the tailor and I had a good laugh, for Gerskov had really put on a convincing performance. And performance it was, put on for Dr. Harding's benefit. Mr. Gerskov was indeed an expert tailor and fully capable of producing a hand-tailored suit but he was practicing a sly deception on these people. He told them that he cut out and made these suits at his home at night, especially first-rate, just for them, because he didn't do custom tailoring for just anybody. This was an appeal to vanity.

The truth was that he would take the measurements and send them and the cloth to Baltimore to a company that sold made-to-measure suits. This company cut the coat and basted it in with temporary stitches and mailed it back to Gerskov, who would then call in his fine customers and explain that he had gotten so far along with the garment and had to have them in for a try-on, so as to check his work for proper fit. This pleased the customers greatly, and they were certain that old Gerskov was indeed dedicated to his humble craft.

Mr. Gerskov's performances at these try-on sessions were indeed works of art that would excite the jealousy of a practic-

ing actor. He set the stage properly for this by having an exact
appointed time for it. Chalk was laid out on his table, a little
box filled with pins, two or three pairs of scissors, and a pad
and pencil for taking notes. Then his customer in place by the
window, for light, and his coat removed, Mr. Gerskov stooped
and gently took from its place under the counter the skeletonized garment to be fitted. This he slipped on his customer
with utmost care so as not to disturb the temporary stitches;
then there was much smoothing of the garment with his hands
and a slight pull here and a little tug there so as to get it to hang
just right. Then with lips drawn tight, he would step away five
or six feet to the back of his customer and survey what stood
before him, and, with a sidelong glance at me, wink his eye and
nod his head. He had a way of bending his knees backward
farther than anyone else I have ever seen, to the extent that his
legs appeared to have a backward bow in them. This, together
with the way he placed both hands on his hips, his somewhat
stooped shoulders, and his wire-framed bifocals perched far
down on his ample nose, gave to his customer the impression
of an artist lost in thought for the creation at his hands.

Dr. Harding was much impressed with all this and spoke not
a word lest he distract the tailor from his artistry. Standing very
straight, an unnatural pose, for he, too, had the stoop of age
upon his narrow shoulders, the little professor clearly nourished some hope that in Gerskov he had at last found hands
that could give him the build of a Greek god. So he stood tall,
as tall as five feet six inches could reach, and took delight in his
delusion.

Gerskov, too, was having the time of his life as he put on his
show, as much for his own merriment as anything else, for he
was much given to good humor. With his customer standing
stock-still, under strict admonishment not to move a muscle,
he then placed a number of pins between his lips, and, with

chalk in hand, proceeded to take a little tuck here or there and secure it with a pin, sometimes removing the pin and replacing it two or three times. Then the chalk was moved up and down in his hand just out of reach of the garment so as to get the exact place for a mark before he brought it in contact with the cloth. Finally, with many pins in place and chalk marks visible in several locations, he announced that that would be all he would need to do.

Getting this "hand-tailored" suit was for Dr. Harding a landmark achievement in his sartorial experience, and he wanted to be sure that everything would be perfect. Also, he was not accustomed to spend so much money for such magnificence as he was having readied for himself. He had given careful thought to that subject before venturing into this extravagance, and he had now come up with an idea that would assure him of getting sufficient wear from this expenditure to justify it, at least partially.

The solemnity of the try-on ended, and with Gerskov's mind free to accept his idea, he let the old tailor have it straight between the eyes with his proposal: "Now, see here, Gerskov," he said. "When you put the buttonholes at the front of this coat I want you to set them back some distance from the edge."

"And vhy do you vant such, Dr. Harding?" asked the astonished old tailor.

"Well, you see, this coat I'm wearing has become badly frayed at the buttonhole edge and I want the new one fixed so that when it becomes frayed, that part can be cut away and a new seam put along the front and still have room for the buttonholes."

This idea really startled Mr. Gerskov, because, in the first place, he wasn't going to make the button holes at all, and this was such an odd request he was sure the company he was ordering from wouldn't comply with it. Something had to be done quickly. Then, his wits about him again, he stepped back and looked at his customer in mock amazement and inquired of him, "Just how long do you think you are going to live, yet?" Dr. Harding gave this some thought and guessed that, after all, what with the fine material he had, this wouldn't be needed.

Everything settled now and Dr. Harding gone, Mr. Gerskov carefully removed the pins from the garment and brushed away all the chalk marks and readied it for mailing back to Baltimore to be finished according to the original measurements.

Dr. Harding entered the barber shop one day to get his two-week trim. At the time, I was cutting Mr. Blythe's hair, or rather trimming it around the edges. He, like Dr. Harding, had hardly any hair on the top of his head. With this type of customer, a good deal of scissors snapping went on about his head without actually cutting any hair. This was to impress him that he was getting something for the twenty-five cents he was paying for a haircut. Both of these men were noted for nursing a dime and I was careful to seem extra painstaking when attending their tonsorial needs, as if some special expertise was required to get their hair just right. Both of them were quite vain about the way their hair was cut, as if anybody could tell the difference.

Mr. Blythe was a professor at the college also, and he and Dr. Harding were old friends. They immediately struck up a conversation concerning some technical aspect of a football game. Knowing both of them as I did, it seemed odd to me and completely out of character for these two to be so engaged. But it developed that Mr. Blythe had been named to a committee that had something to do with the athletic program at the college. Dr. Harding was taking this opportunity to quiz

him on some hypothetical situation that might arise during a
football game. It was apparent that Mr. Blythe considered the
matter of no importance and his reply was superficial. Dr.
Harding, on the other hand, considered it of some importance
and restated his question with some insistence for an answer
implied. Mr. Blythe's reply to this was a testy one and indicated
that he preferred not to pursue the subject further. This was
getting funny, because each of them was visibly struggling to
keep his professorial dignity intact.

Dr. Harding then assumed something of an attitude that
perhaps the profundity of his question was out of the range of
Mr. Blythe's comprehension and proceeded to explain at length
what he had in mind. This further honed Mr. Blythe's indignation. Whereupon, Dr. Harding took a stance in the middle of
the floor and, pointing to the front and to the back of the
room, laid out an imaginary football field, replete with goal
posts. He then restated his proposition, with some pointing of
his finger. He was wearing his clawhammer coat and his anger
was showing as he drew himself to full height and declared,
"Now, Blythe, I have repeatedly asked you an intelligent question, and you have repeatedly refused to give me an answer."

To this Mr. Blythe replied sharply and succinctly: "Dr.
Harding, I have answered you two or three times in language
simple enough for a child to understand." This stung the little
old man deeply and he lapsed into silence while Mr. Blythe
paid for his haircut and walked stiff-backed out of the barber
shop.

I was silent while Dr. Harding removed his coat and took
his turn in the chair. He said nothing at all during his haircut,
but his brow was furrowed and I knew his feelings had been
hurt and his dignity badly ruffled. When I finished with him,
he went over to the mirror on the wall and began adjusting his
celluloid collar with the turned-down points under his chin.

Midway in this, he turned and peered carefully about to satisfy himself that Mr. Blythe had left the room before addressing himself to me: "Well," he said, looking straight at me and with his chin bobbing up and down, "old Blythe thinks I am a fool, and I know for a certainty that he is one."

One summer when it had not rained for several weeks and the farmers and gardens were much concerned about their crops, a series of prayer meetings was started at the Davidson College Presbyterian Church to pray for rain. Dr. Harding was a member of this church and was in regular and faithful attendance at the late afternoon sessions to pray for rain. It was also noted that he carried his umbrella as he strolled leisurely to the church to pray in the heat of late afternoon. This was the measure of his faith in the efficacy of prayer.

After these meetings had gone on for a week or more and still no rain, Dr. Harding arose one day between prayers and remarked that it was something of a commentary on the faith of those gathered there to pray for rain that he was the only one to carry an umbrella to the meetings. And, further, that in the face of so little faith it was no wonder that it was still dry. His observation, delivered with conviction in his somewhat raspy voice, was met with complete silence. Even the preacher had not bothered to bring his umbrella to the meetings.

Dr. Walter L. Lingle came to Davidson College as president about 1928. This tall, cheerful, goodhearted man was soon known as easy to approach and interested in the problems of the people in the community. Because of his friendly disposition and his patient willingness to help, many Negroes found their way to his office to lay their burdens in his capable hands. They felt free to call at his office or home at any time "to speak to Doctor a little bit about a matter," or to meet him walking across the campus, or on the street in town, and talk with him about whatever happened to be of concern at the time. As a result, he was acquainted with the intimate details of many lives. He knew most of the Negroes in town by name, young and old.

I had the good fortune to have this fine man for a friend and as a customer when he needed a haircut. His visits to the barber shop were special events for me, because he always had a lot to talk about concerning just about everything. He also had a store of really funny stories that he liked to tell, and, when there was no other conversation piece, he turned to these. He had a rare gift for storytelling, and his stories were always amusing and meticulously clean.

On the first day of the bank holiday declared by President Roosevelt in 1933, Dr. Lingle came in for a haircut. During the course of conversation, he mentioned that he had been caught in a very embarrassing condition in that he didn't have any money and couldn't get any. There was something he needed a little money for and he was vexed that he couldn't get it at the bank since they were all closed that day. As hard as times were at the time, I had some cash on hand in my pocket and offered to make him a loan, in addition to letting him have the twenty-five cent haircut on credit. He seized on my offer immediately and wanted to know if I could spare him a few dollars until the bank opened again. I was glad to do this, and he promised to pay it back as soon as possible.

Dr. Lingle was gone from the shop about an hour when his good friend and golfing partner, Colonel Cochran, who was head of the R.O.T.C. Department at Davidson College and also my customer and friend, came in and called me aside. He said Dr. Lingle had told him that I had some money, and would I let him have a few dollars because the bank's closing had caught him "without a damn cent." The colonel's vocabulary was somewhat different from Dr. Lingle's, but he was essentially the same sort of person. He knew just about everybody in town, black and white. He had many friends among Negroes in every age bracket. I made him a loan of a few dollars also, for which he wanted to give me a post-dated check. I refused the check, preferring to lend him the money as a favor. He seemed very grateful that I would trust him so, which was amusing to me coming from a man who was the soul of generosity and honesty.

One of Colonel Cochran's staunch friends was Ritch Heath, the same old Negro man who was put on a diet by Dr. George Withers and continued to eat his regular meals and then his diet. Each spring, Colonel Cochran planted a vegetable garden in his large back yard, knowing that he would be away in camp at gathering time. He planted it and left it to Ritch so as to be sure he had fresh vegetables to eat during the summer. Once in a fit of anger and vexation at the behavior of some of his friends, he made the remark that if it became his duty to kill all the Christians in Davidson, he would take his shotgun and kill poor old Ritch and then throw the damn gun away.

Once in the fall when the weather had turned chilly, he came to the barber shop and wanted to know if I had seen Ritch. He expressed the opinion that it was time for Ritch to change into warm underwear. Then he set out to Ritch's house to take him underwear and other warm clothing. About the same time that year, he came across the street one day to see two little Negro boys whose clothing seemed too light for the weather. He took them by the hand and went into Johnny Brown's store, where he bought each of them a complete outfit from the skin out, and new shoes. It was "a shame for them chaps to be walking around with their behinds out," he said.

Once the colonel became intensely interested in a young Negro man who had a serious drinking problem and who had been abandoned as worthless in the community. After much talk and persuasion, this man was finally able to perform satisfactorily in the job the colonel had secured for him. Then, at the colonel's urging he joined the Army. A year later, he had become a sergeant. Colonel Cochran was very proud of this man's achievements, and went about town telling what a fine man Harrison had become. But he neglected to tell the part he had played in this.

Now, getting back to Dr. Lingle. In addition to giving advice and listening with sympathetic ear to problems, he also carried on an extensive small loan traffic with a number of Negroes. These loans were made strictly on the basis of helping out a fellow in need, and were for amounts ranging from fifty cents to several dollars. Of course, no interest was thought about on either side, and repayment was conditioned on the ability and willingness of the borrower. Many of these loans were conveniently forgotten on both sides, and new loans made at a later date without regard to the outstanding obligation. Each understood the other in these matters.

During the early years of Dr. Lingle's tenure as president of Davidson College, the "Wildcats," as the college's athletes were called, had quite a spectacular football team and drew large crowds to their home games. The little town was often filled to overflowing with these Saturday afternoon crowds. There was also a great deal of drinking bootleg whiskey at other colleges during these big games at this time.

Dr. Lingle, an ardent dry, a minister and president of a church-related college, was strictly opposed to any drinking at the games at Davidson, or anywhere else. Davidson College's policy of not permitting drinking at its games was widely known. It was also commented upon, both favorably and unfavorably. Many chose to ignore it.

Dr. Lingle felt secure in the belief that there was no drinking at Davidson's games and was proud of that fact. But he was being deceived by the sneaking behavior of the spectators. Workmen on campus gleefully remarked after one Homecoming game that a one-horse wagon-load of empty liquor bottles was picked up about the stadium.

Another situation was kept strictly from the attention of Dr. Lingle. It was said about that some of his professors were supplying themselves surreptitiously with bootleg whiskey at a highly respected and never suspected business establishment that dispensed the illicit goods by wrapping it as other merchandise and passing it to the professors as a favor to them. This was "graveyard doings," and nobody was to know. Especially not Dr. Lingle.

A black man named Oscar was already well established in his situation as janitor at the college when Dr. Lingle came. In a little while, like everyone else, Oscar knew Dr. Lingle well. A while later, he was promoted to head janitor in Chambers Building, the main administration building and where Dr. Lingle had his office; the relationship flourished, with Oscar being the beneficiary of some largess, along with good advice about a small vice he had that had come to the attention of Dr. Lingle. Oscar, as good a man as he was, was known on occasion to drink a bottle of beer. This was of concern to Dr. Lingle, because he thought even that little bit of alcohol robbed Oscar of his good sense and reliability. What Dr. Lingle didn't know was that Oscar was being robbed of his good sense and reliability by considerable amounts of hard liquor.

As chief custodian of the large administration building, one of Oscar's responsibilities was to make certain that everyone was out of Chambers Building and the door securely locked on Sunday nights. He performed these services with care and much important jangling of keys about his person.

One Monday morning, Dr. Lingle stopped in the barber shop to tell me that it was a great pity about what had happened to Oscar. I had seen Oscar on the afternoon of the day before. The vein in which Dr. Lingle spoke led me to speculate in my mind that maybe Oscar had had an accident in his car. Dr. Lingle went on to say in a very serious manner that Oscar had drunk two bottles of beer yesterday, according to his own admission. Late in the afternoon, as it was getting dark, he had set out to get everyone out of Chambers Building and lock up for the night.

He somehow wandered seven miles away, and, as he was driving by the hospital in Mooresville, he had decided this large building was his destination. Many people were about in the hospital and lights were on everywhere. Oscar went about the business of getting them out of the building and putting out the lights. But they would not listen to him when he told them that this was Chambers Building at Davidson College, and that they had to get out so he could put out the lights and lock up the building.

Someone called the police, and Oscar was locked up tight in the Mooresville jail until morning, when he got word to Dr. Lingle about where he was. That's when Dr. Lingle was told about the two bottles of beer. Since so much had happened, it is presumed that Oscar thought one bottle of beer was not enough to report on this occasion.

CHAPTER THIRTEEN

World's
Fair

During the early part of the summer of 1933, when I was working on the last assignment of the commercial art course, two of my white friends proposed that we go to the World's Fair being held in Chicago. I wanted to go the Fair, but I wanted to finish the drawing lesson I was doing before going, as it was the last one in the course. They agreed to wait until this was done, and we set about making plans for the trip.

Paul Williams and JC Washam and I had been friends for a long time. Paul had a '29 or '30 model Ford cabriolet, a front-seated affair with a cloth top and a rumble seat in the back. This was to be our means of transportation, with JC and me paying a flat ten dollars each to Paul to defray our part of the car's expense, which included gas, oil and everything. I considered this a real bargain, even in 1933, for a round trip of sixteen to seventeen hundred miles.

Since none of us had any money to speak of, we were going to camp out going and coming and while we were in Chicago. Accordingly, we began to assemble such camping equipment as we could borrow. One of our prime prospects for this was Sergeant Burton, who was stationed at Davidson College as a part of the military training program there. "Sergeant," as he was called, was an extremely friendly and cooperative person and well-liked in the town.

He listened to our request with the wry grin on his face that was characteristic of him and agreed to supply us with pup tents and camp cots if we were careful not to let it be known that he was doing this, as it was against military rules to lend equipment.

That part of our needs settled, we began getting together other items that we had to have. This included a camp stove, which we were unable to borrow, mainly because we couldn't find anybody that owned one. We inquired diligently after this, but for this item we had to expend six dollars and a few cents at Sears Roebuck in Charlotte for a two-burner model that burned white gasoline. At our homes we rounded up pots, pans, and other utensils for our kitchen. Among these was an aluminum coffee pot that mama let us take with us, and it proved such a popular part of our equipment and made such good coffee, she gave it to Paul as a keepsake when we returned.

During these preparations a student at Davidson College who was still in town after college had closed for the summer came one day and asked to go with us. I don't remember his name now, after forty years, but he was a pre-ministerial student and we called him Parson, which is probably why I can't remember his name. The other two were reluctant to take him with us, what with his being practically a preacher and all. But after we had talked together some, Parson was included in our party. He had some money to chip in on the car-fare, too. This was no little inducement.

On Saturday night after I finished working in the barber

shop all day, we were ready to go. The other three had spent the better part of the day packing all the gear we had assembled on and about the car wherever it could be put, together with our personal belongings, such as clothes, which were not many. When this was all done, the car looked like the conveyance of a traveling carnival.

We set out that night in high spirits, with two in the front seat and two in the rumble seat, the running boards loaded down with our paraphernalia. We were going to take the World's Fair by storm.

By early morning before daylight, we were well into the North Carolina mountains. Our initial jubilation had subsided by now, and we had gotten sleepy and a little tired from being cramped in the car with our baggage. Paul was driving, and, since it was dark, there was nothing we could see except what was illuminated by the headlights.

Then all of us saw it. We had just rounded a curve, of which there were many in the mountain roads of that time, when we saw it standing there by the side of the road. At first it was so unreal and we were so startled by it that we could say nothing at all. It was only after it had vanished from the light as we passed that we spoke. All of us had seen what appeared to be a pretty young woman with long, light-colored hair about her shoulders and dressed in some loose, filmy, white material that covered her body to the ground. We looked back but could see nothing but darkness. We had suddenly come wide-awake at this strange apparition, which disappeared as quickly as it had come into our view.

There was nothing to explain how and why a young woman would be by the side of this mountain road in a dark and isolated area where there were only thick bushes and trees. Nor why she would be dressed in such white and filmy material in the pre-dawn darkness and the chill of the mountain air. We thought we had seen a sight that was unreal. Until this day, we have not decided what it was we saw that night.

The next morning, we stopped at a place by the side of the French Broad River, high up in the mountains, and cooked our breakfast on the little camp stove we had bought for the trip. Then we started again to drive all day that Sunday.

During the day, JC's ears began to ache. He had previously had trouble with his ears at home. We thought the mountain altitude was contributing to his present discomfort, which was considerable. Then his nose became sun-burned and the skin started peeling from riding in the rumble seat. All in all, he was fairly miserable. We decided that he should ride in the front seat, which had a top over it, with Paul who was driving. This left the rumble seat to Parson and me, instead of rotating around as we had been doing.

We drove all day in this manner, enlivening ourselves by singing songs. At least we called it singing, but it was a poor performance, for none of us could carry a tune in a bucket. Anyway, we were making happy sounds to the countryside as the little Ford maintained a lively pace over the hot roads in the direction of Chicago.

As the afternoon wore on, we started looking about for a likely place to camp for the night. We had traveled all the night before, and the little sleep any of us had gotten was small naps taken as we drove along the highway.

A man at a roadside service station told us that a mile or so farther on we would come to a farmhouse set some distance back from the road. He said the people who lived there would probably let us spend the night in the large yard about the house.

When we drove in at this place, two men were standing out waiting for us. The man at the service station had telephoned and said we were on the way. They were very cordial and told us we could camp anywhere in the yard that suited us. While we made ready to prepare our evening meal on the camp stove, they went to the house and presently returned with a pitcher of milk and some eggs which they gave us. This was a gesture of their hospitality. Two or three younger males came, also, and they sat and talked with us while we fixed food and ate and made ready to spend the night.

This was our first night camping out, and since the weather was warm and clear, we didn't bother to put up the tents. We slept on the cots under the starry sky, and were awakened early the next morning by flocks of jaybirds and their noise. This gave us an early start on the road, and we arrived in Chicago in the afternoon and established ourselves at a campground on South Halsted Street.

This was a large vacant lot behind a service station. There were many other campers there, some with fancy camping equipment in the way of tents, and a few motorized campers. They were all very friendly and, as we learned later, borrowed things like sugar or salt and coffee from each other when they were unexpectedly out. Everyone was very neighborly, and we left our tent flaps open during the day when we were gone, without fear of losing our possessions. One morning a neighbor apologized for having gone into our tents the afternoon before to put down the flaps when it looked like rain.

Soon after we arrived, the owner of the service station informed us that if we were going to need anything to drink we should let him have our order then so that delivery would be made without fail the next morning before daylight by a member of the Capone organization. He said he drank a quart of it a day and that it was good and it was safe. He looked healthy enough, so we told him to get us a bottle for the next day. We thought this made us look like real smart guys. We hadn't been in Chicago more than three hours, and already we were doing business with Al Capone's mob.

The next few days and nights were spent seeing the fair and some of Chicago. During this time, we managed it so that most of our meals were cooked and eaten at the camp. But one day, we decided to eat the evening meal at a cafe.

Late in the afternoon, we entered a restaurant and seated ourselves at a table. Our order was taken, and, while the food was being prepared, a man, who appeared to be of Greek background and who obviously had some connection with the business, came to our table and engaged us in conversation. After a few minutes, he said he had some really good native Greek wine that he kept for his own use, and he would give us some of it, if we liked to have it, before eating. He then invited us to come with him to a little room to the side of the dining area, where he poured each of us a glass of the wine and talked with us until the food was ready. We were at a loss to understand why he chose us from his many customers for his hospitable act.

The fine experience of the fair at an end, we loaded our many pieces of equipment on the car and set out for home. But our good luck was about to play out on us.

We were rolling along the road in high spirits, with much laughter and recounting of our experiences. For a group of green country folks, we thought our excursion into the big city had been quite successful. After all, we had gotten lost three times, and only once had we taken the wrong streetcar. We corrected that mistake by getting off quickly and chasing the right car down the middle of the street at a dead run until we caught it.

Then we knew something was wrong. A noise was coming from somewhere. It was a slight whining sound, and it was coming from the direction of the rear end of the car. At first, it was intermittent, and we thought each time, when it became quiet, that it was gone. Then the recurrence became more frequent, and the noise got louder. There was no mistake. It had a message for us.

A mechanic said it was the pinion gear in the rear end. He said if we took it easy, we could make it home. So the next four or five hundred miles home were driven at thirty-five miles an hour. And our singing was done to the accompaniment of a variety of whining, grinding noises coming from the underside of the car, which probably enhanced the tone of the singing. It was hot that day, and, as Paul was driving—it was his sick car—and JC had to sit under the top on account of his sun-burned nose, it was left to poor Parson and me to share the tight confines of the sun-baked rumble seat.

Back home, we counted up our expenditures. Three of us had spent about $22 each. Paul, who furnished the car, came out about even, except for getting the rear end fixed. We had been gone a week, and we had seen the World's Fair.

I was not pleased with the way things had gone at the shop while I was away. Some of the equipment had been broken as if from rough handling or a fight in the place. I thought it probable that this had occurred after business hours. Ed, my helper who had been left in charge, never gave a satisfactory explanation for this. He had for some time in the past become more unreliable. Added to my other problems, which had not diminished, was the prospect of having to get rid of him. This would be difficult and time-consuming, as I would have to find another suitable person and train him as a barber. In the process, the business would suffer.

Ed had developed into an excellent barber and was well received by the shop's customers. But he had taken up with a fairly wild set, and his personal habits were now those of his associates. As a result, there were an ever-increasing number of days when he was not at his best at work.

By now, I was pretty well sick of the barber business. It held so many problems for me that it was almost unbearable. But I was trapped in a whole life situation that bound me to it. First, there was the little business itself. Under fairly normal conditions, it would provide me with better earnings than I could command at anything else. I had devoted several years to building up a trade in the shop that was bringing me continuous income, as small as it was at the moment, and it held some promise for the future if the Depression would ever go away.

Then, there was my commitment at home to take care of my mother and sister, which was a very large consideration in my life. Above and beyond all of this, there was nothing else I could do to earn a living. I had no other skill that I could turn into regular pay. The economy was such that it was worse than useless to try to get a job.

The brief interlude of the carefree trip to Chicago was all too soon in the past. I was back with my troubles. I was very discontented. It seemed to me that a special brand of punishment was being levied upon me because I was trying, trying so desperately to improve myself as well as the conditions which surrounded me and my mother and sister.

I found it a difficult and despairing experience to put forth every effort possible and continually, time after time, to meet with failure, frustration and meanness. Yet there was nothing I could do except to go on. Go on to what? I kept asking myself. Bitterness crept into me. I found it growing and occupying my thoughts more and more. I had arrived at a state of hopelessness. It seemed that all my struggles had been in vain. Why should I try, anyway? What demon possessed me and exacted this penalty of suffering?

But this condition was not all my fault, either. It was not due altogether to an inordinate ambition on my part. True, I had the will to do, but my frustrations, in large measure, lay in circumstances outside myself. I asked myself why I should be denied the right and the means to develop whatever potential was within me. Right here in my hometown were the instruments of learning that could enable me to accomplish my aims of getting an education.

There was an excellent high school and a college that enjoyed a high academic rating throughout the South. Yet both of these were closed to me because of my race. My lot was to serve the white youths that were assembled here from many states for an education. But this church-related school forbade that I should be a part of its student body. What was I to do with a mind cursed with an insatiable appetite for learning? If I put a little into it, it demanded more and more, and I had not at hand the means to satisfy this craving.

Previously I had, at least to some extent, kept out of my mind thoughts of racial discrimination as it applied to me. That is, I preferred not to dwell on this hateful thing. I was ashamed to let the thought surface that other men entertained a low estimate of me because of a circumstance of race over which I had no control.

I had been born under this cloud, and there had been a degree of acceptance of my condition as a Negro. It is true also that I had not been subjected to the harshness of meanly imposed injustices. As a matter of fact, I had been dealt with in some leniency compared to the rigid application of the rules imposed upon most Negroes. I had not been spoken to in rough language, nor had anyone attempted to cuff me around. I think I could not have accepted meekly or passively the hard treatment sometimes imposed on Negroes.

Nor had anyone tried to take an advantage of me in my business dealings with them. Too, I had been the recipient of considerate and fair treatment, even courtesies. And where

someone had found it necessary to apply the prevailing mores
of racial injustice, it had been done with kindness and not
without some apparent embarrassment on the part of the
person who levied it against me. This had been true since my
childhood. There were many instances in my dealings with
white people where I had received preferential consideration.

I am sure this manner of treatment was at the beginning due
in large part to the high esteem in which my father was held in
the community. And later, when I was on my own, I like to
think it was due to my own bearing and the integrity which I
practiced in my dealings with people.

The bitter hopelessness which had lately come over me was
not associated with hatred of individuals as oppressors or
willful tormentors. I looked beyond to the state of things that
functioned according to design and brought this system into
being and perpetuated it. It is true that evil people had
brought the system to fruition, and an evil intent in the mass
of people was responsible for its continuance and its massive
and finely honed oppressiveness. It was the system that I
despised. I knew that white people were maintaining the
system. But white people were also caught up in this evil thing
and brutalized by it. The pressure of the system was upon
them and they individually were powerless to break its grip. So
tightly had the bonds of racial discrimination been woven into
the fabric of living and into the minds of people that it was
regarded as "right" by many. It was a way of life that they had
been born into, and some had not taken the trouble to examine
it in the light of their own conscience, or of abstract right and
wrong.

And there were those who benefited from it, or thought
they did. They were the cruel ones who delighted in the sense
of power they had over hapless blacks.

Regardless of these rationalizations, there was the ugly truth that I and millions of other Negroes were the victims of a gigantic outrage against humanity. The great power and wealth concentrated in the maintenance of this black-hearted structure awakened in me a deep sense of abandonment to fiendish forces that I knew could hardly be eradicated in my lifetime.

I was conscious also that the reason I had not been dealt with harshly was that I had obeyed the rules. I had not challenged the status quo. Acting within the framework of existing, accepted practices, I had tried to advance myself. Had I behaved differently, my treatment would have been shaped to deal with that. What I enjoyed were privileges granted by indulgent whites. They could be withdrawn at a moment's notice. I had no inherent rights or privileges as a human being. Except for those granted me from day to day and subject to withdrawal at the whim and pleasure of the white persons who granted them, I was as naked of human dignity and prerogative as any other Negro. The ground rules were the same for all. The difference was in application.

I tried to do whatever possible within the allowable bounds of my disadvantage. The system was purposely contrived to make it impossible for Negroes to advance themselves or get free from its snares. Hopelessness and despair were its natural result and its allies. For without hope, there is resignation.

Hope for the future had been my constant, sustaining companion. Now this hope was snatched from me by perception. Heretofore, I had been unwilling to accept my perception, and my mind had stilled the thought. But now, it was there in all its might and ugliness. My whole life situation was the product of a purposely designed hopelessness.

Were they, in allowing a little freedom from the unfeeling severity, only baiting me or testing the efficacy of the system to see if it would constrain under softened circumstances? Would they teasingly and cruelly let out the leash to see how far I

could go, then in one awful, devastating blow drive me back
against the wall, when they had destroyed whatever I had been
able to achieve?

Finally, it had to be admitted that all of the white people
were enforcers of the system. They had to be. The system
would be enforced against them if they in their permissiveness
dared to cross the line of demarcation that bound us all. We
were, all of us, locked in the claws of this thing. It was very
confusing, and my mind was tortured with it.

Among many older Negroes of that time, there was still so
much preoccupation with being freed from actual slavery of
the body that there was an acceptance of this lesser brand of
subjugation. They were freed from the time when they were
put to stud at the will of their masters and bred like beasts,
their children taken from them and sold away to other masters
who dealt with them as they pleased. The Negro mind had
been effectively shackled during bondage, and it was slow to
move from its position of thankfulness for deliverance from
this into the area of equality in its fullest sense. This was still
forbidden ground. They were so blessed by freedom from
being owned and sold that this clawing thing that was imposed
in its stead seemed hardly a burden at all. Their immediate
objective had been attained.

There was shouting and rejoicing in the Negro churches.
Negro minds were fastened on the relative freedom of the
body on earth, and the hope of salvation in a visionary para-
dise beyond the skies. The reality of their condition of servi-
tude and despair was shunted into the background. Negro
preachers were having a field day with emotionalism and were
reaping substantial benefits for themselves. This had no attraction for me. I turned away from it in disgust.

When the parts of my life that made up its whole were
examined separately, I found little to console me. The responsi-

bility I had assumed for the welfare and support of my mother and sister bound me to them and to our home. Business in the barber shop was, like most at that time, hardly providing for more than our bare necessities. Ed, the barber whom I relied on for help in the shop, was no longer dependable. I was paying $3.66 each week to the B&L. I had not missed one single payment. This was no small matter in those days of the Depression when millions were without any income at all, and even to get food was difficult.

I had no social life. That had been given up several years before in the interest of trying to educate myself by correspondence study. Most of my former associates now looked upon me as being apart from them and as having no interest in the things that occupied their time. My affiliation with the church for all practical purposes had been severed. I hardly went anymore. This brought me under heavy criticism from churchgoers and preachers alike. I had been reared in the AME Zion Methodist Church, but this organization as a religious body had never appealed to me. So, when I attained the age that permitted me to choose whether or not to attend its services, I elected to absent myself from them.

What was not known, and what I did not bother to explain, was that from my early years I had been a prayerful person, although my conduct at times would not support this belief. This had always been a very private thing with me and did not involve getting on my knees at bedtime, which I have not done since childhood, nor of talking about it. It was done whenever the need in me dictated it, and when I was alone. Sometimes, the words were spoken aloud, but most often they were said in silence. And there were so many times when there were no words at all, only my thoughts directed to God. Many, many times the agony in my soul was prayed out to God in the silence while I lay in bed in the quiet of night. I had never assumed a religious stance in public, if, indeed , I was religious at all. And it was quite generally taken for granted that I had no interest in that direction.

This self-analysis of my situation served not one whit to alleviate the difficulties that confronted me. It did, however, give me a fairly clear view in perspective of the life situation in which I was entangled. And, as far in the future as my mind could penetrate, there was little more than my present lot that could be expected during all of my life. Optimism had vanished in the light of clear appraisal. Henceforth, I would not deceive myself by hiding the truth in a cloud of wishful thinking. Mine was to be a life desolate of joyful living.

Of great concern to me at this time, the fall of 1933, was the breaking-up both morally and physically of my cousin Ed. It is a sad and a terrible thing to watch helplessly while a good friend and a young man of some promise goes progressively to hell. I wondered if I had the strength to avoid the same fate. The first few years after I brought him into the barber shop and taught him the barber trade had been very pleasant ones for both of us. He had developed into a fine workman and was well liked and received by the customers. In addition to this, he and I were staunch friends and went about a great deal together.

But, somewhere along the line, something had happened to him. About the time when I began studying the high school course by correspondence, he gradually fell in with other companions and our outside interests were brought to an end, as I devoted practically all of my time after work hours to studying. I noticed that he became more secretive with me, and I learned from other sources that his behavior pattern had undergone considerable change. He was my mother's sister's son, as related earlier in this writing. Several years after Ed's birth and the subsequent birth of a daughter, his mother

married a man who was a fireman on a Southern Railway train
that ran through Davidson.

Luke Wilson, the man she married, was a good-natured
person, and his job on the railroad paid well. He accepted
Tinnie's three children (she already had Vecue before Ed's
birth) as his own, and they took his name. Luke was a man
who spent his earnings freely, and Tinnie's children made the
most of it. He bought the house next door to us and went
into the B&L and had it remodeled to make a nice home. He
also kept a good car and the boys had access to this. Theirs
was the Negro family with the best income in town. But the
money was spent unwisely in show-off living. Ed, the most
stable of Tinnie's sons, was Luke's favorite. And, having a fine
car to drive and money to spend, he soon became popular with
a set of companions bent on having a good time. It was
leading this kind of life that gradually brought on his ruin.

Luke was unwise in his spending, with the result that he was
deeply in debt when he was let out of his job with the railroad
in late 1932. This was a severe blow to the family, as he had
been earning a high salary even during the Depression. When
misfortune struck, Luke blamed Tinnie and her boys for
having spent everything he had. They soon separated and he
left town when judgments were brought against him for debts
and foreclosure on the house mortgage stared him in the face.

All of this was quite a come-down for Ed. Instead of his
buckling down and trying to assume the payments on the
house, he went further into irresponsibility both at home and
on the job. Then it was discovered that he had a girl pregnant.
This was first brought to my attention when his mother and
the girl's mother called on me one night to tell me of this
situation and to say that they had to get married. The girl was
my father's sister Charlotte's daughter. So the parties directly
involved were my first cousins, and their mothers were my

aunts. Both women were in a state of tearful agitation and their visit was not a pleasant one. Each of them seemed to take it for granted that her child was the one wronged in this affair. And that, somehow, there was something I could do to set things right for them..

This added yet another dimension to my vexations. I had a feeling that Ed would not want to marry the girl, and that, if he did so against his will, the marriage would not be a lasting one and would be a continual source of unpleasantness. The next day, he would hardly discuss the matter with me, and I did not press him. But a few nights later, they went to South Carolina and were married.

Ma died early in the morning of Christmas day. It was a bleak, cold day. And, adding to the general gloom of almost every surrounding circumstance relating to the Norton family, this Christmas day was one especially filled with sadness. There was hanging over them the immediate prospect of being put off the farm for failure to pay the mortgage. I suspected this eviction had been delayed to some extent out of respect to Ma's illness. Now that she was gone, the normal processes of foreclosure and eviction were in the offing. Pa was old, and the fortunes of his family had run full cycle. He had begun as a poverty-stricken tenant farmer a few short years out of slavery. After many years, he had attained the status of a landowner of some prominence and status in the community. Now, in his old age and the frailty of his body, he was destitute again. His wife of these many years lay dead.

The next night, when the last of the few who had come to sit awhile had gone, Ed and I volunteered to sit together the balance of the night in our grandfather's home in order that someone might be awake there and a light burning on the night when Ma "lay corpse."

There was no longer the spirit of gay comradeship between Ed and me that had developed after he came into the barber shop with me and which had lasted for some years thereafter. This had gradually eroded away as our interests went in different directions. And while he was still at the shop, there was no interchange between us that nourished the old friendship. Too, troubles had descended on him in a sudden rush, and he was singularly unprepared to meet them. I gathered from his attitude that he was now resentful and envious of me.

He had, after I began studying and his new friends had made him the subject of their adulation, tended to look upon my efforts at self-improvement as a foolish waste of time that could be more satisfactorily spent in the pursuits of night-time pleasures. Now, the rug had been snatched from under him; the backing of an indulgent step-father had vanished as if it had been blown away by a contrary wind. The car was gone. The nice, two-story home he had lived in with the family was soon to go on the block and his mother made homeless. He had been forced into a marriage against his will and was now living with his pregnant wife in her mother's home in much reduced circumstances. Beyond this, his health was broken by dissipation, and he had become a chronic drinker. I had entertained the hope that his marriage would establish a new direction for him. And for a time, I believe it did. But the health problem and the drinking were too well established, though he was only in his mid-twenties.

When we found ourselves alone, seated before the blazing fireplace to keep watch over our grandmother's corpse that lay in the next room, there was little we could talk about. Except that this house in which we sat was haunted from some years back when it was occupied by a white family and a woman had been killed there. Since that time, it had been reported that there were doors that couldn't be kept closed, that they would swing open unaided and at unexpected times, attended by a swish of cold air. There were also noises that came from over the ceilings as if a chain were being dragged there. Members of my grandfather's family said they had experienced all these things, and there was at times a passing of something from room to room in the house.

On this night, Ed and I heard nothing of these strange noises from within the house. There was only the occasional murmuring of the wind on the outside.

Two o'clock in the morning is a lonely time under these circumstances, and Ed suggested that he go and get us something to drink. He went out into the darkness, and I was left alone before the dancing fire. His footsteps had little more than died away when the thought came over me in my loneliness that I was sitting there in a haunted house with a corpse in a coffin lying in the dimly lighted room on the other side of the door. An eerie feeling came over me, and I listened intensely for a sound.

Ed was gone about half an hour and the first sound of his walking on the porch sent a shock through me. Then we replenished the fire from time to time and drank the whisky and talked until morning. It was a lonesome night.

During this time, Ed made some comments about his way of life. And, as if talking to himself and not to me, he resolved to "straighten up," as he put it. But he spoke as the Ed of a few years ago who was about to correct some minor fault in his conduct. He was still identifying with that Ed. But a new and different personality had grown up inside him, and had taken charge of him, and was now directing him. He was not identifying with this new person that he had become, and with whom everyone else was now identifying him. I thought that until he recognized himself as the person he had become, there was little hope of his making a change in the direction he had taken.

Each of us was a different person from what we had been a few years earlier. We had taken different directions in our development. Both of us were unhappy, but for different reasons. His unhappiness sprang from having taken the easy path of sensuous pleasures and profligate living. They had reduced him to an empty shell of his former self and had brought into his life circumstances that fed misery into his body and his mind.

On the other hand, I had chosen the difficult way. I had dedicated myself to sacrifice and work, and this had produced circumstances in my life that were engulfing me in despair. Both of us had to go on living our lives from where we were at that time. And it appeared that neither of us could do a great deal to alter our ultimate fate.

After a long time, it was dawn. It had been a dreary night. Ma was buried in the afternoon of that day.

CHAPTER FOURTEEN

Burned Out

Somehow, I have always thought there ought to be desirable things accomplished in my life that would be added up into a total of my progress, as if it were necessary for me to account to myself for the manner in which I spent my time and efforts.

It seemed now that the only area in which I had shown any appreciable progress during the last few years was the time spent studying the two correspondence courses. I had finished both of them, and several months had passed since I had an organized program of study. I missed the stimulation and feeling of achievement that had associated itself in my mind with learning. So in the spring of 1934, I enrolled for a correspondence course in law.

This course of study held for me a promise of great adventure into the mysteries of the law. And when I received the first books and assignments, a time of concentrated attention to them began.

The Depression was still very much with us and trade in the barbershop was at a low ebb. The effects of financial disaster were all around. The state of mind of everyone was depressed.

Farms and homes were being lost. Businesses continued to go into bankruptcy. Main Street had almost the appearance of a ghost town with so many empty store buildings. Money was extremely scarce, despite President Roosevelt's Herculean efforts to get the economy back on its feet.

Studying had a two-fold meaning for me now. At once it provided a means of learning, and, while I was engrossed in the books, it was a constructive occupation that kept my mind away from my problems. Many times I worked at this until late at night. So, it was not unusual that on the 12th of July, 1934, I sat at the dining room table and typed on an assignment until twelve o'clock. Then by way of resting myself a little before going to bed, I walked up the highway to a roadside place that was open and drank a soft drink.

In bed a while later, I must have gone to sleep almost immediately. Next, I became drowsily aware that rain was falling on the roof, or so I thought. I could not remember that it looked like rain when I went to bed, and I lay there half asleep thinking about this. Finally, I opened my eyes and saw fire eating its way into the edge of the ceiling above my head. Almost immediately, there was pounding and calling from the outside to wake us up. The blaze had been seen by others when it penetrated the roof and shot into the sky.

I ran across the hall to wake up Mama and Sister to get them out of the house. We caught up the few clothes we could get in our arms and ran outside. There was no time for anything else. By the time we were outside, the whole roof seemed to be enveloped in flames. We had barely gotten out with our lives. People came running to help, and some tried to get inside to save the furniture. But it was too late. The only things saved were a vanity dresser and a mattress from my sister's room and a few items from the living room. The fire had started at the back of the house and the front two rooms were the last for it to reach.

The voluntary fire department came upon the scene with
much clamor and confusion. They were having trouble getting
a hose down that was long enough to reach from the nearest
fire hydrant, which was about a quarter of a mile away at the
point where Main Street ended. By the time they got a hose
together, the fire was far past the time when their efforts would
do any good. We had run out of the house into the front yard
with our clothing in our hands, and I must have presented a
comic figure there in the light of the fire frantically trying to
put on my tangled pants, while Mama and Sister amid their
fright and tears tried to clothe themselves.

After a while, when the big blaze had burned itself down,
Mama and Sister went to Pa's house, which was the fourth
house down the road from ours. The clothing they had on
their bodies was all they had to wear.

I sat on the grass and watched the glowing skeleton against
the black night until the sun came up. What had gone on here
had happened in the few hours between midnight and dawn of
a summer night. I was still in a state of shocked unbelief as I
sat there and looked at the two naked chimneys standing like
lonely sentinels over the hot ashes of what had a few hours
before been our home. My face was wet with tears, and my
heart and my chest were heavy as lead with hatred. This was
not an accidental fire. This was a continuation of the fires that
had been set at the barber shop. It had been set to burn us up.

I went to Pa's house and ate breakfast. Then I went to the
barber shop and borrowed from Ted, my shoeshine man, an
old Boy Scout shirt that had been given to him. The one shirt
I had saved from the fire was soiled.

To leave one's burning home in the middle of the night is a
bewildering experience under any conditions. But to run out of
our burning home like frightened rats under these circumstances was more than that. We knew that out there in the

darkness was lurking a person or persons who had attempted
to burn us alive. The stealth and meanness of such an act is
appalling. I knew that I was the one it was really meant for, but
it made no difference to the person who did this that my
mother and sister were more than likely to be killed also. So
widespread was the conviction that this fire had been deliberately set, that an investigation was begun immediately. An
official of the state whose duty it was to investigate fires of
suspicious origin was called in.

Our first personal concern was to supply ourselves with
clothing. Some items of wearing apparel were given to us by
sympathetic persons of the community, but there were problems of sizes, etc. Also, it must be remembered that, in the
summer of 1934, most people needed what clothing they had
for themselves. I had a few dollars and we went shopping for
things we most had to have. Fortunately, it was summer and
not much clothing was needed.

We would stay at Pa's house for the time. There was nowhere else to go. And besides that, we had none of the things
that were needed to set up housekeeping, not even pots and
pans. After a few days, when we had recovered somewhat
from the initial shock of having been thrust almost naked out
into the world, my mother and sister and I got together to
discuss our situation and to talk about our future plans.

We owned the house on the other side of town that my
father had bought for rental property shortly before his death,
and on which Mama had succeeded in paying off the remaining three-hundred-dollar debt. It was occupied by an elderly
woman who lived alone, and she agreed to move out and let us
have it.

As the days went by, our problems were brought more into
focus and we could see with greater clarity just what we faced.
It was near the end of the time when the six-and-a-half-year

term for the B & L loan would ordinarily mature, and the debt
be paid off on the house that had burned. But due to the
severe economic conditions of the Depression, profits in the B
& L were not as great as had been expected at the time the loan
was made. As a result the term would be somewhat longer.

I had not missed one single weekly payment of $3.66 on the
one thousand dollar loan that had been used to renovate the
house. Many others during this time of great financial stress
had not been able to keep up their payments, and this was why
the usual six-and-a-half-year term had to be extended. It was
determined that I still owed $145 on my loan. I had looked
forward eagerly to the time when I should have this debt paid,
as it was now very hard to get the money to make the payments
each week.

I had carried $2250 insurance on the house, and we consid-
ered rebuilding on the same lot. But the insurance company
came up with a fine-print provision in the policy that reduced
their liability to two-thirds of its face value where the property
destroyed was more than fifteen hundred feet from a fire
hydrant. Our house was outside that limit, so we only received
a $1500 settlement.

I went to work doing and getting some needed repairs and
renovations done on the other house, so we could occupy it as
quickly as possible. I did not like living with Pa and his two
daughters, Mama's sisters. They were expecting momentarily
to be put out of their house for nonpayment of the mortgage.
And they were trying to get us to pay off their debt with the
insurance money and live there. I had no intention of becoming entangled in this scheme and all of us, my mother, sister
and I, wanted out of their house.

On the morning after our house was burned, Dr. Lingle,
president of Davidson College, came to the barber shop to talk
to me about the family misfortune and to offer his sympathy

and help. A day or so later, I remembered that the college had
recently put new beds in the dormitories for the students and
that they had on hand the old ones which were stored in a
building on the campus. At Pa's house there were not enough
beds for all of us, and I had been sleeping on a pallet on the
floor.

I decided to go to Dr. Lingle's office and ask him to let me
have two of these small iron beds that were no longer in use.
He told me to go directly to the office of Mr. F. L. Jackson,
then secretary and treasurer of the college, and tell him to have
the head janitor get the beds for me. To my great surprise and
hurt, when I entered the office and gave him Dr. Lingle's
message, Mr. Jackson assumed a very indignant attitude and
told me that he had no time to be bothered with such as that,
saying that Dr. Lingle was forever getting himself involved in
something like this and that he was not going to do it.

I had not expected such a curt rebuff, and I went blindly out
of his office and back to the barber shop. Later, when I had
regained my composure, I went back to Dr. Lingle's office and
told him what had happened. I think this was the only time I
ever saw him when he appeared to be even a little angry. But a
stern look came over his face, and then he told me he would
take care of it. The beds were delivered to me soon after that.
They were sturdy little iron, single beds with a woven wire
spring made into them and quite comfortable. I slept on one
of them for the next several years.

When the house was ready for occupancy, we had no furniture to move into it, except the vanity dresser and mattress
saved from my sister's room and a piece or two from the living
room, plus the little iron beds that Dr. Lingle had given me.
On the day when we moved, it was discovered that the uphol-
stery on one of the pieces saved from our living room had
been recently damaged. Was this, too, done spitefully by

someone we knew that hated us? The insurance company
hadn't paid us for the burned house yet, and I had spent the
little I had for clothing and paying workmen to help with fixing
up the house into we were going to move. Materials for the
work on the house were bought on credit until the insurance
was paid. I knew I could buy on the installment plan from
furniture stores in Mooresville, the nearest town that had a
furniture store. But in our nearly destitute circumstances now,
we thought it better to buy secondhand furniture and keep as
much of the insurance money intact as possible.

With this in mind, I went to Mr. J. R. Withers, who was
president of the Davidson bank and a friend and customer.
This is the same kindhearted man whose building Uncle Tobe
and I had occupied with our shops immediately before we
moved into the new building where my shop was presently
located.

Mr. Withers was in the back yard of his home on South
Main Street when I arrived, and I went there to talk to him.
He listened quietly while I explained that I wanted to borrow
enough money to go to Charlotte and buy secondhand furniture and pay cash for it rather than buy new merchandise on
the installment plan at a much higher price. I promised to pay
the money back as soon as the insurance company paid off.
When I had finished telling him my plan, he said he thought
this was a wise thing to do and for me to go to the bank and
tell Watt Thompson to let me have the money. On second
thought, he said never mind that; he would call the bank
himself. When I went to the bank, Mr. Thompson had the
money for me.

Mama and I went to Charlotte and looked about in two
secondhand stores before settling on all of our purchases at
the Baltimore Furniture Company, a secondhand store on East
Trade Street. All of our things were bought for $200 and were

paid for in cash. This fact in 1934 made a big impression on the owner of the store, who came to assist personally in the sale when I made it known to the clerk that this was to be a cash transaction provided the prices were right. The next day these furnishings were delivered to the old house in Davidson that was to be our new home.

Twenty-five years years later I was surprised by an elderly salesman in the basement appliance department of Sears Roebuck's store in Charlotte when he asked if I were still in Davidson. Over the years, I had come in contact with many people in the barber shop and other places whose faces I did not remember. But for some reason, I stopped to talk to this man, and he explained that he was the salesman who had sold the secondhand furniture to Mama and me back in 1934. He said the circumstance of our having bought so much furniture at that time and paying cash for it was so unusual that he had remembered the incident down through the years. He even remembered that our house had burned down and asked about Mama.

The many kindnesses extended to us during this trying time did not eradicate the harshness of the circumstances of our lives. As for me, I had been, in a few short hours on the night of the fire, transported brutally from what I had previously considered a difficult and unhappy life situation into a bottomless pit of despair. I knew now that a hatred existed towards me that had demonstrated its willingness to employ any means to destroy me. My very presence in our home, such as it was at this time, constituted a danger to the lives of my mother and sister. Yet there was some feeling that we were better protected from secret assaults in this different neighborhood because there were more houses about us and the likelihood of a prowler being discovered was greater. Too, some of my father's relatives lived in this area and they were friendly and protective towards us.

But our life style and the relative comfort of our former home had been destroyed, and we seemed like half-naked rats that had fled a crib that was burnt down to rid the world of their presence . None of us had done anything to deserve this treatment. I was full of bitterness, and hope had been drained out of me.

At this time, I gave serious thought to leaving Davidson and going somewhere else to live. An influential customer who was concerned about me suggested that I go to Washington, D.C., where opportunities were better for Negroes. He offered to and did consult our congressman with reference to this. But such a course of action would have completely uprooted us and brought about environmental changes that we were not prepared to assume. Too, it was not certain that employment could be secured in government service at that time, as competition for jobs in 1934 was very severe.

After all, this was not much more than an exploration into outside possibilities, because I think, deep down, we were committed to remain in Davidson, whatever such a future had in store for us. So I buckled down once more to try to clear away the debris of negative thinking and fear that had accumulated within me, and to try and see if it were possible for me to bring some semblance of order and direction back into my life. The burning of our house and the narrow escape we had getting out with our lives had practically decimated me, and I hardly knew which way to turn. But I had to go on trying to earn a living, which was more than ordinarily difficult in this time of the Depression.

In the meantime, an investigation into the burning of our house had been conducted, but no evidence was brought out to link anyone with it. The insurance company had paid the claim, and debts incurred for furniture and material for repairs to our present place of abode were settled. When all of this had been paid, $1000 of the insurance money was left.

Prior to the burning of our home, we had been regarded by our near neighbor-relatives with some envy because they were about to lose their homes for unpaid debts and we were not. Their situation was largely of their own making, because if they had practiced habits of thrift and foresight their obligations could have been met. It seemed ironic, though, that they were still in their homes and we had been the ones to lose ours. Especially so, after all the sacrifices we had made and the effort I had put into getting the money each week to make the payment to the B&L, while they did as they pleased, making little effort to clear their mortgages.

One of the threads of my life that I put back together as quickly after the fire as possible was a resumption of my studies in the correspondence course in law that I had begun shortly before the disruption. All of the books I had received for the course were destroyed when the house burned, but the school very generously replaced them without cost to me, and I was able to go on with study as soon as it was possible for me to bring myself back into that discipline. But I found it very trying to study effectively for some time due to my mind's wandering off into my troubled situation.

At the barber shop Ed had further deteriorated in his behavior pattern and could not be relied on. He had separated from his wife shortly after their baby was born, and she was now threatening court action for support for herself and the child. He was drinking more than ever and had lately become involved in a fight in which he was struck on the head by a thrown jar of mustard, a blow which had given him much subsequent pain and seemed to affect his mind. He had also developed a sore on the end of a thumb that wouldn't heal.

This was an ugly mushroom-like, raw sore that seemed to
elongate his thumb and had to be kept bandaged. His physician said it was caused by a disease he had acquired. I had to
terminate his employment and replace him with another man.
This I did very regretfully, because Ed had been my good
friend and had every possibility of becoming a fine and useful
man. But he had dissipated away his life in unproductive living
experiences.

As related here before, Ed was my first cousin, my mother's
sister Tinnie's son. My dismissing him from his employment at
the barber shop promptly loosed a tirade of criticism on me
from his mother and the others of the Norton family. They
had known all along of his behavior and of my trying to get
him into a different way of living. But that made no difference.
I was the culprit, and he was the one wrongfully used. Some
time later, he left town under suspicion of having stolen a
watch and some other articles.

After that his whereabouts were kept secret from me. Then
I heard he had broken into a home and stolen the articles.
This was a serious offense, and he never came home again.
From time to time, I heard of his having stayed for a while
with relatives in other places, but always it was the same--he
had to move on because of some trouble he had gotten into,
or he was too much of a burden to them. Finally, he died in the
spring of 1937 while living with his stepfather's brother in
Pittsburgh, Pa. The circumstances of his family were such by
that time that he was buried there. His sudden death was
shrouded in mystery.

Ed's popularity in the barbershop had gradually diminished
over a period of time before he left the shop. As a result, the
shop's business had declined. When I let him go, there was a
further loss in business. So the fine little business we had
developed a few years earlier had suffered a great deal by the

time of his going. The combination of the Depression years and Ed's breaking up and leaving had caused serious reduction in revenue. It was as if all the time and work put into it were wasted.

One day in the fall of the year after our house was burned, I was cutting Mr. J. H. Withers' hair and we were discussing my living conditions. I expressed our dissatisfaction with the house we were living in and spoke of rebuilding our home. To my surprise he said, "Let me sell you the Otho Johnson house." This was Uncle Tobe's house, the one he had built shortly before his death. I was surprised at Mr. Withers' offer to sell it to me because the man who lived in it had told me that he owned it. Mr. Withers said this wasn't true, that the man was only renting it from him. Then he went on to say how he had acquired the house.

Uncle Tobe had bought lumber from him during the building of the house and had died shortly afterwards, leaving the debt unpaid. His wife died in a matter of another two years. Then her son increased the debt by borrowing against the property, and finally lost it and the house next door, which was on the same lot. I was already familiar with these circumstances, because I knew what had gone on in Uncle Tobe's family with reference to his property after his death. Mr. Withers had, in fact, related much of this to me over several years, out of his concern in the matter. I knew the property had changed hands, but I thought the man who lived in the house had acquired it, as he claimed.

I was well acquainted with this house, because Uncle Tobe had built it as a sort of crowning glory to his success in the dry cleaning business. I knew all about it when it was being built. It was a one-and-a-half-story house with five rooms downstairs and two rooms and a hallway upstairs. The first story was constructed of brick that came from Chambers Building that had burned on the Davidson College campus (the same source from which the bricks were derived to build the downtown building that had housed our two businesses). The half-story was constructed of wood and had shingles or shakes above the brick lower story. This was by far the best-built house in the neighborhood, and I was immediately interested in buying it.

Mama was not enthusiastic about buying this house. It was within "a stone's throw" of where we were now living in the area of town where most Negroes lived. She preferred the location on the highway where there were fewer people and where our home had been before the fire destroyed it. The location on the highway had a connotation of being more exclusive than where we were living now. As a matter of fact, at the time when our house was burned, four of the five houses along the highway were owned by Mama's relatives, and it was considered the elite section of town for Negroes. So, living in the other area was, to her, a loss of prestige for us. This was one of the mentally distressing losses incident to the destruction of our home.

But Uncle Tobe's house was a better one than any of the ones on the highway, since it was constructed of brick and none of the others were. Mr. Withers said he would sell the house to me for $1000. This was a real bargain price, even in December of 1934. And, in addition to this, he said the other house on the lot would go along with the $1000 purchase price.

When Uncle Tobe built the house about 1924, electric lights were not in common use in the homes in this neighborhood, and the house had never been wired for electricity. Of course, there was no running water in it. At my insistence, we decided to buy these two houses.

This decision immediately posed another problem. Money! There were exactly $1000 left in the bank from the $1500 we had received as a settlement for the fire loss. The house we were buying was in need of some renovation, including wiring and running water. There was no sewerage available in the area. We decided to go on renting both houses until the following spring or summer, a matter of five or six months, in the hope that in the meantime I could save enough money to get some necessary things done before we moved in.

I had told Mr. Withers that I would pay cash for the property, and this was probably one of the reasons for the low price. One thousand dollars cash money in the winter of 1934 was some inducement even to a bank president, which Mr. Withers was; in addition he had an extensive farming operation. On the day when he was ready with the deed, I went to the bank and wrote him a check for the $1000 and he gave me the deed. After examining the check for a full minute, he looked at me very solemnly and asked if I thought I would ever again be able to write a check for such a large sum. I realized from his manner that he considered this the high point in any financial matter that I was likely to be able to arrange. Indeed, few people were making $1000 cash purchases at that time. Many were losing their property because they couldn't pay the taxes on it.

The ink was hardly dry on the deed to the property before complications arose. The man who was living in the brick house went around telling people that I had undermined him out of his home that he was buying. He had told it about that he owned the house, and I, along with many others, had believed this falsification until I learned better from the real owner. Of course this was a face-saving device on his part to conceal and cover over the deception he had practiced by telling that he owned the property. But it was believed by many and put me in a bad light in the community as being something of a scoundrel who would do such a thing.

Then the family that lived in the smaller house came up with the announcement that they had previously bought the house in which they lived from Uncle Tobe's son, having paid him $300 towards this purchase. And if I claimed the house and attempted to collect rent from them, I would be doing a great wrong and taking from them property that was rightfully theirs. There was not the least evidence to prove any of this, but it was told in great earnestness. If they had paid Uncle Tobe's son any money whatever, they never produced any evidence to show they had done so. And as far as I know, he never entered the controversy concerning their claim. At any rate, they never at any time mentioned any of this to me until after I bought the property from Mr. Withers, who had clear title to it. If they had been cheated out of money, I was not the one who had done it.

But the result was that after only six months of living in this area, I had a well developed reputation, with some who wanted to believe it, as a sly one who was victimizing innocent people and getting their homes from them. I had only recently come here as the object of a great deal of sympathy. Now it had turned into suspicion and mistrust and not a little scorn. All I had done to earn this was to buy property from the legitimate owner, who had himself asked to sell it to me. I wondered why I was bedeviled in this manner. It seemed that a strange shadow was hanging over me.

Later, in the spring of 1935, we moved into the brick house, using only the downstairs portion since we had not been able to renovate the upstairs rooms and furnish them. We were much better situated in this house, and all of us were better satisfied.

I continued to study the correspondence course in law, carrying the books back and forth to the barbershop in order to study when I was not working with a customer. When it became known that I was studying law, some attitudes changed towards me. As long as I was studying the high school course and the course in commercial art, it seemed all right and, to some, even commendable for me to spend my spare time with my books.

There had never been any effort on my part either to conceal or to draw attention to my studying or the subject of my inquiry. This practice was continued as a matter of course when I began studying law. But now, the subject of my studies was definitely not an approved one for Negroes. Law had the enabling characteristic of bringing about an understanding of the rules by which men are governed. Negroes were not supposed to know these things.

As a matter of fact, most people were ignorant of law and had a sneaky feeling of fear concerning it. The feeling existed, and still does, not without justification, that a knowledge of law gave its possessor an edge of superior inside learning and an unfair advantage. The more ignorant considered it to have mysterious and sinister powers that could be used against them. Obviously, I was considered by many, both white and black, as learning secrets that were for white people only and, perhaps, intended to use the knowledge gained in some way hurtful to the status quo. Many others, however, regarded me as relatively harmless to them in my studies and asked me about some things they wanted to know. There were some, too, who were not critical of my efforts at learning, even law. This was later demonstrated to me by a most unusual offer of help in that direction. I was also a very popular barber, and the quality of my workmanship was in demand.

CHAPTER FIFTEEN

Characters

Somewhere about the mid-1920s, a long, gangling, ginger-cake-colored young Negro man appeared in town. After some odd jobs, he became my shoeshine man in the barber shop and the part-time janitor at the movie house across the street. In practically no time at all, he became a popular figure and well-known to townspeople of all walks of life. He was perhaps twenty-two or twenty-three years old, without ambition beyond his immediate needs of food and clothing, and had the most totally ingratiating personality imaginable. His shoeshine business flourished and he was a welcome addition to the shop. Soon he was well-known all around the area, and customers stopped in just to talk and laugh with him.

Ted came fully equipped with a full-blown taste for beverage alcohol, and quickly became an off-duty drinking companion to many of his customers, who would seek him out and furnish whiskey for the pleasure of enjoying the good fun he provided. But these were not the only ones who liked and enjoyed Ted. Staid members of the community, bankers, doctors, merchants, college presidents and ministers all fell under his soothing spell.

Joined with his fondness for conviviality was a propensity
for getting himself into awkward situations. He was not
secretive about these incidents, and it was his pleasure to
recount them to his friends for their amusement.

A bit of deception he carried on for years had to do with a
fraternity on the campus. He adopted this particular fraternity
as his own and declared himself a member. The student
members in turn adopted Ted as a "brother" and there was
much discourse between them at the barber shop and at the
fraternity house where Ted was a frequent visitor.

Ted represented himself to these boys as being married,
which he wasn't, and as having one child, a baby girl. His
imaginary wife was a very large and disagreeable woman, with
whose meanness he had to live "on account of the baby," as he
told it. Of course he was always in need of money for the
"support of his family," and his fraternity brothers were
understanding about this and were correspondingly generous
with him in their financial assistance. It came finally to a point
where they decided they wanted to do something nice for the
baby. This pleased Ted mightily, and he licked his chops in
anticipation of this unexpected windfall. But then, the boys
asked Ted to bring the child to the fraternity house one night
for them to see it and to receive their gifts.

This posed a problem, but Ted's ingenuity was equal to it. A
woman of his acquaintance had a big, fat, very black baby. Ted
arranged to borrow the child from her in exchange for whatever presents the college boys gave it. Everything all set, Ted
appeared at the fraternity house with his "little Sasparilla"
dressed in her best for the "brothers" to see and admire.

This so pleased the college boys that they gave several
dollars to get "things" needed for the child. Ted gave the
child's mother part of the money and kept the rest for himself.
In the end, everybody was happy. At unexpected times after

this, Ted would appear at the house with "little Sasparilla" in tow until "her mama wouldn't let her visit the fraternity any-more."

One of the stories the lanky, loosely jointed Ted liked to tell was about the day when the visiting school nurse measured his height at nearly six feet tall when he was in the fourth grade. Then she put him on the scales to get his weight. He claimed he weighed exactly one hundred and eleven pounds. The nurse, according to Ted, looked at the scales in unbelief, then back at his half-naked frame before she covered her eyes with both hands and cried out, "My God in heaven."

There were times when the whiskey he was drinking talked to him and gave him advice, not always good. On one such occasion, he was walking along early one night in some happy alcoholic contemplation when he heard a loud noise of quar-reling voices emitting from the home of married friends. These sounds of discord were in harsh contrast to the vast contentment that enveloped his being. He stopped to listen. At that moment, the whiskey said to him, "You ought to go in there and put a stop to that racket."

"Sure enough?" Ted questioned.

"Yes! They ought not to be fussing and carrying on like that," replied the whiskey.

Something back in his mind warned against taking this advice. The man of the household was large and strong and his hands reached almost to his knees. He was known to be a fighter when angry. Ted consulted his liquid friend again to be certain he had heard aright.

"Go on in and stop it," the whiskey urged.

The front door was closed. But a twist of the knob and a shove put Ted into a room filled with unseemly strife. He closed the door behind him and stood with his back against it before he raised his voice above the clamor and ordered the man and wife, under the direction of the whiskey, to "cut out all that noise in here and behave yourself."

The angry husband, startled and indignant at this intrusion, turned his attention from his wife and advanced on Ted, a knife in his hand and an ugly look of determination on his face. The whiskey had not told Ted what to do in this sudden and unexpected eventuality. In one instant, he became sober, cold sober. Sobriety dictated that he get out of there, and get out fast.

He was standing with his back to the door, and it was necessary for him to advance a little on his assailant in order to get the door opened enough to squeeze himself out. This was a hasty, frenzied activity, and he barely succeeded in squirming his body through the narrow opening when he heard the swish of the knife at his back. His long legs got him quickly to the street. He was striding rapidly away with a loudly thumping heart when the whiskey spoke to him again. "Well, Old Boy," it said, "I damn near got you killed that time, didn't I?"

A fairly recent acquaintance was the new minister at his church. Ted had gone to Charlotte on this occasion to make application at a credit clothing store to buy a suit on the install-ment plan. His business finished he went nearby to a place where bootleg white whiskey was sold. There, he treated himself to a couple of drinks before heading back to the bus station for the ride home. He encountered his pastor on the street and was offered a free ride home in the preacher's car. This suited Ted just fine. Quickly he calculated the money he had on hand and realized that, with the bus fare saved, he had enough to buy a half pint of whiskey.

He hurried back and bought the small bottle of whiskey and met the minister at the appointed place, the bootleg whiskey tucked away in an inside coat pocket. They began the twenty-mile ride back home, with Ted chewing a large wad of gum to keep the preacher from smelling his breath. Along the way, Ted's thirst for another drink became more and more insistent. Finally, throwing all caution to the winds, he told the good man that on account of the cold weather he had bought a little bottle of whiskey while in the city, and would he object if he took a small drink of it.

The minister assured him that this would be all right. Whereupon, Ted brought the bottle into view and removed the stopper. Then, to show his good manners, he extended the bottle and offered to share its contents. The minister, without exchanging a word, took the bottle in hand and, while Ted looked on, turned it to his lips and drained its contents down his throat, leaving only a few drops at the bottom. Then, before Ted's astonished eyes, he threw the empty bottle out the window. They rode the rest of the way home in silence, Ted not having much to talk about.

A week later, Ted was back in Charlotte, this time to get his suit, his credit having been approved. The large package under his arm, he went then and had some drinks to celebrate the fact of his being a well-dressed man before going to catch the bus home.

At the station, the bus was already on the yard and he boarded it immediately, although it was not yet time for its departure. As he sat there waiting, a great and over-powering drowsiness overcame him and he dozed off to sleep.

After a mere wink or so, he was again awake and looking around. The bus was still standing, but somehow things didn't look the same, and the lights were on outside. They hadn't been on a few minutes ago when he dozed off. There was this strangeness, too. He went to the front of the bus to look around. He was still alone on it. Then he saw this sign over the bus station entrance and it read "Winston-Salem, N.C."

Something was wrong here, because he knew he was in Charlotte. But, there in plain view, was the sign. He decided to get
off and have a look around on the outside. First, he must go
back to his seat and get his suit, mustn't leave it in there.

Now look here! The suit was gone from the overhead rack
where he had put it when he got on a little while ago. Something was sure enough wrong. He was hungry, too, and it
hadn't been more than an hour since he ate that great big
hotdog with everything on it. A man in the station said, "Yes,
this is Winston," which added to his confusion. Then, slowly
the shape of things began to form in his mind. Had he slept
longer than he thought and ridden a hundred miles without
knowing? And where the hell was his new suit that he hadn't
paid for yet?

The man at the ticket window could tell him nothing, and
was totally unsympathetic to the fact that he had no money to
pay his way back to Davidson. The next bus would leave in a
little while, and, as far as he was concerned, it was no money
no ride, and that was that.

Then, time was running out, the home-bound bus was on
the yard. The ticket agent consistently paid no attention to his
pleas for a ride home. His charm wasn't working. The bus
driver was equally without concern and held his arm out to
block his entrance while other passengers got on. Finally, with
everybody aboard, the door closed and the driver in his seat,
the ticket agent appeared and held up his finger and pointed.
The door opened and Ted disappeared inside. He had spent
most of the night traveling to reach a destination twenty miles
from his starting point. The installment plan suit was gone,
and he had to pay for it at a dollar a week.

After each untoward incident having to do with his drinking,
Ted made fresh resolutions of total abstinence from alcohol.

During one of these times, he sat to the back of the shop near the shoeshine stand, one long leg thrown across the other at the knee, and, with free foot swinging, he read passages in the Bible for solace to his bruised soul. This was accompanied with much pursing of lips and muttering to himself. The Bible was an old one and worn with use, with many slithers of paper and pieces of string marking passages of particular comfort.

In the dungeon of sorrow from his last exploit, there was much Scripture reading, low murmuring, silent contemplation, with lips tightly compressed together and eyes fixed straight ahead, but seeing only the error of his ways. Finally, when the vision of his behavior would not go away, he stood erect, his narrow chest out, and, with strong resolution in his voice, proclaimed defiantly, "Go do it again! That's what I'll do, go do it again!"

And that's what he did, that very night.

He had a room at old lady Charleston Culp's tumble-down house, and when he went home late and to bed he became violently sick to his stomach. Hearing his groans, she went in to see about him. He was sure he was going to die, and urged the old woman to do something for him quick, "cause I ain't got long in this world."

After some frantic doing about, and knowing nothing else to do, she fell to her knees and began to pray. "Oh, Lord," she said, "please do something for poor old drunk Ted."

Ted heard every shocking word she said, and sat up straight in bed and pleaded. "Ma, for God's sake don't do that. Don't tell Him I'm drunk, tell Him I'm sick. Things is bad enough as they is!

Ted treated the matter of his room rent lightly when his landlady made repeated requests for payment. During the summer months, he would say, "Aw, Ma, don't keep on talking about that. I can sleep in a tree this kind of weather."

Well, this carried over into cold weather, and one bitter night Ted found the door locked. Knocking and rattling the knob did no good. "Ma, Ma," he called, "open up and let me in, it's cold out here." He peeked in by the window near the door, and there sat the old lady by the fireplace reading the Bible. The room was warm and cozy.

"Ma, come on open this door." No response. "Ma, I'm going to freeze out here in the cold."

Then a careless voice spoke from the inside, "Go sleep in a tree."

"Ah, Ma, quit your foolishness".

"I said go sleep in a tree. This is good weather for it till you get your room rent paid up," came the reply.

Once I had a big, jovial barber from South Carolina. He and Ted were fast friends and exchanged whopping stories about their exploits in the realm of personal enjoyment. Walter said when he was a young fellow on his father's farm, he and his three brothers were quite some cut-ups. His father was a landowner and a big man in the little country Baptist church. Each fall of the year they had a revival meeting in the church and there was much singing and praying and saving of souls, not to forget the shouting and general bedlam of such a meeting. Well, Walter claimed that he and his brothers had been riding around in his daddy's Ford waiting for church to let out so they could pick up some girls in there, when one of the three got a bright idea to hasten the closing of the service.

They parked the car in a clump of trees nearby and crawled up under the church where one of them let fly with three or four rounds from an old World War I, 45 Colt automatic. The effect, according to Walter, was instantaneous. There was a wild scramble to get out the one exit; some even left through open windows. "Everybody wanted on the outside, right now, and no fooling around." Here Walter would pause, place both hands over his ample stomach and chuckle in vivid remembrance.

He recalled that the preacher was caught up with about half a mile down the road. He was sitting on a rock, out of breath from running, his clothing half torn off from fighting to get out the door, and there was an angry bellow in his voice, as Walter told it, when he cried out, "Damn a man that'll build a church that ain't got but one door." Ted sat in smiling admiration at such fun.

Walter also remembered when some fellows were operating a still down on the creek at the back side of the farm. This was a successful operation that had been going on for quite some time, successful in that the sheriff had not been able to catch them and they were turning out a considerable amount of white bootleg whiskey. The secret to this was, according to Walter, that they used mules for watchdogs.

"You just can't slip up on a mule and surprise him. He's too suspicious," says Walter. "So the boys kept some mules grazin' in the pasture while they ran the still. And, you know something, the sheriff never could catch them makin' liquor. Every time anything got within smellin' distance or hearin' distance — a mule can hear better'n a fox dog— them mules would start throwin' their heads in the air and bellowin' with their big mouths wide open and pawin' with their feet in the ground. And the sheriff never could catch them boys at the still. When the mules started cuttin' up and hollerin' they'd hide the worm and run off in the woods.

"Anyway, he never found the copper worm, and all he messed up was the cookin' pot. The boys had a real scheme for hidin' the worm. They drove a stake down in the bank just under the water's edge, you know, and tied a rope on to it; then they tied the other end of the rope to the worm and let it down in the pond they had dammed up to get water from. Every time they made a run, they'd hide the worm this way and the sheriff never could find it.

"Well, one day the sheriff got lucky and caught sight of one of the boys runnin' through the woods. Him and his deputies took out after him and they was all runnin' and hollerin' at him to stop or they'd shoot him down.

"But they didn't hit him and he kept on runnin' too. And pretty soon they come to this little old house in a clearin,' and they run up on the porch and asked the colored woman settin' inside if she had seen anybody runnin' by there.

"'No, Suh, I ain't.'

"That old sheriff was smart and he thought the fellow what they was huntin' might be hidin' in there. So he asked her, 'Who's in there with you?'

"'There ain't nobody in here with me 'cept my husband and he's sick near to death.'

"The sheriff walked in and saw the woman settin' by the side of the bed fannin' away with a funeral parlor fan and a man layin' there with a sheet pulled up on him and he was sweatin' and pantin' for breath.

"'This is my poor sick husband,' she said. 'He's dyin' wid the fever, and Ah'm jist settin' here a-fannin' him to try to keep him cool.'

"Well, you know what," said Walter, "them white folks fell for that lie, and soon as they was out of sight, that boy and that gal had themselves a big laugh about it 'cause he wasn't no such thing her husband. He had just run in the house ahead of the sheriff and jumped in the bed with all his clothes on, and she pulled the sheet up over him and started fannin' when the law men come up on the porch. That's how come he was sweatin' and pantin' so. He was run near to death."

Walter and I were sitting on our front porch late one hot summer afternoon when we had half a day off from the barber shop. The Methodist preacher who lived across the street came over and joined us. Some bees were buzzing about in the shrubbery and Walter nonchalantly got up and went into the yard where he began reaching out towards different bees and closing his hand rapidly in an effort to catch the insects. This exercise in abject carelessness about whether or not he was stung by the bee excited the curiosity of the preacher, which was exactly what Walter had intended it to do.

Soon the preacher was in the yard watching in fascination as Walter caught two or three bees in his naked hand, then turned them loose again. The reverend became inquisitive about how this was done without getting stung. Walter explained the procedure and led the good man gently to the point of catching one himself.

This was a bad mistake on the preacher's part. The bee he caught didn't cooperate, and the preacher got stung on the hand. He was flinging his hand about in pain from the sting, amid hearty laughter from Walter, when another one stung him on the side of his head. He beat a hasty retreat across the street to his home. Walter said he never did care too much for preachers anyway.

Walter lived a merry life and in the spring of the year married a pretty brown-skinned young woman who idolized him. She treated him like a king, and he loved her for it. The next winter he fell ill with pneumonia and died within three days.

It was a bitter cold night when he lay corpse in their small house, and friends had gathered for the wake, when a stranger entered the room. The stranger was a good-looking woman, and she had two children with her. She asked if this was Walter's home. She was told that it was. Then someone asked if she were a relative. "I am his wife, and these are his two children," she answered.

"What?" she was asked in astonishment.

"I am Walter's wife and these are his two children," the woman repeated.

Bewilderment brought complete silence to the room. Then there was a sigh or two. The stranger made the few steps to the open casket against the wall and stood looking down into it. There was no display of emotion, just a long look at the remains of Walter. Then she took a seat on a politely offered chair, and, with her children about her, she sat impassively with the mourners.

It was a strange wake with two wives present. It hampered conversation. Gradually, one or more persons left the room, and in a very short time what was going on in Walter's house was known to everyone in the community.

After a while, the stranger asked the time and place of the funeral. Having ascertained these facts, she went out and was gone in the night. News of this lady's appearance and her claim on Walter spread on running feet, and speculation ran in all directions as to what she would do next.

At two o'clock the next afternoon, while the bell on the little church tolled the funeral hour, the same woman and her two children walked slowly down the aisle and took a front seat near the coffin. She sat there dry-eyed in her mourning dress and veil until the preacher finished. Then she followed the casket out the door.

The sorrow at Walter's death and the heavy drama surrounding his funeral left Ted in a highly thoughtful state. He made much comment on this matter, but he couldn't do justice to it. This was, indeed, a tall tale, worthy only of Walter's own telling, and he was not here to tell it.

Two weeks later, a strange white man entered the barber shop and asked Ted where Walter was.

"Suh?" the surprised Ted asked.

"Where's Walter, the big fellow?" the man asked.

Ted's eyes were wide and his gaze was steady on the white man's face when he replied, "Suh, you have just asked a question that a lot of folks would like to know, includin' two widows."

Until the years after the 1930's our area was more rural than urban, and the male pursuits of happiness included hunting in the nearby countryside. I never cared for hunting wild varmints in the fields and woods, but there were others who did.

Along with hunting went the conviviality of kindred spirits. Small parties were organized along lines of careful selection of persons for maximum enjoyment. One night, Plato and Dave, both white; Oskeegum, very black; and Frank, yellow, departed in Plato's old Ford, along with an assortment of possum dogs, to the old Fess Reid place to hunt and enjoy the outing.

They were well supplied with white whiskey, a necessary part of these adventures. The night was clear and crisp, and they were old hunting companions.

After some two hours of drinking and walking and talking and listening to the dogs run, disaster struck hard. The dogs had treed a possum in this tall tree deep in the woods. The men hurried up, and, by the dim light of Plato's lantern, saw the possum on a limb some distance up in the tree. Much discussion ensued as to which one would climb the tree and get the possum, with Frank being the most insistent upon going up.

It was thought by some of the others that he was not in the best shape for climbing, what with his being somewhat staggery from the whiskey. But he insisted, and the others stood back while he climbed up the tree. He was up to the limb where the possum was crouching when the small branch under his foot broke and he tumbled backwards out of the tree and to the ground.

Frank was a hundred and eighty pounds. He landed heavily on his back and lay still. Hasty and concerned examination established that his neck was broken and that he was dead.

This sad accident brought deep grief to the three survivors in the hunting party. They thought they could carry the body out of the woods to the car that had been left in the yard of the abandoned farmhouse at the top of the hill. This was some distance away, and they further prepared themselves for this sad ordeal by drinking what was left of the whiskey in the fruit jar.

Dave and Oskeegum were small men, and the limp weight of the heavy dead man on the three of them soon became an unmanageable burden, what with Plato, the only big man, having to use one hand to carry the lantern. At the second rest stop, they agreed they couldn't carry the body out to the car.

Oskeegum was the oldest of the survivors, and Dave and Plato, being more agile, agreed to hasten to the car and to town for help, leaving Oskeegum with the dead man. He was to answer the calls of the rescue party as a voice guide to the spot on their return.

The two white men headed for the car through the bramble and underbrush of the woods, their path lighted by the dim rays of the lantern. This left Oskeegum, the little black man, alone in the dark woods with the body.

All of this latest plan seemed well and good in the low glow of the lantern, and with all of them present. But with the others gone and the flicker of the lantern light hardly visible in the distance, Oskeegum had quick second thoughts about his lonely situation there in the dark and in the presence of the dead. There was only one thing to do, and he did it.

Plato was first to hear the noise in back of them, but

thought it was the dogs. Then the voice came: "Hey, you all wait on me."

"What's the matter, Oskeegum?"

"You all jist wait, that's what's the matter." Soon the little black man entered the small circle of light. He was panting for breath, and his eyes looked very wide.

"We thought you was going to stay there with Frank till we got back."

"You jist think again. I ain't going to stay down here in these dark woods with no dead man."

"But somebody'll have to stay with him. We can't all go off and leave."

"Yes we kin, too. He's dead an' he ain't goin' nowhere. He'll be right there when we all gits back. I ain't stayin."

Now, they had to go back and find the dead body, something of a problem since they had gotten some distance away and the woods were large and dark. But luck was with them this time, and presently they heard a sound. It was like a groan. Everybody stopped and listened, and searched each other's faces. Yes, it was a groan they had heard, and the dogs were going in that direction.

Frank was sitting up and looking around in surprise when they got there. "What happened, what happened? Where you all been?" he asked.

"What happened? You askin' us what happened when you done fell out of that tree and got killed."

"Ain't nothin' the matter with me."

Then Plato's voice broke in, "Aint? Well, then, you get up out of there and let's go home, 'cause there sure is something the matter with us."

And sure enough, Frank got up and they walked back to the car and went home.

They didn't catch a thing.

One afternoon in winter when Plato got off from his first-shift job at the Davidson asbestos plant, he found Oskeegum waiting for him. It was during the Depression.

"Hi, Oskeegum. What you doing out here in the cold?"

"I'm waitin' for you. Want to see you a little bit."

"What you want with me? I ain't got nothin' to drink."

"Don't want nothin' to drink."

"Well, what is it then?"

"I'm hungry."

"The hell you say."

"Yes I am, too."

"Well, I ain't got no money. Ain't got a cent."

"Hmmmm."

"Tell you what you do, come on go home with me and eat your supper."

The two of them got in Plato's old Ford and went to his home about five miles away. Supper was about ready, and they sat and talked until his wife got the food on the table.

Now, Plato was a poor white man and things hadn't gone too well with him during the Depression. He had a one-dish supper—cabbage. They pulled their chairs up to the kitchen table and prepared to eat when Oskeegum noticed the one dish of food before them.

"Don't eat cabbage," he said.

"Huh?"

"I don't eat cabbage. Don't eat nobody's cabbage. Never did like 'em."

"Like hell you say. Cabbage good. Good for you. Anything taste good if you hungry."

"Like I say, I don't eat cabbage."

Plato sat in thought for a minute, then left the table. Oskeegum was sure other food was being provided for him.

When Plato re-entered the room, he was holding a shotgun and pointing it towards Oskeegum. His face was an unpleasant scowl. "Oskeegum," he said, "I brung you all the way up here with me in my car to eat supper with me, then you say you're too good to eat what I eat. Now, you eat them cabbage. Go ahead. Eat!"

With the gun pointed at him, Oskeegum put a generous helping of cabbage on his plate and began eating. When he had finished that plateful, he went back for more. After the third helping, he looked up at Plato, still holding the gun.

"Say, Plato," he said, "you got any more these cabbage? I want to take some home to Mama. These things good. And like you said, I believe they're healthy, too."

CHAPTER SIXTEEN

Health
Worries

From childhood I was considered physically weak or "deli-cate," as it was sometimes expressed. Almost from infancy, I had stomach trouble and was finicky about the food I ate. Although I attained a height of five feet ten inches, my waist measurement was twenty-eight inches and I weighed a hundred twenty-nine pounds when I was thirty years old. Together with the spectacles I had worn since my early years, I definitely did not present a formidable appearance of strength.

Yet, I had had no serious illnesses, nor had I lost many days from work on account of sickness. But lately, I had developed an unusual wide-awake sleeplessness and a feeling of being tired all the time. Formerly, I had been a reed-like bundle of energy. This new sensation of nervousness and lassitude was strange to me. And yet it seemed that I was on fire inside with a strange new energy, an energy that was consuming me and robbing me of my strength.

It is true that, for some time after the fire at our house, I had slept fitfully and lightly. A few times I had jumped terror-

stricken from my bed in the middle of the night when a rain
had come up and made a noise on the roof, a noise that resembled the crackle of fire. But this new thing that had come
over me grew steadily worse, and soon I was sometimes, for no
apparent reason, filled with strange physical feelings that
produced an extreme anxiety and discomfort. There was no
pain in the sense that I hurt anywhere about my body, but I
had feelings of distress, my breath became short and my heart
raced out of control.

Over a period of time, I was examined by a number of
physicians; all of them said there was nothing organically
wrong with me to cause this extreme discomfort and agitation
within me. Yet the distress remained. The attacks were of
varying severity, which ranged from dizziness and blurred
vision to extreme nervousness and a feeling of suffocation,
together with a palpitating heart and a pounding at the back of
my head. On many occasions, I had what was described as
"panic reactions." It is impossible to relate the physical and
mental distress of these attacks, except to say that there is
extreme fear arising from and combined with the other physical manifestations.

Sleep became very difficult and the slightest sound seemed
to magnify itself into a disturbing noise. The ticking tick-tock
of my alarm clock in the room became unbearable in its
loudness and had to be removed. Many times during the night,
I got out of bed to stand up rigid in a certain stance for thirty
minutes or more to give room in my chest for the short, fast
breaths that seemed, each one, to be the last I would be able to
take. Extreme anxiety was a part of this, and when the attack
subsided, I was left weak and spent. The worst time was at
night, and I dreaded going to bed. I had lesser attacks in mid-
morning. Sometimes during these morning attacks, I went to a
nearby doctor's office and he gave me vitamin shots. This

particular doctor maintained that mine was an emotional problem.

I am sure my emotions were severely involved, but I was convinced this was not the primary reason for my great discomfort. Too, I learned gradually that food or the lack of it had something to do with what was wrong with me. I observed that my most frequent attacks occurred late at night. And that I was weak and nervous in the mornings before lunch time. There were times when I was in such a state of agitation at lunch time that I could hardly force myself to eat. But once I had eaten, I became stronger.

It seems incredible to me, even now as I write this, that I worked every day during this time. But there was so much anxiety and agitation inside me that my work suffered from it. My hands were often shaky, and there were times when I could hardly shave a customer because of my dizziness and blurred vision. One year I had my glasses changed three times in an effort to clear up my visual problems.

After the first two years, the attacks became less frequent and, in general, their severity was diminished to some extent. But I lived in fear and anxiety of the next one. I had learned to eat in mid-morning and mid-afternoon and to drink milk at these times. Also I got up in the middle of the night and ate. This enabled me to live in more comfort, but I still had my problem, and I was in a measure of distress and anxious nervousness a great part of the time.

At the onset of these spells of sickness, I was forced to give up my studies, but after a few months I resumed studying, although at a reduced rate of progress. Then as my disease was brought under semblance of management or control, the discipline of studying was again brought into action and most of my spare time was devoted to this, although it was often difficult to keep my mind away from my discomfort. It never occurred to me during this time that I was hanging on for dear life.

There were so many things confronting me that I felt I had to do. There was no time for giving up, and I resented the physical disability that had intruded itself into my life and was interfering with my tasks. Also, I was ashamed of this weakness that possessed me, and I was secretive about it. I had something of a feeling that it was a thing that I should have the strength to throw off from me. As a result, few people knew my problem or its extent. Even my mother and my sister who were living in the house with me didn't know the intensity of my suffering or the nights of agony I lived through, although they knew I was ill, as it was discernible in my appearance and behavior. I never called to them at night, and, unless I became ill in their presence, they were not aware of my distress, since I kept it from them as much as possible.

This body affliction came at a time when I was under pressures of urgent importance at home and at the shop. The man I hired to replace Ed was not yet a satisfactory helper, and I was deeply concerned as to whether or not it would be possible for him to develop to the point that he would be readily acceptable to the customers in the barber shop. It required a great deal of my time to supervise and help him with problems relating to his work.

At home, there was great need for new furniture and further work on the house we had bought. It had been a year since our house burned, and it had been all we could manage to replace our clothing and to get the house in which we were now living into condition suitable for our occupancy. The house was well and sturdily built, but it had not had the best of care since Uncle Tobe's death nine years before. Then this strange malady that the doctors were unable to diagnose and treat had struck me. The illness, the business, the house matters and my studies in the law course kept me well occupied for the year.

One day I was cutting a young lawyer friend's hair; we were talking about my studies in the law, when a most unusual offer was made to me. Howard Arbuckle was a native of Davidson, and we had known each other for years. He had become interested in my studies. We did a good deal of talking about it from time to time; our conversations were valuable help in understanding the subjects I was studying. He had attended high school in Davidson and gone on to Davidson College, where his father was a professor of chemistry. He had graduated from Yale Law School and at this time was practicing law in a very prestigious firm in Charlotte, headed by the Honorable Cameron Morrison, a former governor of North Carolina and former U.S. Senator.

On this day, Howard was particularly interested in my progress with my studies in the law, and we talked at length about that. Then he told me that he had talked to "The Senator" about me, and it had been decided that I could come into the office with them, and they would tutor me in the law.

This was so startling an offer coming from such an eminent law firm that I was speechless with surprise and gratitude. I'm afraid my response was not very gracious, because I was overwhelmed by this kind and generous offer to help me. This meant that I had an opportunity to become a lawyer, a possibility that had seemed remote. And more than that, it demonstrated that there were white people in high places who were able and willing to break with the tradition of the times and offer me, a Negro, a chance to go into a great law firm and study there. This was most unusual in 1936, and Howard Arbuckle's stature grew to heroic proportions in my estimation and has remained so to this day. For it was he who had interceded for me and made this opportunity possible at a time when it was generally thought that a Negro had no place in the courts except as a defendant.

It was as if fate had in one sudden and capricious moment of her extreme generosity drawn back the mantle of darkness around me and dangled this gem before my face.

But there were other considerations than the ecstasy that had taken possession of me, and I felt I had to address myself to them. This unexpected good fortune called for an immediate and thorough examination of all the circumstances surrounding me, for an acceptance of this offer meant that practically everything in my life would have to be rearranged. This realization was a sobering one.

Of first consideration was money. The Depression was still with us, and money extremely scarce. Without the availability of a certain amount of money, most things that have to do with our living and the fulfilling of our expectations will suffer fatally. And so it was in this case. For upon calm reflection of my circumstances, it was apparent that a lack of money would be my undoing. It was as simple as this. I did not have the money to support myself and our home during my term of study in the law firm, a term which must last at least a year. There was no alternative to this need. It was there.

There were aspects of reality that must be met. One of these was that I had only one year to qualify for the bar. The law was changing such that the next year, applications to take the law examination, necessary to practice, would not be accepted from any but graduates of approved law schools. (Prior to this time it was permissible to try for the bar after studying independently or under the direction of a licensed attorney.) This provision would effectively bar me from taking the examination again if I failed it the first time, as many did who had the advantage of law school education.

Also, my benefactors were not aware of my health problem.

In the barber shop, I could absent myself when it seemed necessary to do so. In the proposed new situation, this would be extremely awkward and unfair to the people who had committed themselves to my instruction. I also had to admit to myself that my learning efficiency was diminished considerably by the uneasiness, fear and mental agitation incident to my illness. My inability to concentrate my attention away from my own feelings was quite frequently a disruptive factor in my attempts to study.

Also in the state of my affairs and very important to my decision, was the thought that the barber shop would have to be closed. This was an overwhelmingly dreary prospect in itself, because it was the only means of support that we had known in our household. And once it was closed and this avenue of earnings shut off, it would be difficult to reestablish in case of necessity.

I felt I had to say no to the generous offer that had been made to me. This was a very difficult thing for me to do, because it had the appearance of my having to shut the door of opportunity in my own face. This after so much struggling to achieve. But when one is poor, it is often necessary to hang on tenaciously to the little that one has rather than to venture its loss in search of a greater advantage that may not materialize. I would go on as I was and hope for the best from what I had in my hands.

So I went on with my studies in the correspondence course, and with my work in the barber shop. But I had now a new sense of being trapped, and of the futility of my trying to better my condition in life. It seemed that this was impossible for me to accomplish. In this mood, searching for answers to questions that I did not know how to ask that pervaded my thinking, I became confused and very nearly lost my direction and the strict control that had previously guided my actions.

My illness was keeping me in a condition of nervous exhaustion and my thinking was not of the finest quality. I guess it was more from established habit than from anything else that I was able to go on.

This has been a very difficult episode for me to relate. And because I believe they will have a bearing on a better understanding of my reactions to events in my life, there are some things that should be said here. I have been described as moody. I have also been depicted in print as "taciturn and seldom smiling." These are observations which I am not prepared to affirm or disavow. But there is a characteristic which I have observed in me and of which I am conscious and will mention here. I can and do experience great depths of despair. On the other hand, it is possible for me to know great heights of elation. Perhaps my range of sensitivity in this area is greater and more intense than with many people and is observable in my demeanor.

In more recent years, when events became very trying, I have tried to suppress these emotions, as I realize that each is an extreme and to some extent undesirable. This is especially true in situations which tend to generate despair, as I have no desire to live in a joyless world. It is true also that events and conditions of grave import to us are almost always accompanied with a mitigating force that alleviates to some extent the blunt blow of misfortune. To illustrate: when our home was burned, all of us escaped with our lives, and there were no injuries to our bodies.

In the matter of becoming elated over actual incidents or circumstances that relate fortuitously to me, I am very guarded now towards giving away to pleasant emotions, lest they fade away into disappointment. The mere contemplation of some good fortune that might bring me profit or pleasure is fraught with a fear that forbids it.

Thus, again, I found I had to disembark from my momentary flight into fancy, a career in the law, and lower myself into the awkward reality that surrounded me. The painful transition, however, left me with the pleasant knowledge that there were people in the world who had a high regard for my strivings, whether or not they were ever to gain fruition.

In the everyday world of my life, conditions were unchanged. The house still needed much work. There was furniture to buy. I could not abandon my studies. My health problem was causing me much concern as it was lowering my efficiency at work and in my studies. My deteriorating health was well into a second year by now, and none of the doctors I had gone to had prescribed a course of treatment. Most of them said I was emotionally disturbed, and told me to "get a hold of myself," whatever that means.

Dr. Wrenn, a surgeon friend, diagnosed my trouble finally as neuro-circulatory asthenia. He had a very thoughtful expression on his face as he made this weighty pronouncement, and gave the impression he was reluctant to come to this decision. He went on to explain that this was a condition sometimes found in soldiers who had undergone stressful situations on the battlefield. He was being kind to me in his explanation, because I learned from other sources that this was a disorder commonly attributed to cowards who had no stomach for war. He advised me to get plenty of rest and not to worry.

In the nature of my disease, it was impossible for me to do either of these things. How does one rest in a condition of extreme agitation? Or, keep from worrying when there are whole half-hours when he thinks each short breath will be his last? When his heart is racing, and there is a pounding inside the back of the head? When confusion settles over his mind and vision becomes blurred? Fear takes hold, stark, naked fear, and perspiration seeps out of the pores. This was my condition, and, as much as I tried to do so, I could not by the force of my will drive it away.

It went on of its own accord. It came again and again. And I endured it in silent terror. I had the audacity, the very great audacity, to hope that I would not die, that I could go on living in this miserable condition.

There was little planning for the future at this time, a circumstance at strict variance with the earlier years of my working life. I was startled when it became apparent that planning or even hoping for the good things in life had somehow faded from my habit of thought. This was a drastic departure from the exuberant and hopeful attitude characteristic in me just a few years ago. I had drawn away from projections of happiness or easier circumstances that might accrue as a result of diligent application to the tasks that were set out before me.

Instead, there was now a plodding day-to-day acceptance of the dutiful performance, in so far as I was able to do so, of the obligations that I had assumed with reference to my work and studies. But it was a flat, dispirited, consciously forced effort that drove me now, rather than the high-spirited venturesome approach that had previously been a part of the joy of doing things. A great weariness was in my body by day and night. Fear and anxiety were constant companions, whereas, in former years, they had been virtual strangers to me and there had been a spirit of optimism and a feeling that, with effort expended, a way could be cleared and objectives reached. But something was eating away at me now, eating away at my body and eroding the clarity of my thinking.

This mysterious something that had taken possession of me in mind and body and baffled physicians was nonetheless a reality. It was gradually, slowly and surely destroying the person that had been me. More that a year had passed since it had become a serious factor and the many changes that had occurred in that time were apparent when I made an accounting of its deteriorating effects.

With the full realization that something most assuredly was not well with my person came a determination to drive to the extent of my energies to do the things that I had set out to do. This had the effect of creating nervous energy that further depleted my strength, but it carried me on in a driven sort of way, like beating a tired old horse.

Eating my meals became a serious problem. I had developed what seemed to be a fear of food. And when I sat down to table with my mother and sister and took food on my plate, a highly nervous and fearful emotion enveloped me and my throat seemed to constrict in a manner that prevented any but small amounts passing into my stomach. This caused a half-choking sensation when swallowing was attempted. My whole body became tense and there was a feeling of being rigidly mechanical in my movements. This attracted the attention of Mama and my sister. When they cast anxious glances in my direction, my state of agitation became greater. It seemed that eating could have been better managed had I been alone at table, with no one watching me or trying to observe my actions without appearing to do so.

Conversation at these times was extremely trying, as the sound of voices grated on my nerves and caused more tension to develop. Out of this came a plan to eat alone as much as possible and to take small amounts of food several times a day so as to avoid the necessity of eating full meals in the company of others. For some reason, I was most reluctant even to try to discuss the sensations that became a part of my daily living pattern. A major factor in this reluctance was the circumstance of my being somehow and quite unaccountably ashamed to even accept my illness as such, probably because I was conditioned to regard pain as a necessary part of any legitimate malady. Since there was no actual pain in the accepted sense, I had a feeling this was not a conventional or usual sickness and no one would understand my problem.

This conviction was reinforced by the attitude doctors took in their appraisal of my condition. All of them were united in their diagnosis that there was nothing organically wrong with me to cause the symptoms of which I complained. Yet some malfunction raged intermittently inside me. A curious thing about this, too, was that I maintained a calm, even placid facial expression. There were no grimaces or other indications outwardly apparent to the casual observer except that my face had become tired and gaunt in appearance.

My usual amiable attitude and approach to dealing with customers in the barber shop had become courteously matter-of-fact in most instances, because of preoccupation with thoughts of my own discomfort, which was often quite severe as I carried on my work and tried to conceal from my patrons that anything was out of the ordinary with me.

My studies in the correspondence course in law were continuing. This was not as trying as it might seem because, during those times when my body sensations were at ease, studying provided a means of escape from thoughts of the conditions that surrounded me on every side. Too, I was fascinated with the study of law, and each new assignment was something of an adventure in the realm of unexplored knowledge. Also, I had decided to take the next state law examination to see if I could pass it. My grades in the correspondence course were excellent, and I had begun to study state statutes and precedents on my own as a means of preparation for the bar examination, which was fast approaching.

A new factor now entered the picture; a third barber shop opened several doors away from my location. Two white barbers were in this shop and making a strong bid for patronage at a time when business in the barber shops was still in a drag from the Depression. Previously, white barbers had never been successful in Davidson, although from time to time one or more had tried to gain a foothold. But regardless of whether or not they were able to remain in business permanently, this coming always had the effect of splitting the business between three shops instead of the two shops that existed before the new business opened.

These young men were real go-getters and some of my business was drained off to them at a time when I needed all the customers I could get to do the things at home that required money. It meant that now it was necessary for me to put forth greater effort in the barber shop at a time when my physical condition was such that it was taxing me severely just to keep the reduced pace that had been forced upon me by my illness.

When time for the law examination arrived, I went into it with much self-doubt. I had not been able to complete the correspondence course, nor had I studied extensively in state precedents. Nevertheless it was time for the testing, and I entered into it with fear and apprehension. Assembled with me to take the examination were young men who had the advantage of college degrees and law school education from the finest universities.

A week later, I was notified that I had failed. It was small consolation that many of the others had failed also. They could try again next year and most of them did. But as for me, the door was permanently closed.

The bubble was broken. Whatever aspirations or hopes had been generated in me were now completely dashed insofar as a career in law was concerned. It was not until after the examination and I had been notified of my failure that the full import of this settled over me. Then I realized that some-

where inside me there had been kindled the hope that this was
an avenue of escape from my life situation. It seemed that,
without fully realizing it, I was clinging to this straw for liberation. Now the straw was gone and in its place, nothing.

That is, there was nothing but the hard reality that whatever
efforts I had made to dig myself to higher ground had been of
no avail. My strivings had served only to humiliate me in
failure. A gleeful man came into the barber shop and announced that he had heard I had some law books for sale. I
wonder if he knew how much that hurt, or if he cared.

At any rate, I must again clear my mind of hopes for bettering my situation and set back my thinking into the struggles of
my present condition. My desperate trying had been attached
to a flimsy thing. It had faded into nothing.

For the past several years the focus of my attention had
been on studying and learning. My failing the law examination
brought me face to face with the realization that there were
other areas that needed my urgent attention, areas that had
been shunted to the side in my quest to learn. Of paramount
concern was the state of my health. While I had done whatever was possible in this direction, consulting doctors and
doing the things that seemed to lessen the severity and frequency of my attacks, it remained true that I was a long way
from well. The attacks still came at intervals, and constantly a
feeling of apprehension was with me. I was weak and without
energy, easily discouraged, and I lived in constant fear of the
next severe attack, whose time of coming was unpredictable
but certain of arrival. I was afraid of these hard attacks which
brought so much fear and suffering to my mind and body. The
racing heart, the shortness of breath, the constricted throat,
the bloated stomach all combined to bring me an indescribable
sensation of terror and discomfort.

One of the first things I decided to do in reference to this was to lessen the pressure of studying. The spur for this had been torn away with my failure of the law examination and the knowledge that this held no future for me. A tremendous vacuum was left here, both in stimulus to study and the dreary emptiness left in my mind. I questioned myself as to whether or not I had used studying as an opiate to ease the pain of a frustrating life situation, over which there seemed no way for me to gain mastery.

At any rate, the condition of my health demanded that I funnel my attention in that direction. What to do was uncertain since the doctors were offering no help. But at least I could stop driving myself towards goals of achievement, for there were none left in my horizon.

Modern Appliances

By now we had replaced much of the secondhand furniture purchased for the house we moved into after the fire. One of the first of these items replaced was the wood-burning kitchen range. The used one we had bought was a complete disappointment in that it smoked and the oven failed to heat properly.

The ice-using refrigerator had served us well, but its use was the base for an unsatisfactory condition that had developed around getting ice to use in it. In 1937, there were few electric refrigerators in use, but they were taking on in popularity to the extent that the ice companies were making a concerted effort to combat the purchase of these machines by offering new designs and more efficient and attractive models that used ice as a coolant.

In our area, we were served twice each week with delivery from the icewagon. The source of our dissatisfaction was that the white iceman refused to deliver ice to the back door. He insisted upon carrying the dripping ice into the front door and all the way through the house to the back porch where the refrigerator was located. This was the custom with deliveries to Negro homes in the area, and he was adamant in adhering to it. Always before, when we lived on the highway above town, before our house was burned, ice was delivered to the back door as a matter of course. He ignored requests to deliver to the back door after we moved into the all-Negro section of town, and often caused inconvenience by not stopping at all as a punishment for our asking him to come to the back door with the ice.

Disgusted with this needless effrontery, I dispatched Mama by train the twenty miles to Charlotte to buy an electric refrigerator from Sears Roebuck's store. In a few days it was delivered and installed in the kitchen. On the iceman's next visit, he was met at the front door where he stood holding his melting ice and was told that we no longer needed his services as we were now the owners of an electric refrigerator. He was really set back by this revelation, for he had apparently not considered the possibility of losing a customer to the hated electric device in the Negro section. He equated my purchase of the refrigerator as a pretension to superiority over the other Negroes. He was quite indignant at this idea and told it about town.

The white barbers who had moved into town were making an aggressive bid for patronage. Of particular interest was a contrivance they had installed to promote the growth of hair on bald heads. This consisted of a metal cabinet about twelve inches square and standing some thirty inches in height from the floor. Impressive-looking gauges and handles for adjustments festooned one face of the cabinet, from which protruded a length of rubber hose. This, in turn, attached to a helmet-like piece that fitted over the head.

The mechanism in the cabinet activated the head-piece to produce an intermittent suction and release on the scalp. This was supposed to exercise and stimulate it, and grow hair on heads where none was presently growing. With the head-piece in place and its movement up and down as the suction was applied and relaxed, the customer had the appearance of a fictional out-of-space robot.

Through this to-do, my competitor gained considerable publicity, as well as some of my bald-headed customers. In order to combat this growing menace to my business, and the much favorable comment accruing to my rival, I found a similar device that operated on the same principle of pull and relaxation, except that mine was operated by attaching it to the water faucet for pressure to activate it instead of to the electrical outlet, as was true of the other fellow's apparatus.

Rivalry between us for the bald-head business became fairly intense, with the relative merits of the two machines being discussed and brought into question. Somehow the question of safety became involved in this, and it was noised about that if something should go wrong with that electric outfit it could become quite dangerous, what with that thing fastened onto the head and all. Of course, there was no danger from my water-propelled contraption except perhaps getting wet if anything went wrong with it. This was a long way from getting electrocuted, and much to be preferred. As a result, more and more customers sought my "safe" treatment and abandoned the dangers of that electric contraption. There is no record that any hair was grown by either method.

With respect to growing hair, I once had an interesting experience with an Army officer stationed at Davidson College.

The captain had a little hair growth around the edge of his head, but he was slick bald on top except for a little fuzz that was barely visible on close examination. He became desirous of having a full growth of hair on his bald pate. I was cooperative in this venture and, over a period of a year or more, used a variety of nostrums having their manufacturer's strong recommendation in an effort to effectuate his wishes, and at the same time to strengthen my own financial assets.

Finally, when I had done my best, with no resulting hair, this gentleman resorted to his own resources, and one day brought into the barbershop a small bottle of a preparation he had himself bought in answer to an advertisement. He presented this to me with the admonition to read the directions carefully and follow them strictly, in using this medicine on his head. I had heard of this high-priced remedy, but had not actually seen or tried to put it in practice, having from experience no faith in any yet known remedy to grow hair.

Anyway, this set the stage for a continuation of applications to the shining skin on top of the captain's head, this time with his own prescribed lotion, which relieved me of responsibility in its effectiveness. These treatments continued regularly twice each week until the time when he was transferred to another station. On his last visit to the shop, when he was leaving and I gave him the final treatment, he told me to keep what was left in the bottle and maybe it would do someone else some good. With a broad smile and a wink, he left it at that.

The next time I saw this fine man was several years later, when, on a visit, he came into the barbershop to speak and to chat awhile. He was still bald, and commented on that fact. This time he was wearing the star of a general of the Army.

Business was picking up some in the barber shop in 1938, the ravages of the Depression having been tempered by a slow but steady rise in the general economic condition. Also, my white competitor in the barber business decided that the pickings in this area were not as promising as they were in a nearby town. Needless to say, I was not one to discourage this idea. When he moved away, my business showed an increase in volume, but not as much as I had thought it would. However, his going away left only two shops in town and this was better than three.

Fred Buff, the local shoemaker, had his shop just up the street from the barber shop. During the hard times of the Depression, he had secured part-time work as a brakeman on the railroad yard in Charlotte by way of augmenting his earnings. Fixing shoes, like cutting hair, had suffered a sharp decline during these difficult years.

Fred had grown sufficiently affluent with the income from both enterprises to indulge himself in the luxury of a fifteen-cent barber shop shave about three times a week. One day when his face was one big blob of white creamy lather and I was shaving away at his beard, a stranger entered the shop and took a seat on the shoeshine stand which was against the partition wall and faced directly toward the barber chair where I was working. I couldn't keep from noticing that this man's attention was unduly drawn to me, and I wondered at his evident curiosity. This was explained shortly when he put his question to me. My fellow barber at this time was a very black man. My complexion was light and my hair was somewhat long. He was not accustomed to seeing this combination of skin colors working together as barbers, and while there was no doubt as to one racial identity, there was, on the other hand, my appearance, which left some room for question in his mind.

I was shaving around Fred's chin when the question came, and an accident was narrowly averted when I answered because of Fred's sudden and violent movements. The stranger uttered his perplexity with a courteous query.

"Barber," he said, "eh, what nationality are you?"

His question was no sooner out than the answer floated into my mind and off the end of my tongue as I turned in his direction and replied, "I am Scotch-African, sir."

Instantly bubbling over with mirth, Fred Buff went into jerking, wriggling, sputtering laughter that blew lather from his face and nearly caused me to give him a bad gash with the razor. The stranger seemed embarrassed by my answer and the hubbub it had caused and left the shop with an unsmiling expression on his face. All the time, Fred Buff thought this so funny that he couldn't stop laughing. I joined with him in this merriment, and we agreed that maybe that fellow wouldn't ask such questions in the future.

It was perhaps a year later when a mutual friend hurried into the shop one afternoon to tell me that Fred had fallen from a freight car on the railroad yard and the wheels had passed over him and both of his legs had been cut off almost at the hips. The stumps were so short that he was never able to manage artificial limbs, and he spent the next few years of his life in a wheel chair and died of a heart attack.

But always, after the incident related above, I was known to Fred Buff as "that Scotch-African."

During the past year, I had not forced myself into intense and lengthy study periods, although I kept at the correspondence course in law and had finished it. This more leisurely pace of study and the knowledge that there was no longer any reason for urgency had the effect of easing my tensions, and I was able to sleep better. Now that I had relaxed the unrelieved driving of myself it became clear to me in this better perspective— even the perspective of failure—that it was imperative for me to bring what I had been requiring of my body into line with its abilities to perform in a reasonable degree of comfort, else it might soon fail me altogether.

There had been too little regard in my thoughts for anything except to fulfill the desires of my ambitions. But the body must be attended also, and had been screaming to me for a long time now that something was badly amiss. So I resolved that I would be kinder to myself, that I would rest my body, that I would not drive my mind into tortuous thought nor make heavy demands of retention on it.

Then I tried to assess what all this hard trying and almost complete subjugation of self to an ideal had gained me. For one thing, and of eminent importance, I had a serious bodily impairment, to whatever cause it might be attributed. The doctors said it was mental in origin, since they could find no organic cause to explain it. But whatever the cause, I had been unable to gain such mastery over it as to bring it under my control.

Instead of devoting all spare time to study, I made a practice now to sit quietly and do nothing. At times I dozed off to sleep. In this manner I discovered the healing power of sleep, just sleep. I also discovered that there is a proper attitude of mind to induce sleep. It does not come easily in a state of agitation or worry.

Out of my struggles, I had learned not to be deluded by suppositions. I had learned that always it is necessary to discover as nearly as possible the exact facts related to any undertaking. To do this, it is essential to be critically analytical and not blinded by preferences or hindered by prejudices either for or against a given element. In short, the thing must be seen in its entirety just as it is, in the stark, unconcealing light of reality.

In the cool glow of this reasoning, I tried to put myself together at the point where I stood. At the outset, some factors stood out prominently on the side of gain. In the past ten years I had completed three correspondence courses that, in the aggregate, were of inestimable value to me, both at the present and for the duration of my life. This was the greatest gain.

This had been accomplished while I carried on the business of running the barber shop and earning a living for the three of us, Mama, Sister and me. This enterprise had been carried on at times under excruciatingly distressful circumstances. But the fact had to be considered that it was impossible for me to dictate the conditions under which I lived. I had to work within the framework of the circumstances which surrounded me.

I had to accept my defeats and frustrations realistically, in the full understanding that I had exerted energetically and almost to unbearable limits whatever capabilities lay within me, considering always the opportunities that were available for the fulfillment of my desires. Better than this, I could not do. There must be no guilt feelings if at this moment my quest for achievement must now be abandoned. There must be the knowledge that I was possessed of a yearning after something that lay beyond my grasp.

It was in this manner that I tried to come to terms with the inner me, at a time when my body had become rebellious to my will, either from disease or from thoughts encamped deep in the subconscious that brought only frustrations and their disconsolate brew to the surface. The intense, hard driving and the unmitigated seeking after must be at an end.

Looking about me now, somewhat as a stranger examines a new setting, I discovered that in the past several years I had put many things out of my life. I had thought just to lay them aside until another time, but I had in the interim become a changed or different person, and they no longer fit in the old places. In their stead were new or different thoughts or ideas. It was as if I had suddenly returned to my old home from a distant place and found that many things formerly large and cherished in my life had become dwarfed and dowdy and miserable in my absence.

I had become almost totally separated from my association with the young Negro men and women I had grown up with. They had gone their individual ways, and I had gone mine. A gulf had been established between us that could not now be bridged over, due in large part to their having followed in traditional paths for Negroes and having made little effort to advance themselves either economically or educationally. It was a lonely feeling to have persons of long acquaintance regard me with guarded reticence to let me into their lives again. I had abandoned them to fish in strange streams, and their lives had entered ever-deepening channels that led further and further into shallow physical satisfactions. We met now as virtual strangers, none of us really able or caring to become better acquainted in the new circumstances that had intervened in the passing years.

Long absent from regular attendance at church, I decided, along with my mother's urging, to go there more often, partly, I am sure, to remove me from the isolation that I had voluntarily chosen during the years when I was engaging in intense concentration on studying. This, too, had changed. The emotionalism had subsided almost to the vanishing point. But the nature of my illness was such that the rise and fall of the minister's voice put me in great discomfort. This was further aggravated by the knowledge that I was in propriety required to remain until the end of the service. My discomfort was so great that the sermon had no meaning for me, other than a feeling of imminently impending suffocation. It was impossible to explain to others that I had such a sensation merely sitting quietly in church. At least, I thought it was impossible to explain, and didn't try to do so. However, I lapsed again into very sparse attendance at religious services. Indeed, this was true of attendance at any gathering of people where I had the least feeling of compulsion not to leave at will, because the same discomforts and feeling of being trapped overcame me.

During my growing-up period, there had been little time for play. Mine was a work-a-day world from early childhood. As a result, I never developed a familiarity with sports that led into going to games, nor any participation in them, although I was reared in a college town where athletics were a topic of conversation and enjoyment to most of the people. This was especially true in the barber shop where games were talked about at length. But to me such conversation was a distraction. I had no interest in any athletic contests. So going into any sort of crowd had no particular attraction for me. It was then no hardship to avoid gatherings of people, since I had never developed an interest in those things which ordinarily brought large numbers of people together.

The one exception to this was going to the movies, and the circumstances under which I went there were quite different from other public gatherings since I was in a private place, removed entirely from the others in the audience. This movie house was located diagonally across the street from the barber shop and was attended by large numbers of college boys, as well as the townspeople. It had a justly deserved reputation for showing the best and most popular movies of that time. The variety of these fine shows was enhanced by the fact that the program was changed every other day, allowing three different shows each week.

Segregation was the rigid order of the day, and there was no balcony or other arrangement to accommodate Negro patrons. But the Stough brothers, owners of the theater, were my customers in the barber shop, and they had years ago, before the onset of my illness, offered me the use of a small room adjacent to the projection booth where I might go and see the shows at any time and at no cost. Access to this space was obtained by use of a stairway just to one side of the main entrance and was the one used by the operators of the projectors. This was a fine arrangement for me and satisfied the requirement of segregation since I was alone there. This had been for several years my only form of diversion, and many afternoons when business was slack in the barber shop, and I wanted a rest from studying, I went there for the matinee or at times to the night show.

After the trouble with my health began, I continued to go to the show at those times when I was relatively free from symptoms of distress. I discovered that there was something quieting to my body about becoming engrossed in a good movie there in that quiet place. I could leave this place of isolation at any time without observation or curiosity as to why I was doing so, a necessary advantage to me after my illness began. Now that there was more free time, I went to the movies more often. This was my only form of participation in any public recreational activity, a fact which further solidified my reputation among Negroes as a recluse, a self-sufficient loner, aloof and withdrawn. There was a complete lack of understanding of my reasons for my behavior.

Sometime after I had settled into this less stressful mode of living, I began reading widely in books of psychology. This was largely a response to the doctor's insistence that my health problem had its origin in an aberration in that area. Personally, I did not subscribe to this belief. But it was a fact that I was subject to very intense fears and apprehensions, apparently without cause in my physical being as far as they could determine. It was my belief that my trouble was physical and that this was the cause of my mental distress. This seemed logical from the sensations that wracked my body, although there was no pain as such. The doctors were the experts and they all said it was the other way around.

Whatever the cause, medical men had given me no relief. And, except for one who sometimes gave me vitamin shots, none of them had prescribed any medication to relieve my suffering. In their lack of knowledge there seemed to be an unwillingness to admit that there could possibly be some physical reason for my condition. Although they attended me courteously and with an apparent degree of perplexity, it seemed to me that they regarded me as a malingering hypochondriac.

It was apparent also that the doctors who knew me well were hesitant in applying this stigma to me. Yet, as far as they were concerned, I was displaying all the symptoms of that unenviable condition. None of them had suggested any treatment at all for me, other than the advice that I get a hold on myself, a very disconcerting response to my appeals for help and relief from a condition that caused me such intense suffering. I came now to realize and accept that they didn't know what was wrong with me, and that there was no hope for any cure from the medical men.

Reluctantly, and with my apprehensions heightened from this conclusion, I gave up seeking their help. This left me on a further island of desolation, for somehow, without actually being conscious of it, there was before this a basic belief that in time the doctors would do something for me, or that my body would throw off or overcome this thing that had come into it. The first belief was now dispelled. As for the second hope, there was the stern realization that this condition had been with me for some years and was showing little indication of going away, although I had made some accommodation to it.

In part, my accommodation consisted of coming to terms with it by reason of a familiarity with its pattern of operation. Its symptoms were so well known to me that there developed some actual lessening of fear at the time of attacks. This tended in a measure to reduce the extreme mental agitation, and, I believed, reduced the frequency of severe attacks. But I could never free myself of all, or nearly all, of the fear and mental distress. At times when the physical manifestations became well developed, the knowledge of past experiences had no effect to mitigate the suffering, for my mind was so occupied with its present turmoil that there was no room for it to grasp anything else. At these times, an indescribable frenzy went on inside my body and my mind.

There was the feeling of haste and urgency in my body, as if its processes were going at high speed and it was impossible for me to slow it down, that all this ungoverned activity inside me was somehow using me up. And there was an attendant sensation of lightness or being weightless.

When I stood or walked, it felt as if my feet hardly touched the surface for support, and it was difficult to keep from staggering. At night, I had so much a feeling of being glaringly and intensely awake, as if any sleep at all had forever gone out of my being and left instead this acute and highly stimulated awareness that raced in my brain. My heart palpitated wildly, and my belly became bloated and seemed to fill me so full that there was hardly space left in my lungs for the shallow, quick breaths that were a part of these severe attacks. A throbbing set up at the back of my head and upper neck, and my vision was disturbed. Any noise was greatly magnified, even the ticking of a clock was unbearable. I had a compulsion to be alone during these distressing seizures. The presence of other people seemed to heighten my agitation, and I was ashamed to be seen in this weakness. There were varying degrees of these attacks, ranging from comparatively mild to heavy, with either all of the symptoms being present or only a part of them. But I never knew what was in the offing.

Experience had taught me that there was some relation between this and food. Slowly, I became aware that I no longer felt hunger, in the sense of emptiness, or the usual sensations of hunger. Instead, I became nervous and apprehensive. This knowledge had led me into eating small amounts several times during the day, and at night I formed the habit of getting up to eat after midnight. In the household they became accustomed to my nightly forays into the kitchen, where I often cooked the food of my choice. I could tell this brought relief from frequent, hard seizures, and this manner of eating was adopted as a way of life.

In the meantime, we had incorporated the upstairs portion of our house into our living space. For sometime after we moved here, this part of the house was unused. It had never been finished. This story-and-a-half house had five rooms downstairs, and two rooms and a hallway upstairs. Flooring had been put down in the hallway, but the two rooms had only the subfloor.

By working at night and on Sundays over a period of time, I was able with the help of some common labor to raise the ceilings and put down the floors. Then I bought a new spool bed, a cotton-padded mattress, along with a chest of drawers, and moved my room upstairs. I had been sleeping on the little cast-off single bed from the college that Dr. Lingle had given me when our house burned in 1934.

We also wanted a bathroom, but this was another matter. It had to be built at the end of the hall and would necessitate putting a dormer on that part of the roof. This required a carpenter, and had to be put off until later.

In a year or so, we decided to go on with this project. I had some savings, but it was decided to get five hundred dollars from the B&L for this undertaking. Prices for building material, carpenter work and plumbing were relatively cheap at this time. Even so the five hundred dollars were quickly spent, although we used a secondhand tub and kitchen sink.

There was no sewerage in the Negro area and none in contemplation, so it would be necessary to construct a septic tank in the ground to take care of this need. I spoke to some of the town officials concerning the lack of sewerage facilities but heard nothing of it. It was not usual to put sewerage in Negro neighborhoods. After several complaints and my pointing out that it was the town's responsibility to provide this service, I had a man make the excavation for a septic tank and begin its construction.

When the town's officials discovered what was being done at our house, they came forward and told me that further work on the pit would be unnecessary as they had decided to extend sewerage facilities to our section of town. This was a pleasant surprise, and work was started a short time afterwards to put down municipal sewer lines in the Negro neighborhood.

Business continued to increase in the barber shop, and my competitors, realizing that they could not starve me out with low prices, and, what was more to the point, that they were suffering more from this policy than I was, became agreeable to a raise in haircut prices. So in 1941 the price for a haircut was raised to thirty-five cents.

As long overdue as this price increase was, it was met with considerable protest by customers in the barber shop, especially from the customers from the college. They assumed that they had a right to cheap haircut prices, without regard to the welfare of the barbers. At thirty-five cents, our prices were still lower than in the surrounding towns, but that seemed to make no difference to the college people. They thought they were a special breed entitled to have their work done for them at lower prices than the prevailing rate elsewhere. Our price had remained twenty-five cents up to this time.

Together with this insistence on cheap prices for barber service, they were more demanding than other customers in the kind of service they received. They wanted more time taken with them than it was necessary to take with other people. I had always insisted on top quality of workmanship in our shop, with special favors and consideration to any special customers ruled out. We took the attitude that everyone was a special person and served him accordingly. This policy had attracted many patrons to the shop from a wide area. Since these people were twelve-month-a-year patrons, their patronage in the shop was very desirable. Naturally I was very concerned with the cultivation of this business.

This proved a happy choice of emphasis, because, as the population in the area increased, more people were coming to the shop from out of town. These people were glad to have the benefit of our good services and were willing to pay a fair price. This gave us twelve-month business and tended to free us from the more arrogant domination of any special group by scattering our patronage so that it came from an extended area and lessened the importance of a concentrated few who wanted to force their terms on us.

This attitude of dominance fully flowered in the faculty at Davidson College during the Depression when their salaries remained largely stable at a time when most other people were experiencing much greater financial distress. The behavior of these people in such a situation of relative security and affluence during that period naturally left a residue of distaste in the community. Many had taken full advantage of the hard times to work people in their homes at the lowest wages. For instance, they paid $3.00 a week for a full time "maid" of all work, which included cooking, cleaning and child care, not to mention washing and any other tasks that could be imposed upon them.

The manner of many had become arrogant and condescending to the community. But with the bettering of the general economic picture and the corresponding price increases, they were fast losing their position of dominance over the prices they could pay for help and services and commodities in general. The reaction to a price increase for barber services was but one of the ways they tried to maintain for themselves a system in which they could have more for their money at the expense of unfortunate people who had previously found it necessary to accept arbitrarily established, extremely low pay for their work.

But work opportunities were expanded by now, and the general level of the economic condition of workers had improved to the extent that they could free themselves from these unjust conditions. This was true in the barber shop, also. My business was now being expanded by people outside this narrow group who wanted to maintain a condition of economic deprivation in the community that would benefit themselves only. Their self-importance and influence were wearing thin in the face of the rising ability of people in general to protect themselves from abuses.

I was no different from the others and carried my own vivid recollections of impositions. So it was with a feeling of relief that I was once again able in some measure to support my business with patronage from outside this influence.

My competitors in the barber business had for some years made a noticeable practice of showing traditional great deference and submissive respect to this group in the college faculty. For a time, this seemed a successful means of attracting patronage for them. But this very evident favoritism and bowing and scraping to this select few had the effect of alienating other people of the community from patronage. These circumstances helped the trade in my shop, and I was doing a fairly brisk business. Then, one by one, the favored few began coming to my shop, but, because of my failure to truckle to their wishes and cheap prices, I was not personally popular with those in this group that wanted special treatment.

I had bought a car a few months before the price of haircuts was raised from twenty-five cents to thirty-five cents. It was a used car, two years old, in good mechanical condition and appearance. This was in 1941, at a time when few Negroes owned cars in our area, and the ones who did had old and ramshackle vehicles as a general thing. My car being a good-looking one was evidence to some that I was prospering out of proportion to other Negroes, and this was not considered a good thing since it raised the expectations of the others and made them dissatisfied with their low pay scale.

It was also regarded as positive proof that I didn't need to raise prices for haircuts, unless it was to pay for the car, which idea was not regarded favorably. According to this reasoning, my owning a good car was a measure of affluence I had no right to achieve.

But, on the other hand, I was convinced that my buying the car was one of the prime reasons why my competitors had agreed to raise the price of haircuts. My seeming prosperity at a time when their business was declining and they had growing families that required more money was a strong motivating force towards their decision. This reasoning was not lost on the faction that was trying to maintain low prices, and I was seen as the influence that was disturbing the status quo among Negroes.

What was not realized at the time was the fact that they were experiencing a fast-rising general impatience among Negroes with the existing conditions that were being imposed upon them. Promises made to lift racial inequities callously broken over many years had finally congealed mass Negro thinking into disbelief and disillusionment with further promises. War was raging in Europe, and its effects on the home economy gave impetus to Negroes' hopes of being able to do something on their own to alleviate the imposition of racial injustices. This was reaching into our lives, and no wall could be built around our community to keep its influence away.

With all of this going on around me, business continued to be good in the barber shop and my earnings were improved accordingly. I and my family were able to live more comfortably on the increased income.

The problem with my health was still with me, but much diminished in its severity. By being careful in my living and eating habits, I was able to do the increased work in the shop in relative comfort. I was still subject to the attacks, but they were milder and came at less frequent intervals. But I was tired most of the time and had not much energy to spare. My outlook, however, was brighter, and the abusive driving of myself had been lessened to tolerable limits. The easier, less compulsive way of living better suited the needs of my body.

I was still impatient to get ahead, and there seemed nothing I could do to satisfy the urging inside me. A good deal of frustration was a result of this, but, by now, I had come to regard my present situation as one of marking time until I could gain some mastery over my body and the conditions that imprisoned me.

Hope for the future was returning. With this resurgence of hope came the realization of how deep had been my despair, of how far I had sunk into hopelessness, without daring to raise my eyes to the chance of a better tomorrow.

CHAPTER EIGHTEEN

Resignation

The increase in business in the barber shop during the war years brought with it more activity on the part of that faction of the Davidson College faculty that was dedicated to the control of community economics, which certainly included control of prices of barber services. Some became obnoxious to the extent that their patronage was no longer desired in my place of business.

At the time there was a World War II Air Force training program in effect at the college and the cadets were required to get frequent haircuts, a circumstance which brought a great deal of additional work and required special evening opening of the barber shop. In the intensification of the faculty group effort to control the barber shop, it became apparent that the officers attached to this cadet training program were being influenced to interfere with our business.

At first, they were cooperative and seemed well pleased that the required services were available to the cadets. Then they became intrusive and attempted to set up conditions unfavorable to our effective service to the cadets. This included sending them in for work in large numbers at inconvenient times during the day, and frequent changes in hours when they were allowed to come to the barber shop. Then came an attempt to get a kickback of ten cents on each haircut, the ten cents ostensibly to go into an "entertainment fund." According to this plan the cadets would pay for their haircuts on the campus to designated personnel who would then pay the shop for barber work done, less the ten cents per haircut kickback.

This plan would take control of the barber business out of the hands of the shop owners and place it in the hands of the group that wanted to dominate it. It became necessary to make it very plain to the officers that if they wanted service for their cadets in local shops it would have to be on terms agreeable to the shop owners, that we would tolerate no further interference from them. This brought a threat to import barbers from an Army base to attend to the needs of the cadets and thus deprive us of this business. We did not give in to their demands and heard no more of bringing in barbers from out of town.

I felt I was the main source of resistance to these efforts at regulating the barber shops. My competitors seemed so dominated by the college that they were fearful of taking a stand against anything the people from the college said. I found myself walking the tight rope of persuading my competitors to resist the take-over tactics, on the one hand, and keeping the aggressors at bay on the other. I never knew if or when my competitors would give in, which they seemed strongly inclined to do. But they were pressed by their own needs now and followed my lead in holding out against unfavorable and detrimental working conditions for all of us.

In proportion as my small business prospered, I seemed to fall further and further into unpopularity with the faction that had apparently prescribed limits of success beyond which I must not go in my quest to expand my earnings to exceed what would provide the meager necessities of life. I was working hard at my job and by this means trying to increase my income.

This, however, appeared contrary to the design that had been established for me. It was entirely permissible, and even quite proper and fitting, for me to work beyond the endurance of my body, but for this effort to bring financial rewards beyond certain low limits was not acceptable. There was talk about my earnings per hour, which had to be an estimate. But the estimate was always higher than it was thought proper for me to earn.

I heard persistent rumors that my competitors were quarreling among themselves. Instead of patching up their differences, the rift grew wider, culminating in a complete break-up of the business partnership. The resulting litigation left Hood as owner of the shop; his brother, Rutledge, was out.

Rutledge was the older of my mother's two brothers, whom my father had taken into his barber shop and taught the barber trade years ago. After my father's death, Rutledge managed the shop for my mother. During this time, he taught his younger brother Hood the trade and took him into the shop as a barber.

When Rutledge was inducted into the Army during World War I, Hood assumed management of the shop. He was managing to suit himself and ended this relationship with my mother by renting the building where the shop was located and setting mother's barber shop equipment in the street. Hood then went into business for himself where my father's barber shop had been.

Rutledge was taken in as his partner when he came back after the war. This partnership had lasted until the mid-forties, at which time the rupture came between the Norton brothers, and Rutledge found himself also in the street without a place to work.

A period of about twenty-five years had elapsed since my
mother had been treated so shabbily by her brothers. Much
bitterness had existed in the family because of this episode.
But time has a way of lessening old hurts. Their parents, Ma
and Pa, had died, and Rutledge and my mother had a better
relationship. He had not been a part of the initial acts of
callousness, which left her in destitute circumstances with two
small children to support.

A short time after the separation of the Norton brothers in
the barber business became final, Rutledge asked me for a job.
He pointed out that he had no place to work and was in need
of means of supporting his family which now consisted of his
wife and five children. I had misgivings about the desirability
of this arrangement. Past history did not encourage such a
step. On the other hand, there was the possibility that if I
didn't give him a job, he would set himself up in business as an
independent competitor and further complicate the barber
business. My mother and I talked over this matter and agreed
to give him a job and await developments. If it turned out
unfavorably, his employment could be terminated.

At this time, my helper in the barber shop was a young man
who had come to me via a circuitous route and out of an
unfortunate personal background. Henry Jackson was born
into the household of sharecropper parents on a farm in South
Carolina. As a youth he had polio which left him with a de-
formed leg that caused an impediment in his walking. When
times became particularly bad for his family during the Depression, he left his father's home and came to Charlotte, N. C., a
distance of about sixty miles. He had left home in the middle
of the night because the landlord on whose place he lived
didn't like for his farm help to leave. He had no money, and a
thrifty uncle gave him the total of his savings, a twenty-five
cent piece. With this he walked and caught rides, but mostly

walked, until he reached Charlotte. In Charlotte, he found his way to Woods Morgan's Barber College, where he bargained with Mr. Morgan to work about the school in exchange for his room, board and training in the barber school. His school requirements met, Henry came to my shop upon Mr. Morgan's recommendation.

Since he was trained in a segregated school on Negro patrons, I had the usual task of retraining him in the techniques of cutting hair for white patrons. This is a difficult switch, as it involves starting the learning process all over again. At the time when Rutledge came with us, Henry had become a good barber and proficient at cutting white people's hair.

For some weeks, it seemed that Rutledge's coming in with us was going to work out all right. Then he became very aggressive, especially towards Henry. It was plain that he intended to drive him away if he could. This I would not tolerate. Also, he brought habits into the shop of showing favoritism to certain customers. This was foreign to my way of doing business. I had never seen such exhibitions of servility and grasping after patrons by a barber as was his practice. This led me to believe that he and his brother might have been hard put for business and that this could have had much to do with their business separation. In every respect, his performance became unsatisfactory, and I had to tell him he could not work with me any longer.

A short time later, he attacked Henry and beat him up with his fists. This was completely uncalled for and without any kind of justification because Henry had been kind to him while he was in the shop and had never given cause for hostility. Rutledge now became hostile towards me, and I was told that he made some threats about getting even with me.

Henry had been with me something more than five years

when Rutledge came to us. He had married during this time
and was doing well in the shop, but his marriage had run onto
rocky ground, and his wife was continually having him in
domestic relations court for non-support. This was a matter
that gave him great concern. They could live together in har-
mony for a short while; then there would come a dispute and
separation. Next would be a summons to court. It was an
unhappy way to live.

One Monday morning several months after I severed relations with Rutledge, Henry failed to come to work. This was
unusual for him, and, when he had not come in at lunch time, I
became concerned and made inquiries. He was at the time
living apart from his wife, and I thought he might have had to
answer another summons to court. The next day he was not at
work again, and nobody I asked knew his whereabouts.

After several days, a man came to me and said he had seen
Henry get on the northbound bus late the Saturday night
before and that he had a heavy suitcase with him.

So this was it. He had bought himself a bus ticket divorce, a
type of divorce in somewhat common use among Negroes at
the time. The procedure was simply to buy a ticket, the longer
distance away the better, and ride the bus to freedom from
marital difficulties.

Three weeks later, I received a letter from Henry, written
from Jamaica, New York. He said he wanted me to know
where he was and to thank me for all the things I had done for
him. Then he said he had gone away in secret because he didn't
have the heart to talk to me about it. It was a very nice letter,
and I was glad to know where he was.

But his going left me again in the situation with no help in
the barber shop. This was very depressing because there was a
good two-barber business in the shop, and I knew from past
experience what difficulty I would have replacing him. Negro

barbers who could work white trade were scarce indeed, and it
had been necessary for me during the past several years to train
each one for the job, since legislation had been passed that
made it almost impossible for a Negro barber to learn white
trade.

Before 1929, a barber in North Carolina could learn the
trade by going into a shop and working as an apprentice under
a skilled barber until he became proficient. In 1929 legislation
was passed establishing a Board of Barber Examiners and
requiring persons aspiring to become barbers to attend a
barber school or college that provided the necessary training.
Once the prescribed training was completed in the school, the
applicant must then go before the Board to pass an examination as to his proficiency. If this test was passed successfully,
the applicant was given an apprentice license which required
him to work for a period of eighteen months under a registered master barber. At the expiration of this time, he was
required to go again before the Board for a second examination. When this final test was passed, the barber was given a
Master Barber Certificate which entitled him to practice
barbering as a full-fledged barber without restraints.

This legislation was to have the effect in a few years of
almost entirely eliminating Negro barbers from working on
white patrons. This was accomplished by requiring Negro and
white barber students to attend separate schools. Under this
arrangement, the Negro student in the Negro barber school
could learn his trade only on Negro patrons, and the white
student learned on white patrons. Prior to passing of this
legislation, most barbers in North Carolina, and the South as a
whole, were Negroes. But white men were going into the trade
in increasing numbers, and the passing of the barber law
favored the white barber for work on white trade.

After the passage of this law, the number of Negro barbers

working white trade gradually decreased until after a few years there were not many of the old ones left. The result was that Negro barbers who owned "white" shops found themselves in troubled times for getting barbers. This was my situation. In order to get a Negro barber trained for white trade, it was necessary for him first to attend the segregated Negro school where he had only Negro patrons to practice on, then go into the shop that worked white trade and start learning all over again because of the difference in cutting the hair and shaving white customers.

Under this system the Negro who wanted to work white trade had to learn the trade twice, at considerable expense of time and money to himself and the Negro shop owner who wanted to employ him. I cannot say what the new law was intended to do, but I know its end result was the beginning of the end for Negro barbers who worked white trade.

Even when I started in business, it had been difficult to get experienced barbers to come to Davidson because of the eight-month college term and the low prices prevailing. After a few years, when the effects of the barber law made a scarcity, it was extremely hard to get Negro barbers who could do white trade. Young students were reluctant to try to learn because of the hardship imposed upon them.

Henry's sudden and unannounced going away at first filled me with dismay and fear, fear that I would be unable to carry on the business alone. While the condition of my health was considerably improved from the time of its lowest ebb, I was by no means entirely free from the debilitating attacks. They were by now less frequent and not nearly as severe as they had been at the beginning, but there was still the need to be on constant guard against over-fatigue and to adhere to a strict rule of frequent eating.

I realized that I had depended heavily on Henry in the shop

because his presence afforded me the opportunity to regulate the pace of my work to the needs of my body and to absent myself at times for a sandwich or a glass of milk. I discovered in the course of my illness that a lack of taking food several times during the day produced in my body sensations of extreme discomfort. It was as if my body required the constant flowing of energy into it that resulted from always having in my stomach enough food to keep a never-ending digestive process in effect.

The sensation of hunger as such was gone from me. I had not felt it for many years. Instead, mine was a feeling of distress, of dread and terror because of the sensations that took possession of me.

Being in the shop alone and with more business than I could serve offered nightmarish possibilities. But I would have to face them now. First, I resolved firmly that there was just so much that I could do. There was no need to try to delude myself. Either I had to accommodate myself to the requirements of my body's capacity to deliver for me, or I could eventually do nothing at all. My rigid adherence to this rule allowed me to carry on the work in the shop.

But it was a trying experience, because there were so many instances when the number of customers waiting for service tempted me and caused me to over-do myself beyond the ability of my body to function in comfort and at a rate that I could maintain from day to day. Then came the inevitable falling away of customers because of my inability to serve them. This was a matter of concern and heartbreak to me. I had seen this happen again and again over the years when I lost my helper for whatever reason. And always it was burdensome and filled me with frustrations at helplessly watching as the business so painstakingly nourished and built up gradually vanished for lack of help to serve its needs.

It was several months before I had another man to work with me in the barber shop. This time, the young man had attended barber school in a northern state and had learned something about cutting white people's hair. He had not had a great deal of experience with serving white patrons, but he had some familiarity with the techniques of this work, and this made it much easier to train him than it had been with the others who had experience only on Negro patrons.

Rutledge had by this time established himself in a shop of his own in an adjoining town only two miles away. As could be expected, he was hostile both to his brother Hood and to me. Since there was no communication between any of us, there was a complete lack of any kind of business cooperation. But a strange and quite unexpected situation developed out of this. Hood had for years been the one in the Norton brothers' partnership to consistently exhibit towards me and my mother and sister an attitude of dislike and disdainful scorn. All of a sudden now, he made overtures towards me for cooperation between us. He had, in fact, been helpful to me in securing my latest barber.

This was a radical turnabout in the relationship between us. I knew that his change towards me was for one purpose only and that was to present a combined force against his brother, for whom he now had a greater dislike. But whatever the reason, our working together in business agreement was helpful to both of us and established a favorable condition under which it was possible to gain a considerable mastery over the forces which had previously promoted competitive rivalry between us in the hope of maintaining cheap barber prices.

The fact that the brothers were now in separate shops of their own placed each of them in the position of having to get barbers to work with them. As long as they were together, they could each depend on the other in the shop to relieve the pressure of having to work alone. This had been my unfortunate situation all the time. Now it was in their experience. They were finding that to get barbers, they had to charge approximately standard prices. Other barbers didn't care about a college professor who deemed it as his right to dictate the price he would pay for his haircut. Nor did they concern themselves much about college students who wanted cheap haircuts so they could accomplish the dual purpose of having a few cents extra to spend for something else and keeping the Negro barbers working for low pay.

A generally better working condition was established in the barber shops as a result of the quarreling and separation of the Norton brothers into individually operated shops. In a wartime economy, further increases in need for our services placed us in the price range of other barbers in nearby towns. But each time there was a small increase, it was met with opposition from the usual source.

Then there was a comparatively new group in the town that had joined with the college people in the effort to regulate the barber shops. These were some of the people who considered themselves the town's big shots. (The population of the town was about two thousand, or a little better.) A number of these were fairly recent arrivals, and they had cloaked themselves with a mantle of would-be authority over the economics of the town insofar as they were able to exert themselves.

These two groups acted enough in the same order and behavior pattern to indicate that there was an agreement among them. These people represented among themselves the highest salaries and earnings in town. They were the leaders in trying to set up oppressive pricing conditions for Negro barbers.

At each small price advance, they complained the most, or

extended the time interval between their haircuts and insolently said that we were not going to make any more money from them by raising our prices. Some went to neighboring towns for their barber services in reprisal. More often than not, they paid more in the out-of-town shop than we were charging. But this was a part of the oppressive tactics, as they tried to infect others of our patronage in the community to behave as they were doing. Prices in all other lines of work were continually going up, and there was no other way for us to meet our needs but to increase the price of haircuts.

One man, an official in the bank, became vocal on the subject to the point of saying vehemently to me that price increases for haircuts were not needed because I already had plenty of money in the bank. This and further conversation with him implied that I shouldn't have money in the bank. I had only a few hundred dollars on deposit. I knew if I wanted to keep it and add to it, as I hoped to do, it was necessary to do what had to be done about prices in the barber shop.

Anyway, why all this agitation about a dime? I was certain it wasn't the amount of money involved, or that this small increase would in any way affect him. I didn't consider his banking connection as a circumstance that brought the management of the barber shop within the scope of his authority. But I realized from his attitude and remarks that it was not wise for me to have money in that bank, since it appeared to be a personal affront to an official there. I withdrew my small savings and deposited them in an out-of-town bank.

Members of the student body at Davidson College became involved in this, and they either developed on their own initiative, or were coached in it, their brand of juvenile harrassment. This included ways and means of getting the barber to spend more time with them than was needed. There was a customer's sudden discovery that his hair had not recently been cut the way he liked it best. Then would follow much combing and fixing to demonstrate his wishes. A favorite trick was to wait until the barber had finished cutting his hair and then decide that he wanted a little more from the top. "Just a little, now, not too much." When this was done, he could then decide that it was too short!

There was more than enough of this pattern of behavior to tip the barber off to what he was dealing with. And the pattern was so general with certain ones that it seemed hardly the result of individual design. These contrivances did serve to take more time and to vex the barber. They also served to get that patron a less than perfect haircut.

Prior to this time, I had felt no pain in my body from my illness. There were sensations of distress only. But recently I had begun to experience aches in my joints, and particularly in my feet and ankles. At first, I tried to cast this out of mind as of no consequence. As the months went on, my body became more painful. This new thing was invading my body. Its pain and discomfort was increasing in severity just when the health problem that had tormented me for several years was, at last, becoming to some degree manageable and fairly tolerable under a strict regimen of controlled eating and conservation of energy.

Later, my knees began to hurt, especially in bed at night, as did my shoulders. All of this was progressively becoming worse.

For my feet, I tried a variety of arch supports. At first there were elastic bands, two inches broad, that slipped on the foot and gave support. Then elastic ankle supports. These gave some relief for a time, but they were not enough. Then I went to metatarsal supports. These, I thought, were the invention of the devil himself. The kind I started with had an elastic band that fitted around the foot at the instep; to this was attached a piece of leather about an inch wide that extended forward along the bottom of the instep to the soft indentation just back of the ball of the foot. At the end of the leather, there was affixed an additional dome-shaped thickness of material about an inch and a half in length, an inch wide and about a quarter of an inch in height at its thickest.

Altogether these were innocent-looking contraptions, and when first put on were deceptively comfortable. Then the fun began. The longer I stood on this thing, the bigger the "dome" became until there was something of a sensation of having a walnut in this soft place in the foot. All of the body weight rested on the walnut and it became embedded in the flesh and the foot folded its soreness around it. The elastic band part of this support was another interesting and unpredictable phenomenon. They had to be just the right size. If they were too large, they didn't hold position properly. If the band was too small, all sorts of sensations began to take hold on the feet. At first, I felt the constriction exerting itself over the breadth of the band. As time dragged on it narrowed until it felt like a rope tied securely about the middle of the foot dividing it into two numb and swollen parts, except for that place where the "dome" was supporting the tender, pulsating metatarsal arch.

I was desperately determined to find a way to alleviate my suffering.

CHAPTER NINETEEN

Home
Remedies

About a year after the aches and pains started in my body, they had developed into a real problem of serious dimensions. In addition to the hurting in my feet and ankles, the pain in the joints of my shoulders became more constant. I found there was hardly any comfortable position that I could assume to sleep at night, since any way I lay put pressure on my shoulders and increased the pain. My spine had become involved from a point low between the shoulder blades to the back of my head. There were times when I could turn my head only a short distance from side to side.

Again the doctors said they found no reason for this condition and gave me no medication for it. Abandoned to my own devices in this, I used a variety of rubs, liniments, and other nostrums for external application said to have some benefit in the relief of pain. I had a sunlamp, two infra-red heat lamps, an electric heating pad and a hot water bottle.

One of my favorite rubs was a certain liniment, a white liquid of fairly thick consistency and a strong odor. Because of

the odor, I only used it at night. I didn't want to smell like it in
the barber shop. I called it my horse liniment because my
grandpa Norton always used it on the horses when they had a
limp, and I remembered the smell from those childhood days. I
never considered it as having an offensive odor, but it was
pungent and pervasive. It gave some relief from discomfort.

Somewhere in my search for relief from pain in the upper
portion of my body, I discovered an apparatus. In desperation
I thought it might give some help. This was a shoulder brace
of unhappy memory. Since I was receiving no help at all from
medical sources, what comfort I was able to achieve resulted
from my own improvisations. This had been and still was true
of my original illness, which, under a fair degree of control
now, was still with me. Shoulder braces, in the first place, are
skeletonized straight-jackets, except that the arms are left free.
Their purpose is to maintain the upper part of the body in an
erect position, shoulders back and no slump. And this they will
do, too.

But the body rebels at rigidity. If it is painful besides, the
brace soon becomes an instrument of torture. After much
adjustment and wear, it becomes more comfortable, and the
body derives the support benefit it was intended to give. I
broke myself in to this thing and wore it for many months,
although it is doubtful that it helped as much as it hurt.

Simply said, I was miserable again! Before the onset of this
latest condition, I suffered untold and unimaginable horrors of
internal distress, though I had become relatively and sometimes
almost entirely free from pain. Now there was the torment of
aching and hurting from my feet and ankles, and from my
shoulders and my spine. There were days when I was in pain
from the bottom of my feet to the back of my head. But I
don't recall that I ever missed a whole day from work. I had
dark circles under my eyes that wouldn't go away. My eyesight

was so affected that I had my glasses changed three times during one year.

One day at the hospital in Mooresville, the physician who examined me expressed surprise that I had just left my work to come to his office. He told me that I must prepare myself for the time in the very near future when I could not work at all. He said that my spine was becoming rigid, and that there was nothing that could be done for this. My other aching he dismissed without comment. He gave me no medication for anything.

My mental state was pretty bad that night when I lay in bed with my hurting body and my dismal thoughts. The next morning I went to work as usual.

Meantime my car suffered, too, due to an unfortunate situation that occurred in its mechanical innards.

One day in my zealousness to keep the my car in good working order, I decided that the radiator needed flushing out to remove any sediment that might have lodged there. To aid in this cleaning-out operation, I put in a considerable amount of caustic soda and left it for several days. It did the job all right. It also ate away gaskets in the engine and let water mix with the oil in the crankcase. I was totally unaware of what was going on in the machinery until a rattling took hold under the hood. Then it was too late. The engine bearings and cylinders had been damaged.

It was near the end of the war, and automotive repair parts were scarce and difficult to get. So I decided to sell the car and wait until new ones were again available. This was a longer wait than I anticipated, but I got a real good deal on the old car when I sold it. It was a 1939 model Nash Ambassador four-door sedan. I had bought it in 1941 as a used car in good condition for $500. It gave excellent service all during the war years and I was sorry to see it go. But in its present condition, I thought it best to sell it if I could.

Accordingly, I set out to Charlotte one day. My destination was the lot of a secondhand car dealer who advertised extensively for cars. They were hard to get during and at the end of World War II. His lot was in sight when the engine coughed and stopped. On raising the hood, I discovered a blaze licking at the side of the carburetor. Frantic at this sight, I looked around for something to put it out. There was nothing available, not even a handful of dirt, so I beat at the fire furiously with my hat until it was out. Then I limped into the car lot, afraid the engine would cough again and destroy the car before I could sell it.

The owner himself came out of his small office to talk to me. First he looked at the worn-out tires; no new ones had been available during the war. Then he inspected the exterior and interior of the body, both of which were in good condition. He must have taken it for granted that things were amiss under the hood because he didn't even raise it to look at the engine. Then he made his offer. He said the best he could give me for the car was $750. This so startled me that I sat there without uttering a word. He misunderstood my silence and said he was sorry but that was the best he could do.

He paid in cash, and I hastened away, lest he change his mind. And so I was reduced to riding the bus.

During the hot, dry summer months the aching in my body came at less frequent intervals and was less severe. On Sunday afternoon, July 20, 1947, I felt I needed a diversion, so I took the bus to Charlotte to visit a friend. Later in the day when I was ready for the return trip home, my friend walked me back to the vacant lot used by the small bus line as a terminal. Standing there was every long, gangling foot of my ex-shoeshine man and friend, Ted. The reunion was pleasant. I hadn't seen him for several months. The three of us stood and talked, waiting for the time for the bus to leave. Cigarettes were passed around. Ted refused. This struck me as odd, because I had seen few times when Ted didn't want a cigarette. Later, when I passed mine around and he refused again, it was cause for comment.

He answered quite casually, and I thought more than a little smugly, that he hadn't smoked since back in March. This revelation so startled me that I found myself staring in his face as if I had not previously seen him that day. Taking note of my surprise, and enjoying it too, Ted repeated his statement that he hadn't "smoked a one since back in March." This was the 20th of July, four whole months. Impossible, I thought. But he hadn't had a drink, either. At least none was smelling on his breath. And that was something else again.

Maybe, just maybe....

We had a pleasant visit all the way on the bus till we got to his stop at the hospital where he worked. There was smoking all around us on the bus, but Ted never once lit up. He appeared complacently unaware of it. This whetted my thoughts considerably. I thought I knew Ted's weak will better than that.

That night at bedtime, I sat on the side of my bed and thought of Ted. If he could stop smoking, why couldn't I? Many times I had tried to quit and, indeed, had stopped for periods varying from a day or two to three weeks. Always I had started back again, much to my later disgust. But if Ted could quit—good old Ted of little resolution—surely I could. And I was convinced that this was a thing most needful for me to do.

One thing that concerned me immediately was that cigarettes had for some time past affected me strangely. They seemed too strong for me now, made me dizzy and brought on some of the symptoms of my old malady. This was particularly noticeable before lunch. As a result, I had almost stopped smoking in the mornings, and did so with some anxiety about it in the afternoons. But I still smoked, and was smoking as I sat there on the bed.

I came to one firm conclusion, and it was to be irrevocable. There was one other Lucky Strike in my pack. I would smoke this last one, and, with the help of God, I would never smoke another one. Then I sat there and thought of all the reasons why I never wanted to smoke again. There were many reasons for my not smoking, and not one for doing so. At the time I was forty-three years of age, five feet ten inches tall, and weighed one hundred and twenty-eight pounds. There was something seriously wrong in my aching body, and I was certain that cigarettes were not doing me any good.

The next morning, I felt strangely clean and strong. The glow of satisfaction with myself was upon me for my separation from tobacco. But I was to discover a week later that, while cigarettes were making me sick, it seemed that some substance derived from smoking them had penetrated the cells of my body and, now that the constant supply was cut off, there was an actual physical craving for it.

This was decidedly different from the psychological vacuum produced by not going through the motions of smoking. This was a need to have restored the daily trickle of poison my system had become accustomed to. It was very real and becoming more insistent each day as the accumulated supply dwindled inside me.

Mr. John Payne, alumni secretary at the college, came in at this time for a haircut. He seated himself in my chair and offered me a smoke. When I declined, he insisted.

"Aw, go on," he said. "You can smoke while you cut my hair."

"I don't think I want one just now," I said, but this was certainly not the truth. He probably detected a wistful note of

desire in my voice, for he came back with the question I had
hoped to avoid.

"You haven't quit, have you?"

There it was, five little words. And my yearnings had become such by now that it was difficult to say whether I had or
not.

"I just haven't smoked any for the past week," I faltered.

"What! You haven't smoked in a whole week?"

I admitted as much. Then came one question after the
other. "How do you feel? Do you want one? Are you going to
quit for good?"

To the first question I answered truthfully, as I did to the
others. "Awful. I sure do. I hope so," and so on.

I finished the haircut and he left the shop. Later in the
afternoon, he was back again. "You know my daughter, who
was in here yesterday with her two little boys to get haircuts,
well she is a heavy smoker too, and when I told her you had
quit smoking, we had a long talk about it, and we believe if you
can quit, we can too." Then following some more questions,
he was gone again, this time with his chest pushed out and a
confident look on his face.

"We are not going to smoke till you do," were his parting
words.

Two days later, he was back. "Have you smoked yet?" was
his opening remark.

"Not yet," I answered. "How about you?"

"Not a one. We've quit."

I could tell he wanted one, though. As for me, the going was
rough. I had been without about ten days now and the urge to
smoke was my constant companion. There was one noticeable
change in me. The air I breathed seemed fresher and my
capacity for it was greater. There was a sort of empty feeling
about me, and my mouth felt clean and fresh. But deep in the
emptiness nestled a clawing after me to smoke.

Mr. Payne came by regularly every day or two to see how I was getting along and to inquire whether I had smoked. In a week it was apparent that it was going badly with him. His face was haggard and he complained of not being able to sleep nights. His daughter was having the same trouble, and both of them were irritable and cross. He questioned me closely as to whether I had smoked, and there was skepticism and unbelief in his manner when I said that I had not. The next day he was back and said he had just been to his doctor and had been given codeine for his nerves. The next time he came, he had a burning cigarette in his hand. He and his daughter had both given up and gone back to smoking.

When I had been three weeks without a smoke, I was still having problems with something inside me that kept up the urge and the need for me to smoke and restore to the cells of my body whatever substance my smoking had fed into them, and for which they were now starving.

This condition, I believe, is definitely more severe for some than for others. This accounts for the fact that it is almost impossible for some smokers to quit the habit, while others have very little trouble getting detached from it.

I was one who had a hard time of it, and for many weeks I resorted to a variety of expedients to divert my attention from the craving inside me. The first four or five weeks were the difficult ones. After that, it was easier. Then I felt so much better, and so much cleaner inside, and the air I breathed had a strange new quality about it. The taste buds, long smothered by cigarette smoke, became active again, and food had a good and pleasant taste.

It was during the third or fourth week of my abstinence from smoking that looked up one day, and who do you think was entering the door? It was none other than Ted!

The first thing I noticed about his smiling face was the

cigarette drooping from his lips and the delicious curl of smoke wafting upward to his eyes. He was utterly unconscious of the cigarette, as if it were a natural fixture to his mouth. At once I realized I had been duped by that long-legged wretch. Here he was in the fullness of his enjoyment, while I sat there torturing myself in self-imposed denial of a smoke. And he was the one who had started it all when he told me on the twentieth of July that he had not smoked "since back in March."

But despite his smiling face, Ted had problems to relate. He had two years ago taken to himself a wife. This, he admitted now, was a serious mistake. One of the most serious errors he had ever made, he thought, especially since there was a certain degree of enforced permanence in the bonds of holy matrimony. This fact was continually being brought to his attention by an unsympathetic judge in the domestic relations court at Charlotte.

I listened as any good friend should while he unburdened himself of his woes, but all the while I was conscious of the burning cigarette in his hand and the smoke that emitted from his mouth at intervals. And it was comforting to me to think that after all there might be something to this old saying about poetic justice.

My mind was filled with what he had done to poor Mr. Payne and his daughter, and to me, with his glib mouthing about quitting smoking. In my half-hearted and not altogether guileless commiseration with Ted's plight, I mentioned that there were people who seemed to enjoy being married. To this he gave a memorable reply.

"Walter," he said, calling me by my middle name as he usually did, "when I first married that woman, I could have eaten her." Then he thought a minute and added. "Now I wish I had." He spoke earnestly and with vehemence. I thought what he said was amusing and laughed. But he didn't. He had intended no witticism.

As I write this, it has been twenty-five years and some months since that Sunday night the twentieth of July 1947, when I gave up smoking. I have never put another cigarette to my mouth. Now I give thanks to my friend Ted, who is long dead.

In the next few months after I gave up smoking, incidents occurred which were to have a dramatic impact upon my physical problems. It is strange that the first of these happenings should arrive as a toothache, of all unwelcome things.

I was lying in bed late in the night, awake and aching in my joints, when I realized that there was a new source of nagging pain. This was coming from the tooth farthest back on the lower right jaw. This was the same tooth that had given me so much pain in my boyhood during and for some weeks after Dr. Voils' procedure of "killing the nerve" and filling it. In later years, it had become the far terminus of a dental bridge that spanned a vacancy resulting from the extraction of two teeth adjacent to it. This gave added significance to the importance of my retaining this tooth in my mouth, for, if it had to be removed, the bridge would also have to go. This would leave me without lower back teeth on that side.

I had enough troubles and aches and pains and discomforts without that. So, early the next day, I was in Dr. Fred Hartness' dental office just over the barber shop on the second floor. Dr. Hartness, who had put in the bridge, was busy. But he said that Dr. Tom Bell, a young dentist in his office, could see me.

Dr. Bell poked about the tooth and tapped on it and said he could find nothing there to give me trouble. I was glad to accept the idea that this was perhaps nothing more than a sympathetic aching or, better still, a mirage. But a week or two later there was a definite, prolonged, throbbing aching there. Straightway, I went back to Dr. Bell. This time, he became somewhat miffed at my insistence that the same tooth had been aching. After another examination, he said there was nothing there to cause it to ache.

I had recently been in considerable discomfort with pain in my body, and my patience was short to the extent of my speaking sharply and to the point that I was sure the tooth was hurting. Then he directed me to another seat and said he would make x-rays of the tooth and show me there was nothing wrong with it, just to satisfy me.

When the pictures were taken, he told me just to wait a minute and he would develop them. Shortly, he called me into the little darkroom where he was holding the film up to the light. There was a look of sober perplexity on his face as he told me the picture showed a considerable involvement in my jawbone. He handed me the filmstrip, and I could see the root of the tooth that should have been embedded in the jawbone was extending into a hollow space in the bone. The hollow space was fully an inch in length and deep enough for practically all of the root of the tooth to be seen hanging off into it. The tooth was being held in my mouth by only a thin shell of the jawbone.

At once I was filled with a horrible apprehension. Only a few months before this, a man of my acquaintance had, in this same office, been found to have a jawbone condition that was cancerous and resulted in prolonged surgery and eventual removal of the jawbone. Dr. Bell said they could do nothing there for my condition, but that he would make an appointment for me with a dental surgeon who was competent to take care of it.

In a few days, he told me that Dr. Vaiden V. Kendrick in Charlotte would see me in three weeks. This was a long time to wait, filled with anxieties and foreboding of certain impending disaster as a culmination of all my physical problems.

On the morning of my appointment with Dr. Kendrick, I took the bus to Charlotte and walked from the bus terminal to the multi-storied downtown building that housed his office. I rode the elevator upward with a sinking heart. Here I would find the answer, and I was fearful of what it would be.

In the office, more x-rays were taken. Then Dr. Kendrick said the only way he could be sure was to go into the jawbone and see what was there. He said he could do this by making an incision back of the tooth. I gave my assent to this and he went to work. In a matter of minutes he was chiseling on the bone, and I could feel the impact of the tapping of the little hammer on his instrument. I was not put to sleep.

Finally, he told me there was no malignancy there, but the affected area in my jawbone needed cleaning out. This, he indicated, would require an extended procedure, and he suggested that I go home and come back at a later date for this operation.

I was so pleased with his finding no malignancy that, after a minute to think, I asked if he would go on with the operation at once and get it done with. He agreed that there was not much need to let his present incision heal and then go back in to do what was necessary. So he set to work again, this time in earnest.

This was more of an ordeal than I had thought it would be in my moments of elation at his happy findings. It was prolonged, uncomfortable, sometimes painful, and a few times I became very hot. The doctor was considerate, and stopped occasionally to allow me to rest.

The operation completed, he put packing in my jawbone and admonished me not to remove it from the incision back of the tooth. This was to insure that the healing was from the bottom to the top; otherwise he might have to go in and open it up again. As for the tooth, he had his fingers crossed. It had practically no support, and, unless the bone reconstructed itself quickly, there was a strong chance that it would have to be removed.

When Dr. Kendrick let me go, I walked the four or five city blocks back to the bus station, stopping once at a drug store to buy a mouthwash. A friendly bystander, hearing me tell the druggist what I wanted and why, suggested that I use iodine in my jaw. I thanked him for his advice, but didn't get the iodine.

Back in Davidson an hour later, I went directly to the barber shop. I was in no condition to work, so I went home and to bed, where I stayed for two days.

The toothache, which at first seemed a baleful thing, had led to the discovery of the condition in my jaw. This would prove to be one of two milestone events that were eventually to bring a much improved physical condition into my life. But for the immediate future, it brought only another problem. A few days after the surgery on my jaw, I began having weak and dizzy spells. There was no apparent reason for this from the operation. I began to suspect the dressing the doctor had put into my jawbone as a possible source of this sickness. With a small tweezers I got hold of the ribbon-like dressing and removed it from the cavity in my jaw. There was an odor on the bandage of medication that was sickening to me. Also, there was the stink on it from the place in my jawbone. The bandage was acting as a wick to release these substances into my mouth and cause me to become sick.

When I went to the doctor after ten days, he was of the opinion that the bandage hadn't caused my trouble and replaced it, saying it was necessary to the proper healing of the incision. The next morning, I was sick and removed it again. Once the soreness from the operation subsided and the sickness from the bandage went away, there was no noticeable discomfort in my mouth.

There was, however, the uncertainty as to whether the bone would reconstruct itself fast enough to save the tooth involved. After three months I had reason to be hopeful as the cavity appeared to be healing quite rapidly and the tooth was holding its own.

Once the operation was done, and no cancer found, I began some speculation with the idea that perhaps the aching in my body had its origin in the infection found there. However, during the first few months after the operation, the aches in my body seemed to intensify. Then, gradually, I began to feel better, and the aches and pains slowly drained away until in two years' time a great deal of it was gone, and I was able to do my work in the barber shop in relative freedom from pain.

I had had a most difficult time standing and holding up my arms to cut hair when my body was host to so many aches. At one time, my discomfort became so severe that I considered seriously the purchase of a recently introduced seat arrangement that would allow me to sit at my work. I was in so much pain when I stood at work that I thought it was unbearable any longer. The idea was abandoned when I discovered this device to be cumbersome and impractical to use.

As the pain subsided in my body, hopes for the future increased proportionally. Just being free from the agonizing pain was a thing of merciful liberation for me. I had hopes that it would go away completely, since by now it seemed fairly certain that its cause was the infection in my jawbone.

Business had remained reasonably good in the barber shop during this time, and my latest helper had by now become proficient in his work. But there was the continued petty harassment by the group at the college and in the town that wanted to dominate the barber business and impose long hours of work and low prices on us. This harassment and interference was brought to new and sudden intensity in 1950 when I and my competitor bought new cars shortly after our latest ten cent raise in haircut prices.

It made no difference that our prices were still lower than in towns nearby, and that prices were generally advancing. We were guilty of the cardinal sin, showing a flagrant disregard for our college guardians' authority over our lives and business, and compounded it by exhibiting a measure of prosperity in the purchase of new cars. Further, we barbers were the only Negroes in town to do this.

Fortunately, this indignation was not shared by most of my customers, or at least they gave no indication of such feeling. Quite a few people were buying new cars as they became available again after World War II, and most of them seemed not to care if I had one.

I had by now become accustomed to the usual withdrawal of some patronage when the price of haircuts was raised. More and more people were coming in from areas outside the town and they were not concerned with whether I had a new car or not. Furthermore, they expected increases in our prices as costs in general went up, and our increase was only ten cents on the haircut. Their attitude diluted the effectiveness of the complaints and other tactics of that group of college professors and townspeople who were bent on exerting control over us.

All the faculty members of Davidson College were not a part of this highly vocal group who sought to control and regulate my business, but most of the others on the faculty and in town who didn't actively belong to that group were glad enough to accept any price advantage that might accrue to them as a result of the activities of the more aggressive ones.

Nor is there a record of any opposition to pressures that were exerted in efforts to lower the price of haircuts.

Soon after this latest eruption, the pattern of a new stratagem began gradually to emerge. At first, its intent was almost imperceptible, and the practice was initiated so subtly that it easily could have been mistaken for a naturally growing popularity of my barber helper. But as this latest scheme grew in its application, its pattern and purpose became increasingly apparent.

This became especially noticeable when a rapidly growing number of college students preferred the services of my barber helper. It is normal for a young barber to attract more customers as his abilities increase and he becomes better acquainted with the people. This is expected and encouraged by the shop owner because it increases the shop's business and enables the new barber to build a practice that will support him.

But this recent surge in my helper's popularity assumed abnormal proportions. And it was to me an equally glaring incompatibility, that my own desirability as a barber should decrease among these same people in proportion as my helper's popularity increased. I was aware of my helper's deficiencies as a barber. From this awareness, it was not difficult to conclude that his suddenly accelerated acceptance was artificially induced.

I learned also that the same pattern of preference for the hired barber had recently developed in the other shop, and that it was of the same mold as that which had arisen in my shop and was practiced by patrons from the same source.

This was a new way to attack. They would penalize the shop owners for raising prices by showing favoritism for our helpers and withholding their patronage from us, and at the same time create an impression of the shop owners' incompetence as workmen. In this petty way, they were applying economic sanctions against us in order to limit our income, which was meager at best. They had no concern for the fact that we shop owners had to keep prices reasonably in line with other places in order to get barbers to work for us, and that we were paying the barber seventy percent of what he earned on his chair. Their one purpose was to make it as difficult as possible for us.

Another disadvantage to the shop owner in this practice of customer favoritism toward the hired barber was that it gave the barber a false sense of his worth, because his favoritism was due to the purely vindictive intention of bringing pressure to bear on the shop owners. This made discipline difficult for the employee who now felt that he was very important in the shop and could do whatever he pleased.

I could not help but reflect that, during all the years of my considerably lowered efficiency due to my long lingering illness and, more recently, to the debilitating effects of the aches and pains that pervaded my body as a result of the infection in my jaw, I had retained a high degree of desirability and popularity as a barber. This was true even during the years when my hands were often shaking and trembling from internal torture due to my long-standing illness, and years before the trouble with my jawbone. Now that the pains and aches were fast receding and I was in much better condition to perform my duties, I found that my services were shunned by these people for whom I had many times worked in great discomfort, but apparently to their satisfaction.

There was a circumstance, however, by which this latest assault on me was mitigated. This had to do with the personality characteristics of my barber helper. Soon after he came to me, it was apparent that he was of a gloomy and morose temperament. He had become imbued with the idea that as a

World War II veteran he was entitled to continued remuneration from the government. This he tried to effect by claiming war-related disabilities. He became increasingly sullen and dissatisfied as his efforts failed to bring his aim into reality.

He was given to long periods of silent pettishness. In addition, his working discipline deteriorated, and he was frequently absent from work, a situation which I was unable to remedy. His new-found acceptance seemed to establish in his mind the idea that now that he was in demand he could shirk his duties and further nurse his grudge against humanity.

These habits were not endearing ones and served to reduce the effectiveness of the desired shift of patronage to him. However, the system was in operation and was to grow as the years went by. It was to become a vicious thing in later years and more widespread as the shop grew in popularity and the demand for our services became greater. This seems a contradiction, but, as business increased in the shop and as prices continued to rise, as they did for all commodities and services in the post-war economy, the opposition became more bitter and hostile. It was as if the very idea of my having a prosperous business was one that could not be tolerated.

CHAPTER TWENTY

Tragic
Accident

Sick of the whole thing, and wanting to establish another source of income, I decided to set up a grocery store in the Negro neighborhood where we lived. This seemed a good idea because I could locate it in the heart of the Negro community, at considerable distance from any other store. Accordingly, I had a building built and outfitted with the necessary shelves, counters, and other equipment required for a small grocery, including a meat department.

My sister, a beautician in Charlotte, agreed to come home and take charge of the store. This would allow her to live at home as she preferred to do. We opened a completely new store in the spring of 1951, with high hopes for its success. But it was destined during the fifteen years of its operation never to pay its way, and, instead of bringing in additional income, it cost me several hundred dollars out of pocket each year. The only advantage was that my sister could live at home and derive some income from it.

The failure of the store was attributable to the refusal of

many Negroes in the community to trade with us. They had long been accustomed to buying from the white-owned and operated stores some distance away. And, even though our store was more convenient and the prices no higher, they refused to trade with us in numbers sufficient to make the store's operation a profitable one.

It became apparent that a great deal of the reason for their not patronizing us stemmed from resentment at our owning the store and further setting ourselves apart by becoming merchants and "trying to make money off of us," as was said. It did not matter that there was a greater convenience of closeness to the store, nor the fact that with sufficient volume of business we could have employed a Negro person from the neighborhood as a clerk, an unheard of thing in the white-owned stores at the time or since, for that matter. The great concern seemed to be that they might add a measure to our prosperity by trading with us.

There had been for many years a feeling among other Negroes of our community, and indeed of the area, that the family to which we belonged had set itself apart from them and that we thought ourselves their superiors. This idea was perhaps buttressed by the fact that the men of our family, on both my father's and my mother's side, had been self-employed either as tradesmen-businessmen or as land-owning farmers. They had in this way escaped the onus of being employed by others in the very low paid and often hard and dirty work usually assigned to Negroes.

Thus our industry and resourcefulness had placed us in a better economic situation which in turn reflected itself in better homes and living conditions for us than were possible for other Negroes. It had also brought with it a considerable measure of trust and respect from the responsible white residents of the community. These factors had, indeed, set us apart, and for as long as I can remember there had been these distinguishing characteristics that displayed the members of our family in a different light from other Negroes in the town.

One other consideration in our being regarded as different was the fact of our being light in complexion, and that we did not join freely in social activities. All of these circumstances added up to an unwillingness on the part of our fellow Negroes to buy from us, and perhaps increase the economic breech between us. We did learn, however, that there was a great willingness to do business with us when credit was needed. We also learned that we could not rely on payment when we extended credit in emergencies.

Some said then they would not trade with us because we would not allow them credit, but, when we did allow credit, they got in our debt and quit trading with us. Of course, they did not pay up before they quit us as customers. Then they spoke against patronizing the store at every opportunity. We finally came strictly to a cash and carry system out of necessity.

An interesting sidelight on the extension of credit had to do with a man who frequently bought items in the store. One day he came in and bought a chicken. When the chicken was brought to the checkout counter it was discovered that he lacked two cents of having enough to pay for it. My sister told him to take it and he could pay the two cents later. It was a whole year after that before he came again to the store and then only because it was late in the day and he didn't have time to get to another store to make his purchase. The first thing he did upon entering was to pay the balance he owed on the chicken. He had remembered it all that time and had stayed away from the store a whole year to avoid payment of two cents.

This reminded me of something that had been told me by a customer in the barber shop about an experience he had while

working in his uncle's grocery store located in a Negro neighborhood in Charlotte. This young man said that after he had
been working in the store several weeks and knew many of the
regular customers by sight, he would, when they lacked a penny
or two of having enough money, let them take the merchandise
with a promise to pay the small balance next time. His uncle,
observing such a transaction, admonished him never to do this
as it was a sure way to lose a customer. He said he had tried
this and found that the customer so favored would often stop
trading at the store to avoid payment of even one penny.

But getting back to the store as a possible means of increasing my income, this, too, was a dream of no substance, and I
found myself not only without prospect of financial reward,
but, instead, saddled with a continuing deficit that I had to pay
in addition to the considerable investment I had made in
establishing it.

Sometime in the early 1950's, I sat one night reading a
newspaper. On the printed page before my eyes emerged a
bombshell that caused me to leave my chair and wander about
the room in amazement and wonder.

In the health column, I had just read of the discovery of a
disease or malady that affected large numbers of people but
which had not until very lately been diagnosed and treated for
what it was. The symptoms described in the article were so
nearly the ones that had plagued me for many years that I grew
excited in my sudden hopes of getting permanent relief from
the distressing tortures that had been a part of my life for so
long. And for the relief of which I had found no help from
any other source than that which I was able to devise from out
of my own suffering and inept hit-or-miss experimentation.

The disease was described as being the medical opposite of
diabetes, and the news story indicated that the only known

treatment was diet. The article stated further that extensive experiments and investigation of the disease had been carried on and a book, *Body, Mind & Sugar*, written by Dr. E. N. Abrahamson and A. W. Pezet which explained the disease and its treatment in terms that a layman could understand and apply.

The very next day, I made a trip into Charlotte to Smith's Book Store in search of the book. They had never heard of it, but, after searching in a catalog, they said they could order it for me and that it would take about three weeks for delivery.

In my impatience, this seemed an interminable time to wait. But there was no alternative, so the days dragged slowly into weeks as I waited, hopeful from the first that this was to be the means of my deliverance from the torment that raged so often in my body and mind. Three weeks was a long time to keep in suppression my almost jubilant expectation of a miracle to come out of this book.

Three long weeks, indeed! But here for the first time in fifteen years of intermittent endurance of horrible fright and body sensations was a promise of relief.

There had been so many, so many nights when I had wakened with a heart that had begun to race for no apparent reason, and my breath came in shallow jerks, each one seeming to be the last I could ever take. I had stood many nights in the floor in a certain stance that I had learned, afraid to move for more than thirty minutes at a time while my heart beat madly, and I was hardly able to breathe. This was often accompanied by a pounding at the back of my head, and always with a consuming apprehension of impending catastrophe. Three weeks to wait, pitted against so many years of fruitless searching for something to end the horrible fright and the indescribable sensations that every so often took hold of me.

When the book came, I devoured its contents hungrily, as a

starving man consumes meat. I found that my own discovery
that food had something to do with the control of the attacks
was correct. But my error was that I didn't know the foods to
use or to avoid, and as a result some of the items I was eating
were perpetuating and intensifying my trouble by delayed
action instead of correcting it. The book set me straight on
this and gave reasons why its information was true. It also
enunciated another great truth, that my body could not tolerate
caffeine. I knew that coffee kept me awake nights, but its other
and more serious effects in producing and maintaining my
health problem were unknown to me.

The more I read in the book, the higher my expectations
rose. The explanation of what was wrong inside me that
brought such distress and why it did so held me to the pages
until far into the night.

Apparently for all these years it was not even considered
that there might be a disease that was just the opposite of
diabetes. Even after the discovery of insulin, and its production by the islets of Langerhans, it appears that no one reasoned that, if there could be a disease resulting from the
under-production of insulin, diabetes, there could also be a
condition resulting from its over-production. If pancreatic
glands were capable of an under-production of insulin, they
could also be capable of an over-production.

A group of cells in the pancreas called the islets of Langerhans are responsible for the production of insulin. When these
cells fail to produce enough insulin, diabetes results. Diabetes
as a disease has been recognized for three thousand years, but
its cause was not known until the early part of the twentieth
century when it was discovered to be the result of a deficiency
of insulin in the body.

The over-production of insulin was the subject of the book.
This condition resulted in varying degrees of insulin shock in

the sufferer depending upon the excess amount of insulin being produced. In the diabetic, the under-production of insulin causes an increase of sugar in the blood. In the opposite condition, where there is an over-production of insulin, there's too little sugar in the blood. This is called low blood sugar, or hyperinsulinism.

This explanation would seem to indicate that a very simple solution would be to eat sugar or something sweet and restore the balance. Doing this would give relief, but, while the sugar or sweet would raise the blood sugar level and dissipate the distressing symptoms, it had another effect. It in turn stimulated the islets of Langerhans to produce more insulin and set up a vicious circle, so that the apparent remedy would cause more and often worse attacks several hours later. It was this delayed effect of certain foods that made it almost impossible to know the foods responsible.

Once I had an understanding of the chemical reactions resulting from taking certain foods, and the prescribed diet was followed rigorously, there was a corresponding improvement in my condition. There was no sudden routing of symptoms, for my condition was of long standing and my body required time to adjust itself to the new regimen. But continued application of the principles advised brought slow and sure improvement.

Even before the ravaging effects of my disease were greatly diminished, the fact of knowing what my trouble was and what was causing it robbed it of its devastating mystery and some of its capacity to instill in me a paralyzing fear when I was held in its throes. The fear was not so much centered upon death as a physical fact, in the sense that one no longer had a future on earth, but upon the sheer unrelieved and agonizing distress of body and mind. In a matter of months, there was a noticeable leveling off of symptoms, and I could feel my body responding favorably to the dietary treatment.

As my body was responding favorably to the diet, my helper in the shop was responding to some inner urge that was not to the benefit of himself or to the business. He had lately become unbearable in his conduct. Knowing I was depending heavily upon him in the business, he grew progressively worse in every respect. He regulated his hours of work not according to the needs of the business but to his own whim and convenience, and he had lately begun to take Mondays off, saying that he didn't feel like working on Mondays. When he was absent for two weeks on a stretch, I hired another man.

This was an elderly man who had long experience working white trade, I was assured. But his work was not up to the standard of our shop, and he seemed unable to adapt to the challenge to bring his work into conformity with our high standards of excellence. Though he was unsatisfactory from the first, he was the best I could do at the time, and he was retained, in the hope that he could improve. But he was too much set in his ways for too many years and could not change at his age. At this time a rift developed between my competitor and the barber he had working for him. After waiting for some time and being assured that he was not going to return to this employment, I hired him to work for me.

Soon after this, the ROTC Department at Davidson College began a strict policy of requiring the cadets to have haircuts at frequent and regular intervals. This was a boost to business in the barber shop. That and increasing patronage from surrounding areas resulted in almost continuous work every day in the week.

The aching in my body which had been caused by the infection in my jaw was about all gone now, but the permanent impairment in my feet necessitated the continued wearing of arch supports, and a painful spot in my upper spine wouldn't go away. My old illness of low blood sugar continued to respond to the diet treatment. There was still considerable residue of fatigue and other manifestations of the low blood sugar condition. These were to continue for a long time, but the severe attacks and the constant apprehension were so much improved that, by comparison with previous times of discomfort, I felt myself able to carry on the much increased load of work in the shop. Altogether, my health problems were much improved. I felt in better physical shape for work now than I had for several years.

The fact that business was good had an exhilarating effect on me. For the first time it seemed that I had at last gained some mastery of the barber business and that it would provide a much improved and faster growing economic base, which I was anxious to achieve and for which I was willing to work very hard.

As my goals took form and began to materialize, there was a good feeling that perhaps it was possible for me to bring to realization a fair degree of prosperity and security for the years to come. For so very long, every way I turned, I seemed thwarted and met failure and disappointment, but now it seemed that there was a glimmer of hope. I was almost afraid to trust it.

My new-found exhilaration was soon to be dimmed by a resurging sense of hostility towards me. At one time this had seemed to become less noticeable, but, with the increase of business in the barber shop, resentment towards me rose to new and heretofore unknown heights. This resentment was not directed towards any helper, only against me. It took the form of refusal to patronize me as a barber.

This behavior was centered in the students and faculty of Davidson College. They came into the barber shop one after the other and in groups and spurned my services. This could have been understood to some extent as a normal preference for a certain barber, had my most recent helper enjoyed such popularity and favoritism in his previous employment with my competitor. But, according to him, this was not the case. I knew from experience what confronted me.

Business was brisk in the shop and I was kept busy with other customers, but it was more than ordinarily noticeable that this college group made a point of ignoring me and giving patronage to my helper. This practice was disconcerting to me and to other customers, as it was intended to be. When I finished with a patron and called "Next, please," these people would not even do me the courtesy of noticing me or saying that they were waiting for the other barber. They just sat silent, as if I were not in the room. Because of this, many customers who would accept my services were at a loss to know when their turn came in my barber chair.

Such confusion caused me the embarrassment of some-times taking a poll of each person in the shop to establish who was next in my chair. This behavior seemed to give the perpetuators a feeling of satisfaction as they sat in their petti-ness. The impression of lack of customer acceptance was to have the effect of influencing new people who came to the shop not to get into my chair. If all those people preferred the other barber, it was easy to infer that he must be the best barber, and I the unacceptable one.

The resentment towards me seemed to increase as the business grew in volume. Or maybe it was the other way around, and business increased from other areas in proportion as resentment grew towards me. Anyway, business in the shop continued its upward swing, however much the effort to create an impression of my unworthiness.

During this time, Hood Norton reverted to his traditional role of hostility towards me. This put me at odds with both of the Norton brothers again, since Rutledge was still angry with me from the time when I discharged him. Their anger was not hurting my business, and I was little concerned with it. I attributed a great deal of their attitude towards me at this time to jealousy over the very patent fact that mine was now, without question, the foremost shop in the area.

Now that I was working harder than ever before and my business was doing quite well, more people found fault with me. It was said that I was greedy and wanted to make money, and that I worked all the time and spent nothing. Among some college folk, who knew big words, it was said that I had a monopoly on the barber business. The word "monopoly" was intended to convey the impression of something sinister in my activities and to render me all the more reprehensible. Anything, I gathered, beyond subsistence earnings was too much for me to earn, regardless of how much effort I put into my work.

In spite of the attitude towards me of a certain faction of our patronage, it was conceded without debate that I had the best barber shop for many miles around. Barbers in neighboring towns became concerned when their patrons stopped by to patronize my shop. Word-of-mouth advertising by satisfied customers spread the fame of my barber shop over the surrounding territory. The "flattop" was a popular style of haircut at that time, and we were so good with this style that customers were attracted from a wide area to enjoy the unsurpassed perfection of our work.

It seemed to me that this was a proper time for expansion. So I set about the tedious business of getting more barbers. I had visions of building the shop into a large one, even if it were located in a small town with a population of about twenty-five hundred.

I had no illusions about the seriousness of the problems

confronting me in this self-imposed new enterprise due to the segregated barber schools and the necessity of retraining men to cut the hair of white patrons. At first I tried to find young Negro barbers who were working Negro trade and induce them to train with me for work on white people. Then I tried for trainees in the barber schools who would come directly to me when their course of instruction was completed. Both attempts proved unsuccessful. Members of the first group knew the difficulties of getting started in shop work and didn't care to begin again in their training. Students in the barber schools were in most cases committed to jobs awaiting them in shops serving Negro patrons in their home communities.

This left one alternative that I could think of, to try to interest some local persons to go to barber school with the intent of coming to a job with me upon graduation. Finally, I had one young man in school. A few months later, another one went with a commitment to come back and train for work with me.

With two men in school, I was now confronted with the not altogether pleasant question of whether the business could be increased enough to support four barbers. I would also need to expand the size of the shop by adding equipment to provide work space for the extra men. The latter would entail considerable expense.

When the first young barber came out of school to work for me, I found that it required all the money he could earn at his chair plus a supplement from me to pay him. I had also to spend a considerable part of my time coaching him. This reduced my time at gainful work and resulted in a loss of income for me. I thought, however, that this was worthwhile from a long-range point of view when he, hopefully, would make a contribution to the business.

A few months later, it was time to install equipment for the second barber trainee. By this time the first young man was showing progress in his work and was not such a burden to me in terms of supplement to his pay or in time required for supervision of his work.

The second trainee was more of a problem than the first. He needed more discipline and was harder to teach, and there was the additional question of whether or not the business could afford him. But a helpful aspect developed with the coming of the second young barber. The first one had advanced far enough to be a real help in training him. This relieved me to a considerable degree and gave me more time to devote to my own patrons. But I had two of them to pay, and neither one was earning all I paid him. However, their being on duty in the shop increased the volume of business, and this was helpful in carrying the extra load of expense.

With the coming of summer and the closing of the college for that season, we were faced with a corresponding drop in business. Not many of those who left patronized me personally, but their business increased the shop's volume of income. These college patrons would take a trainee's unpracticed services in preference to mine. They wanted the work rendered in our establishment, but they had no use for me. I was not their kind of nigger.

Strangely, a great deal of the recent resentment towards me sprang from the ROTC Department's strict requirement that cadets have a haircut every eight days. I had not influenced the directive, nor could I have done so, so far as I know, but this circumstance added fuel to the already bright flame of indignation against me.

Compounding the strangeness of their attitude towards me at this time was the fact that, if the barber services required were not supplied locally, college customers would have been at considerable expense and trouble to go elsewhere. As it was, they had the option of going somewhere else anyway, even to the other shop in town, but my shop had acquired a widespread reputation for the excellence of its service. They apparently wanted this service, and, as they and others desired it, the business grew. But the resentment towards me seemed to intensify because of the freedom from their domination this growing business afforded me.

In this summer of 1957, when there were four barbers in the shop, a shocking accident disrupted our lives.

My one experienced barber had made plans to visit New York City that summer. After working all that Saturday, July 20th, in the barber shop, he and his wife along with their two young children set out to drive in his car to New York, a distance of about six hundred miles. It was to be a joyous vacation trip for all of them.

The next afternoon I received a long distance telephone call telling me that his car had been involved in a head-on collision somewhere in New Jersey and that his five-year-old son had been killed outright. His wife and daughter were injured, his wife seriously. He had to be cut out of the twisted wreckage of the car and it was thought doubtful that he would live. A few days later, the young son's body was brought home and buried while his father and mother were still in the hospital in New Jersey. Jack's legs were so mangled and his other injuries so extensive that he remained in the hospital all of the next year, and when he came home he was a cripple walking with braces on his legs.

In a week or two, after the initial shock and sadness of Jack's accident, business in the barber shop settled down to the three who were left. By this time, my first trainee had a little more than a year's experience and was able to carry on his work without too much supervision from me. The second one needed help and was getting it from the two of us.

CHAPTER TWENTY-ONE

Real
Estate

I was determined, more than ever now, to increase the number of barbers in the shop, so that when one was lost for whatever reason, his going would not create so much of a disruption in the business. This kind of disruption had been one of my major problems through the years. When I lost my helper, the business suffered until there was a replacement. Now a new condition had sprung up. There were more people in the area and prospects for increasing the size of the shop seemed good, although my personal acceptance as a barber was badly deteriorated. The relentless campaign against me had brought this about.

Renewed efforts to get and train barbers and to bring more customers into the shop resulted in a steady growth. So that, by the end of the next four years, the shop had a bustling business and a staff of seven barbers. It was the largest barber shop anywhere in the surrounding area, and people came from everywhere to patronize my popular place of business.

All new equipment from work stands to barber chairs had

been installed, making the shop the most modern to be found. Our space had by now become too small for the volume of business we were doing. The partition that divided the building into a front and a back section had been moved to the back as more barber chairs were added, and now there was hardly enough back room space for the barber staff to hang their coats or for other needed facilities and storage of laundry and supplies. Practically all of the long room was now being used as the customer service area.

During this time of rapid growth for the barber shop, my personal popularity with that certain faction in the town had not grown. The same was true of the college people who set the pace for an element in the town to follow. They now developed and practiced a superficial veneer of strict courtesy towards me. As far as the students were concerned, this courtesy was dictated in part by their desire to have me cash checks for them, which I did, and by my routine practice of ignoring their presence unless they spoke directly to me. They now called me Mr. Johnson.

The people from the college maintained an arrogant assumption that their business was the chief support of the barber shop, and that I was engaged in a practice of very doubtful morality by making money selling haircuts to them. This was not true by any means.

But as usual, the college people were so taken up with their self-importance that they engaged in the fantasy that the barber shop was wholly dependent on their trade. Many of them asked if we closed the shop when college was not in session.

During the time of the shop's rapid build-up, I launched another venture by acquiring some rental property in the Negro section of town. This was modest, two ex-Army duplex buildings, moved from another location. When these apartment buildings were completely renovated in their new location, they were the best and most modern rental property available to Negroes. They had underpinning all around the foundations, instead of being set up on pillars and the undersides exposed to the weather as most of the other Negro houses were. This made them warmer in winter. They also had indoor plumbing with full baths, another innovation. This was in 1958, and few Negroes had full baths in our community. Most had only a toilet stool installed in an enclosure built on the back porch, an inconvenient arrangement that was plagued with freeze-ups in cold weather.

Three years after my apartments were in place, one of the structures had to be moved from its location because water from a power company dam was going to inundate the area. I had an option to retain the building if I could move it somewhere else. This would have posed a problem had I not a year or so earlier acquired a vacant lot nearby.

Having this other lot solved one problem for me, but it opened up an unexpected new one that for sheer, cranky meanness was hard to equal. The two families occupying the apartment building elected not to move out during the short distance move to the new location and the reconstruction of the foundation and other necessary procedures, including electric, sewer and water line connections. This was expected to take only a short time, and I made every effort to keep their inconvenience at a minimum by planning the work for as rapid completion as possible. Too, their election to remain in the building was forced upon them because there were no other places available for them to move into.

With the building in place and lowered to its new foundation, I made application to the town for immediate connection of utilities. After a few days when nothing had been done, I went again to see about the services. Still no action was taken. Then I discovered that F. L. Jackson, who was mayor of the town and its only executive officer, had not given the order for the work to be done.

Everywhere I turned, I was met with frustration in my attempt to get these services connected to the building. The town's crew members who must do the work said they had to wait for Mr. Jackson's order before they could proceed, which was true. When the days stretched into weeks, I realized that I was confronted with an episode of stubborn meanness that was directed at me.

In the meantime, there were two families stranded in the apartment without water, sewer or electricity. They had to depend on the kindness of neighbors for the use of their facilities. One of these families had children and this depriva-tion was particularly inconvenient for them. This made no difference to Mr. Jackson. Apparently he had to demonstrate to me that his was a position that enabled him to deal with me as his fancy dictated, and there was nothing I could do about it.

This state of affairs had gone on for nearly six weeks, when one morning Mr. Carr McCormack came in to me for his usual haircut. Mr. McCormack was an elderly very wealthy man who was originally from Birmingham, Alabama. He had come to Davidson in retirement a few years back and built a large new home in which he and his wife lived. Because of his fine personality, Mr. McCormack had justly become known to most of the persons of our little town as a kind and considerate man. I had always enjoyed our good conversations when he came to the barber shop.

On this day, I was not in a good mood, and he asked what was troubling me. I told him the whole story of Mayor Jackson's withholding the permit for utilities to be connected to my apartment building. He expressed surprise at what I had told him. And when I had finished cutting his hair and he was

ready to go, he told me that Mr. Jackson was a friend of his
and that he would go by his office and talk to him about the
matter.

It was only a two-minute walk from the barber shop to the
mayor's office. But it was thirty minutes before Mr.
McCormack returned and stalked the length of the shop to
where I was working. I could tell by the purposeful manner in
which he moved his tall, angular body that he was tense and
angry. His face was set and stern as he motioned me aside from
my customer with a quick movement of his hand. I had never
seen him in this state of anger before, and I had no idea what
he would say to me.

He looked hard in my face as if he found it difficult to
speak before he said these few words: "You go on and do what
you are doing about your houses. You will get your services
from the town." With that, he turned and stalked out again.
The next day the needed utilities were connected to the building.

It was sometime later when I learned from a reliable source
in the town hall that, when Mr. McCormack left the mayor's
office that day, Mayor Jackson's eyes were wet with tears, and
he was heard to remark that it looked like he was going to lose
all his friends over that matter. I am convinced others had
spoken to him about this, but evidently those who spoke on
my side before Mr. McCormack's visit had not moved him.

Mr. Jackson was not "home folks." He had come to
Davidson a long time ago to work at Davidson College, where
for many years he occupied a major executive position with
much ceremonial pride of position. Upon his retirement from
the college, he became mayor of the town, where he continued
his autocratic reign, but on a reduced scale. He was now past
seventy years of age.

I was definitely not Mr. Jackson's kind of nigger. He was

frequently my customer in the barber shop, except during those times when he was, along with some others, engaged in trying to bring pressure to bear on me.

At one time, I cut his hair regularly for a period of six months without uttering a single word to him. This was contrary to my custom of always speaking to a patron as he seated himself in my chair, and, if nothing else passed between us during the haircut, I always thanked him when he paid for my services. But for a whole half-year I devoted myself strictly to trimming Mr. Jackson's hair in silence and otherwise ignored him completely. This was after our second encounter. It resulted from another interference with my property rights and in regard to his position as executive officer of the town.

Several months after the first unpleasant official encounter with Mayor Jackson, I bought two other duplex apartment buildings that had to be moved from the proposed backwater area. Since the lot mentioned before was of adequate size, my plan was to move these two buildings to the same lot where the other recently moved duplex was located.

The man from whom I bought these buildings was a professional house mover, and I was much surprised some days later when he came in to tell me that, when he applied for the usual permit to move the buildings, he was told by Mayor Jackson that he wasn't going to allow those buildings to be moved. No legal reason was given when the permit was refused.

My own talk with Mr. Jackson got no further, except that he exhibited anger that his decision in the matter was being questioned. I gathered also that he found it particularly distasteful for me to speak to him concerning the matter of moving the buildings, since he curtly informed me that he had made his decision known to the man who was to move the buildings and that there was no need for further talk about it. When I insisted, he became angry and said that all I was trying to do was to get rich. This last was in the indignant tone of an accusation of some wrongdoing on my part. I listened to his fuming, but told him flatly that I intended to move the buildings. I then tried to get the house mover to move the buildings over the mayor's objections and without a permit, but he refused to do this. Instead, he sent his attorney to talk to Mr. Jackson and try to get the permit. This failed too.

Since all of this was an extra-legal affair that had to do only with the stubborn recalcitrance of an autocratic old man, I was determined to force the issue. After these exchanges had gone for nearly a month, I decided one day that I had had enough of Mr. Jackson's extremely brusque and arbitrary behavior, and that I would go to court if necessary to move the buildings. When I went home to lunch that day, I picked up the telephone and called Mr. Jackson at his home, where I presumed he would be at lunch. When he answered, I identified myself and then told him that if by tomorrow I didn't have a letter from him authorizing the movement of my buildings I was taking him to court immediately. Then, without waiting for his reply, I hung up, bang. The next morning, the authorizing letter was in the mail. It is one of my keepsakes, along with the one from the bank demanding that I give up my lock box there.

Several days after I received Mr. Jackson's authorization for the relocation of the duplexes, and before they were moved, he strode self-confidently into the barber shop and informed me that I might as well give up the idea of moving the buildings because he was a director in the bank and that he had seen to it that the bank wasn't going to lend me any money for that purpose. This bit of news was delivered in his characteristic manner of self-importance; then he left the building. I surmised that he had arranged this with the same bank official who had a few years back told me that I had too much money in the bank. I knew they were friends.

I had made no application for a loan from any source, nor had I any intention of doing so. Mr. Jackson had assumed that I would need to do this and that his affiliate bank was the only one in the world.

A year or so earlier, he had entered the barber shop one day after I had recently installed six new barber chairs. He made complimentary remarks about them and speculated that they were quite expensive. An hour or so later, he was back again to tell me quite pompously that he had just come from the bank where he was a director and that he had made arrangements with an official at the bank for me to borrow the money and pay for my new barber chairs. He went on to say that he knew I owned my own home and that if I failed to repay the money the bank would then take my house from me. I never knew whether he intended this as a favor or as a trap. I just looked at him, without giving any answer. I had not asked him to intercede for me.

In due time, the apartments were moved to my location and were ready for utility services from the town. The same stubborn obstinateness was encountered that had taken place when I moved the first building. I could not get water, sewer, or electric line connections from the town. As these buildings were not as yet occupied, there was not the same urgency for the utilities that had existed when the first apartment had been moved. However, this was no excuse for the facilities not being connected. Too, tenants were waiting to move in as soon as the utilities were available. The reason they were not connected was the same as had existed before, Mr. Jackson's arbitrary exhibition of petty irascibility.

Another circumstance had intervened in the meantime that provided an interesting sidelight to this episode. The town had recently begun the extension of a large water main to the outskirts of the town limits to supply an industrial site in which vested local powers in the bank had an interest. As a part of this extension, it would be necessary to cut a ditch and lay pipe across my property, the very same property where my apartments were located and where city connections to utilities were being denied.

Progress of the ditch-digging machinery and the pipe-laying activities towards the spot where it would begin crossing my property opened to me a line of thought that I considered to have some amusing possibilities. So I let fall the information that I was just waiting for the town's machinery to get on my property and then I was going to get a court order and attach the equipment and see how long I could hold up Mayor Jackson's pipe line project to the outskirts of town. I explained that I didn't think it unreasonable for me to refuse to let them cross my property with a water main to extend service to the city limits when I was being refused service to my apartments which were well inside the town.

Shortly, the pipeline activity came to an abrupt halt, well before it reached my property line. Then, after some delay, the equipment was moved to the opposite end of the proposed pipeline and started working its way back. It would now take it some time to reach my property coming from that direction and would cause me further delay in getting service to my buildings. I went before the city council and in the presence of Mayor Jackson, who was presiding, told of my difficulty in getting city utilities to my apartments. I left the meeting with the assurance that the services would be provided, as they were, and with dispatch.

Some weeks later, Mayor Jackson came to me with the information that he was as a special favor to me having a fire hydrant placed at the edge of my lot so as to provide my buildings with special fire protection. I guess this was intended as some sort of appeasement to me for allowing the pipeline to cross my land, which I didn't contest. The hydrant was placed where he said it would be put and is still there.

It was after this that I cut Mr. Jackson's hair for six months without speaking to him, but he kept coming to me for haircuts. However, he managed to convey the idea that he "let" me cut his hair as a favor to me. Later, I was told that Mr. Jackson said of me that I was one of "our very best citizens." He also had said that if I moved the apartments, I would do it over his dead body. He was a remarkable man.

My health problem was by now much improved. The old lingering illness that had given me so much distress was under control. Its terrors were gone. The aches and pains from the infection in my jaw bone were practically all gone, too. I was now not so much concerned with the sensations of my body and could give my attention to things outside myself. Business was still on the uptrend in the barber shop, and I was actively looking about for larger quarters in a building that I could buy, although I said nothing about my ambition to buy a building on Main Street.

It must have been two or three years after this when an old friend and customer in whom I had finally placed my trust and asked about the possibility of my buying a building suggested that I try to buy the Thompson Building at the corner of Main and Depot Streets. This building was ideally suited to my needs, both as to size and location. It was built originally for a young men's clothing store on the most attractive business location in town, directly across the street from the Davidson College Presbyterian Church.

At first, I was not inclined to make overtures to the owner of this building, because I thought it was not for sale, and then I thought it would certainly not be for sale to me. But the more I looked at this building, the more I was convinced that it was exactly what I wanted. So, one Saturday afternoon as I worked along in the crowded barber shop, I decided to go down the street two doors to the real estate office that handled its rental and make inquiries. Anyway, there was nothing to be lost in this. The building had been advertised for rent, and this was to be my approach to asking questions about it.

Yes, the building was available, and they would be happy to rent it to me, I was told by the man in the office. But when I mentioned the possibility of its purchase, there was a foregone conclusion on his part that it was not for sale. So sure was he that the owner would not sell, the possibility had not even been considered. However, he was enthusiastic about renting it to me, pointing out its many advantages to my business needs. But he was sure the building was not for sale. I left the office with the feeling that maybe, after all, I should not have asked about buying the building. It could seem very forward for a Negro to ask about buying property on Main Street.

The real estate agency was owned by a man who had, some years before, come to Davidson from Mississippi. The fact that he was from Mississippi had established in the minds of most Negroes that he was hostile to them. I had had no experience whatever with Mr. Bourdeaux, who was an arthritic and most of the time confined to his home. But I had somehow thought he might not be favorable to the idea of my buying a building on Main Street. The owner of the building was an elderly lady whose conservative trends were well known. And, although she was "home folks," I had my doubts about her willingness to sell her property to me, even if it were for sale, which was extremely doubtful. All told, I had the dejected, let-down feeling that I had extended myself too far in making inquiries about buying the building. But how else would I find out?

My conversation with the rental agent was late on Saturday afternoon, and I was dumbfounded when about mid-morning

on Monday the realtor came to tell me that he had talked to the
"Old Man," as he called Mr. Bourdeaux, on Saturday night
about my proposal to buy the Thompson building. Mr.
Bourdeaux had called Mrs. Thompson, then vacationing in
Florida, and she had agreed to sell the property. He said
further that Mr. Bourdeaux wanted me to come by his house
and see him right away.

Now I had to readjust my thinking altogether. My last
thoughts on this matter had not been encouraging ones. They
had been filled with misgivings about the advisability of my
having asked to buy the property. One thought was not to
pursue the matter further, and probably save myself some
embarrassment. At lunchtime, however, I decided to go and
see Mr. Bourdeaux and face whatever there was to face.

He received me in his bedroom, where he was sitting on the
side of the bed in long underwear and wearing a broad-
brimmed black hat. He was talking on the telephone. That
finished, he was cordial. He was also matter of fact when he
told me of his long distance call to Mrs. Thompson in Florida
and of her decision to sell the building. Then he said that since
I was the first to ask, he was giving me the first opportunity to
buy.

All of this had a good sound to the ear, but I thought the
gimmick might have been in the asking price to me. I had
already decided on what I thought the property was worth at
the time, then what they would probably ask for it. And last,
what I would be willing to pay for it. I could not ask for help in
this matter.

I was greatly surprised when the figure asked was to the cent
what I had thought I would be willing to pay. It was a little
more than I thought the property was worth, but not exces-
sively so. I reasoned that if I wanted this building, which I did,
I had better buy it now and not let it go to the open market
where I was certain someone else would buy it.

Mr. Bourdeaux gave me the key and told me to examine the building. This I did, making some interior measurements to satisfy myself as to its size. Then I went back to him, still not fully satisfied that they would sell the property to me. When I asked point-blank if he would sell to me, he answered that he would. Then I asked if Mrs. Thompson would be willing to sell to me, and if she knew that I had asked to buy the property. Mr. Bourdeaux answered forthrightly that Mrs. Thompson knew that I was interested in buying the property and that she was willing to sell it to me. Furthermore, he said if she were not willing to sell to me that he would buy the property himself and sell it to me. I could not ask for more assurance than this. I agreed to buy and the preliminary papers were drawn up and signed.

It was assumed that finalizing the transfer of title could be completed in a matter of two or three weeks at most, since only one person, Mrs. Thompson, would be involved in making the deed. Our agreement was made on November 1, 1965, and, allowing at most three weeks for completion of legal matters, I thought there would be ample time to renovate the building and move the barber shop into it shortly after the first of the year.

But a word of caution. I asked Mr. Bourdeaux not to announce that the building had been sold to me. Also, during the negotiations for the sale, no mention had been made about how I expected to make payments, so I volunteered the information that I would pay for the building upon delivery of the deed. All of this transaction had taken less than an hour, under cordial circumstances.

I left Mr. Bourdeaux's home in a feeling of high elation. This was indeed a triumph. Now I could own my own building and have the barber shop on the most desirable location in town, together with a building of adequate size and of such a

design that I could make a show place of it. This was a happy
day. But I kept it all locked inside myself, telling no one except
my mother and sister. I didn't want my most recent ambition to
become known to others. There had been too many bitter
disappointments before, and I didn't want it publicly known if
I failed in this.

A week later, it was discovered that Mrs. Thompson alone
could not make a valid deed to the property. The circumstances
of the title were such that she would have to be joined in this
by her children, heirs of the Thompson estate. Then it was
discovered that an agreement had been made between Mr.
Thompson, who had built the building and was now dead, and
an adjoining landowner that the south wall of the building was
to serve as a common wall for any structure the adjoining
owner might build to it. In accordance with that agreement, an
eight-inch portion of the thickness of the building's south wall
was built on land not owned by the Thompsons.

These discoveries quickly and effectively dampened my high
spirits and expectations. Mr. Bourdeaux, however, assured me.
These matters would be straightened out and a title without
encumbrances of any kind furnished me for the property. I
wanted very much to believe this, but serious doubts had taken
possession of me.

The Thompson children who would need to sign the deed
were four in number, and of course their respective spouses
needed to sign. They were widely scattered in the country.
Then there was the question of whether all or any of them
would sign the deed. That settled, it took time to circulate the
document back and forth between the lawyers and the heirs.

In the meantime, negotiations had begun with the adjacent
owner for the land under the common wall. This was the
means by which it became known that I was buying the property. It didn't take long for this information to bring a sneaking

response. A few nights later, blood-red paint was splotched and thrown on the large plate glass windows on the front of the building. This I interpreted as a threat that my blood would be spilled if the transaction were carried through and I became owner of the property.

I went into the street that day with shame and anger in my heart to clean up and scrape away the red paint, symbol of threat of danger to me. The building that I had hoped would be my pride and joy stood defaced and befouled by an act of meanness directed towards me. The red paint threat did not deter me. But it was in this manner that a chain of terroristic events was initiated that was to haunt and vex me continually, and, finally, to drive me out of business.

It was nearly three months before all legal requirements were met to pass title of the property to me. During all this time, I had the feeling that all was being done that could be done to speed up the process. Mr. Bourdeaux called me every few days to report on the latest progress being made. Over the weeks I developed a distinct liking for this man and confidence in his integrity in his dealings with me. He guided the whole transaction through to a successful conclusion, just as he said he would do at the beginning. After that time I enjoyed many conversations with him at his home until his death.

I became so confident of the final outcome of the title transfer to me that I began, at Mr. Bourdeaux's suggestion, the extensive renovations on the building that I wanted to do before moving the barber shop into it. This included the installation of a central system of heating and cooling, now a necessity for a business anywhere in the South. By the time the deed was delivered to me, work on the building had advanced considerably.

On the 22nd of February, 1966, everything was in readiness. The building had a new front, with two large plate glass win-

dows facing east. The entrance to my business was centered
between the windows. The window on the left of the door
from the inside commanded a panoramic view of the wide
expanse of the grassy green, tree-studded Davidson College
campus, with the magnificent Chambers Building in the far
background. The window to the right of the door looked out
upon the Davidson College Presbyterian Church with its
massive columns and grandly presented entrance. The church
faced north, and rising above the three-story columns another
sixty feet, a slender steeple topped by a cross searched high
into the sky, the cross facing to the north and to the south. My
building was on a corner of Main Street. It had a third large
plate glass window on the north side that gave a view of North
Main Street and across Depot Street to the neighboring post
office building. The view from inside my new shop looking out
was beautiful.

On the inside, the building had been completely renovated,
with a new acoustical ceiling, a gleaming new tiled floor, and
new overhead lighting. The shop attracted much favorable
comment and attention from the many persons in the community who had watched the progress of the work being done on
it. I was especially pleased with the surprising interest shown
by the elderly ladies of the community, all of whom were well
known to me. They seemed to have developed a special interest
in this project and watched its development closely.

At the close of the business day of George Washington's
Birthday, 1966, I and all the members of my staff joined in the
moving of the barber shop equipment from the old to the new
location. We worked until far into the night and all the next
day, which was Wednesday and our regular closing day, so that
we could be ready to open for business on Thursday morning.
And ready we were, too, although there were still many things
to be done.

One of the major things to be done was the moving of the gas heating equipment from the old to the new location. This had to be left in the old location for heat until we moved out. A makeshift wood-burning heater had been used in the new location while the work of the building was in progress. This was still in use when we moved in, and, although it was not adequate to heat the building to a comfortable temperature for the barber shop, it was all we had and far better than nothing, as we soon found out.

It was late the next afternoon, Friday, when the workmen finished installing our heat. One of the last things they did in this installation was to take the smoke pipe from the wood heater and connect up the gas equipment to the flue. Then it was discovered that the gas company had not turned on the gas, and, since it was past their quitting time, they had all gone home. The building was still fairly warm from the fire in the wood stove, but this was gone now. And it had turned bitter cold outside. It was our closing time, so we left, hoping the gas people would be there first thing in the morning to turn on the gas. Overnight, the building's temperature became icy indeed. And the next morning, Saturday, which was our busy day, found us with very cold feet and nearly numb fingers trying to cut the hair of warmly clad customers who were undaunted by the cold, while we barbers worked in our thin white jackets.

I could not remember it ever having been as cold as it was that February morning, and this was shared by all of my barbers, one of whom had been stationed in Alaska during the Second World War. At one time I thought I must give up because the back of my head was hurting so from the cold, and a muscle under my shoulder blade felt as if it were frozen. This muscle was to give me much pain for several months afterwards. I don't know why it took the gas people so long, but it was past mid-morning when we got heat into that cold building. Once the heat was on and the building had time to get warm, we passed our first Saturday pleasantly in the new location.

The building was ideal, the equipment modern, and public reaction and acceptance most favorable. Every prospect was for a prosperous business in this new location.

But there were other influences lurking in the background that were soon to strike. Two weeks after we moved into the new place, I arrived at work one morning to find that red paint had again been splattered over the entrance during the night. This time, I called the police, which I had not done the other time when paint was thrown on the front of the building. Both town and county officers responded. One especially diligent county officer was led in his investigations to question closely one individual who was suspected. But there was no direct evidence to connect him to the act.

After that there were no further episodes of paint being used to mar the building or to threaten me. But the incidents were enough to convince me that there was alive in the community a hostile person or group that could be expected to attack me in some manner or other. I had a fear of fire. I had had experience with fire when our home was burned, and I was afraid that some night a blaze would be started and everything destroyed. So the joy at having my own building and a fine barber shop with a prosperous trade was greatly reduced by my apprehension that some night the whole thing might well go up in flames as an act of violence against me. And there was nothing I could do to prevent it.

It was deeply troubling to think about this evil that followed me. Nor could I begin to fathom or to understand the meanness inherent in the cowardly behavior of sneaking in the darkness of night to impose in secret a hurt upon another person. I thought my ambition to have a fine place of business in which to serve my patrons was a praiseworthy one. It was in the American tradition. And yet it appeared that this tradition was not meant for me to follow. For white men, yes. But for me, a Negro, no. There was a different concept of what I ought to want or of what I should strive to achieve. White men could have the things that I was striving for, but they were not meant for me. My ambition, if indeed I should have any, ought to be kept within the bounds set for Negroes.

I had been told all my life by other Negroes that it was dangerous to have ambitions, and more dangerous to seem to achieve them. One must remain in ignorance and poverty and seek his pleasure in things that consumed the mind and the body. And at last, die and be buried in an unkempt field, and be properly forgotten, because there would be nothing in such a life worth remembering.

And yet I had been unwilling to accept this philosophy as a guide to direct my actions. I knew what was expected of me, but somehow I was outside of this looking on as a spectator, as if I were someone else, as if I were someone to whom these rules could not apply. The whole of my life had been ordered around my own concept. I refused to accept the identity that others conceived for me. I had conceived an identity of my own, and, no matter what was done to me, I persisted in clinging to the identity that I had established within myself. This was the real me. This was what I had to be. There were none who could make me other than that regardless of pressures they brought to mold me to the likeness they had chosen for me. They could despise me; they could try to create a sense of worthlessness in me; they could hurt and mangle me; but they could not destroy the identity that I had brought to life within myself. This I would keep forever.

Blood red paint had been put at my door, and I knew it was a symbol of hatred and an attempt to intimidate me. It could and did instill apprehension and dread of what might follow. The demons of hatred had been loosed, and they had their work to do. It was to grow, both in acts and intensity.

In late June of that year, 1966, Mama's brother Rutledge died. He was the one my father had taught the barber trade away back about 1910, just before father died in 1912. Due to a stroke, Rutledge had not been able to work for five or six years prior to his death, and, since he had not accumulated anything to live on, the last years of his life were spent in the deprivation that is the lot of sick old folk who have no money. His barber shop customers, for whom he had worked these many years at reduced rates, had no use for the sick old man he had become, and he was left to fend as best he could for his needs.

He and I never established a cordial relationship after it became necessary for me to terminate his employment when he worked for me after his break with his brother Hood and the dissolution of their partnership. I was in his hospital room along with his daughters a while before he died, and gave what assistance I could to the nurse who tried unsuccessfully to insert a tube into his throat to draw off fluid from his lungs. He died two hours later.

If during his last years Rutledge was abandoned by the white customers he served as a barber, he went at last to rest among their dead. The Negro cemetery which Uncle Will had founded many years ago as president of the Christian Aid Society was in an out-of-the-way place and thought an undesirable place of burial, even though it was now kept up and attended by the town. Accordingly, one of Rutledge's daughters applied for and was sold a plot in the hitherto white municipally owned cemetery. Rutledge Norton became the first Negro to be buried there. He was joined by his wife a year later. And as I write this they are the only Negroes who have ever been buried in Mimosa Cemetery.

Rutledge's death brought into my mind a review of the long years of almost continual strife in the family which had come to my mother and me and my sister as a result of my father's having trained him as a barber and taken him into his barber shop more than half a century ago.

CHAPTER TWENTY-TWO

Blasts
and Bullets

Nearly six months had passed since the last paint smearing on the barber shop building. I began to hope that I would have no further problems in that direction. But this was just a quiet time, an interlude before another and more vicious form of attack.

My attention was called one morning to a small hole in about the center of one of the plate glass windows. The hole came from a bullet fired either from a pistol or a rifle. Police agreed that it was from a high velocity projectile, since it did not shatter or fragment the quarter-inch thick glass. The bullet was fired from the outside, yet we were never able to find it or any trace of it on the inside of the building. It seems that it might have struck something else, or embedded itself in an opposite wall, but search as we did, it was never found, or at least its finding was never reported to me. The hope that it might have been fired at random was soon dismissed in favor of the theory that it was meant for that particular window.

Since the hole in the glass was small, I decided to wait for

future developments, if any, before replacing it. Six weeks later
the hole was enlarged to an opening eight inches in diameter by
a shotgun blast. It, too, came in the night, and was not heard by
the police, although it seems reasonable to assume that a
shotgun blast fired on a quiet street at night could have been
heard some distance away.

I considered it established now that my place of business
was the deliberate target of a person or persons bent on
terrorizing me through the destruction of my property. I ran
an advertisement in the local newspaper offering a one hundred dollar reward for information leading to the apprehension of the guilty party or parties. This brought no results, but
a month later the glass was again blown out of the same
window.

My insurance policy on the building, in addition to coverage
for loss by fire, also covered glass breakage and other forms of
vandalism. But inasmuch as it had been the target of repeated
acts of vandalism, I did not report the breakage of the glass
for fear that all of my insurance might be canceled on the
building, and I would be left without any protection in case it
was destroyed by fire. And I was afraid of this. So I replaced
the expensive plate glass windows out of my own pocket.

Since the breaking of the glass windows was necessary to
the intrusion of any object to the inside, I had a burglar alarm
installed, hoping that the loud noise from its siren would alert
police or others if the windows were broken again. This would
warn, I hoped, if a fire bomb were thrown through the window. I lived in dread of this.

A week later, another shotgun blast in the night blew out a
large hole in the center of the glass. The burglar alarm had
aluminum tape running along the edge of the glass. This tape
had to be broken to set off the alarm, and as it was about four
inches from the edge it was not broken by a hole in the middle
of the glass.

The police had caught no one doing these acts. They had only called to report it after the damage was done. So the ringing of the telephone in the night brought me out of bed in fear of what they had to tell.

I had the alarm tapes placed at twelve-inch intervals, running up and down the glass windows. This would be sure to set off the alarm if a break of any size was made in the glass. This gave the windows of my fine new barber shop the appearance of a jail cell with the bars running up and down. One kind lady remarked about this, saying that it was a shame that I had to conduct my business behind the bars of a jail. I also kept the ad running in our local newspaper offering a hundred dollar reward for any information leading to the arrest of whoever was causing this damage. Nothing came of any of it, and the destruction continued.

Our mother, now nearly eighty-three years old, had some months previous suffered a light stroke. This did not impair the use of her limbs, but, for a while after, she had a slight speech difficulty. Her greatest damage from this stroke was to her memory, which was already suffering from the effects of some hardening of the arteries. Up to this time she had done a part of the housework and helped my sister with the cooking. Now my sister found it necessary to make frequent trips home from the grocery store, which she was running, to check on Mama. But one day Mama attempted to cook something and left a pan of grease on the burner. This caught fire and set fire to the woodwork, causing several hundred dollars of smoke damage to the interior of the house and furnishings before it was extinguished.

All of us were pretty much upset about the windows that were being shot out at the barber shop, and this apprehension extended into thoughts of what other forms of attack might be chosen to strike at me. The fire in our home posed another hazard. We decided that Mama should no longer be left in the house alone, that she needed someone with her at all times.

We decided to close the store, and my sister would stay at home. This solved the problem of needed companionship for Mama. The decision was a sudden one and required a little time to effect. However, in a matter of two or three weeks the store was closed and Sister was home to keep house and attend to Mama.

During the fifteen years of its operation, the grocery store had been a constant financial drain on me. Not a great deal, but several hundred dollars each year. As related previously, we had never been able to attract to it a sufficient volume of business to make it a paying enterprise. It did afford employment and salary for my sister and enabled her to live at home with us, which we found more satisfactory than for her to work in Charlotte and spend weekends at home as she had previously done.

Closing the store was an expensive undertaking. The stock of merchandise on hand had to be disposed of at a heavy loss. Counters, refrigeration equipment and the many other items of furnishings necessary to the operation of the store were locked up in the building and written off, with no possibility of recovering anything from their sale. All told, this had been an expensive venture for me, and I closed out the business with the feeling that it should not have been that way.

During the time when we were occupied with closing out the store, breakage of the plate glass windows at the barber shop went on unabated.

It was nearly Christmas of 1966 by now. The trees were bare across the street from the barber shop on the Davidson College campus. They stood by day in their nakedness in the bright sunlight of crisp winter days, or exposed their branches to dampness under leaden skies. At night they stood like gray sentinels waiting in the dark for the light of day. The hands on the clock in the steeple of the sprawling Davidson College Presbyterian Church silently kept the secret of the hour when my windows were broken under the shadow of the cross that topped the slender spire.

Business in the barber shop was continuing a slow decline. At the time when the shop was moved to the new location, there were seven barbers employed in the business, including myself. Business was thriving, and I hoped in another year to increase the staff to eight barbers and stabilize the business at that number. I did not know of a bigger barber shop in our area, even in the larger towns and cities. I considered it a worthy achievement to have built up such a business in a small town the population of which was less than three thousand people.

There were also about a thousand students at the college during the approximately eight months of the year when it was in session. But four thousand people could not support a barber shop of this size. This was indeed a popular place of business, and customers came from a widely scattered area surrounding us. At times, it seemed that they came from everywhere. A barber supply salesman who traveled a wide territory observed that mine was the best and the busiest barber shop in the state of North Carolina.

I had worked a long time and very hard to achieve this measure of success, and I had a feeling of deep satisfaction at this achievement. It was said that my business brought more people into town than came for any other reason. A very popular young men's clothing store, next door to the barber shop in the old location, found its business in steep decline when I moved to the other end of the street. A dry cleaner found it necessary to move his establishment closer to my new location. These businessmen told me that the whole balance of business traffic in the little town was shifted from the lower to the upper end of town when the barber shop was moved there. Such was the magnitude and influence of my barber business when it was moved to its new location.

In the new quarters, I expected the business to reach new heights of popularity and success. But this was not to be the case. The past months had brought a decline in our trade. This I attributed in large measure to the circumstance of my windows being shot out. This was always done at night, but there was, of course, no guarantee that it couldn't happen during business hours and thus expose patrons to the danger of injury. In addition a certain unfavorable notoriety attaches itself to a place of business where acts of violence and destruction occur. It was widely known that my place of business was under continual attack, having its windows blown out by shotgun fire. This was not a reassuring circumstance to gentle people who had no desire to associate themselves even remotely with such a state of affairs.

The burglar alarm tape running up and down the plate glass windows and spaced at one-foot intervals apart was a constant reminder to all who passed by of the hostile actions against the place. On the inside, customers looked to the outside through windows that gave the appearance of a barred fortress against attack. This greatly reduced the attractiveness of the place and introduced an element of danger into coming there.

There was no communication with me by persons claiming responsibility for these acts of violence. There were no threatening telephone calls, no lettered insults or threats scrawled on the building. There was just silence and the continued shooting out of the windows. The latest offense was an attempt on two of the windows. Before this time, only that window that had the name of the barber shop lettered in gold on it had been shot out. But this time that window was shot out as usual and the adjacent one on the corner in the north wall was also fired upon. Apparently these shots were fired from a car moving directly in front of the building. That way the window bearing the sign was a straight-in, direct shot. But it placed the glass in the north wall at an angle and the charge struck it obliquely and glanced off into the adjoining framework, leaving the heavy plate glass pitted and marred from the impact of the shot. I decided not to replace immediately this one glass that had not been shot out, confident that there was no need to do so because the next attempt would take it out anyway.

But, surprisingly, there were no more shotgun blasts into the windows. After this, the night shooters just stopped. I had no idea why they had begun, nor had I any idea why they stopped. It could have been that more people were alerted by the sound of the alarm siren, as they were. But the police never caught anyone, nor, as far as I know, did they have any suspects.

It took a while for me to conclude that the shoot-outs had stopped. But when several months passed without an incident, I breathed a sigh of relief. Then a cue ball was thrown through the north window, the one marred by the last shotgun blast. A month later, a soft drink bottle tore a jagged hole in its replacement, and I wondered if, instead of a cessation of the damage, another method of achieving the result had been substituted.

Then the attacks with thrown objects stopped. I was afraid of what would happen next.

Business in the barber shop continued to decline, and instead of adding another barber to my force, I lost one. It was obvious that more people were wearing their hair in the new longer style now, but this was not enough to account for all of our loss of business. I felt much of it had been frightened away by the shotgun blasts into my windows. So, little more than a year after I moved into the new location, I found my

staff of barbers decreased by one man, instead of being
increased by one, as I had expected. My anxiety for the safety
of my business property was such that I dreaded the coming
of night. I felt totally without protection.

I thought many times that I might not have been subjected
to these attacks had I not moved into my own building. But,
on the other hand, since I had moved from the other location,
the bank had taken over that building and was asking the
tenants to move out so that the bank's business offices could
have that space. Had I not bought my building and moved
into it, I would have been without a place for my business.
When I moved into the new location, I was told by a man
knowledgeable in the barber business that I could just about
"name your own price for this building and the barber shop."
Now, instead of enjoying my own business in my own building, earned through decades of honest hard work in very
trying times, suddenly I was a sixty-three-year-old man, very
tired and very frustrated with all the trouble my business was
causing me.

There was yet another factor that gave me concern, and I
had no way of knowing to what extent, if any, it had influenced the attacks on me. There was a faction of the public
that saw in my purchase of a building at a very desirable
corner location on Main Street, and the establishing of my
large and well-appointed barber shop in it, as something more
than a community improvement that they could approve and
patronize. They saw in my ownership of this property a
degree of prosperity that they could not concede to a Negro.
Many of these were of that group that had consistently tried
to dominate the operation of the barber shop and confine me
to their own idea of what was fitting and proper for me to
earn and to possess. They wanted the services of this top
quality business establishment, but they disliked the idea that

it was profitable to the extent that a Negro could make such an investment.

As the weeks grew into months without further damage to the windows, I experienced a great relief of tension from the outrage and expense of replacing the costly plate glass. But my relief from the humiliation and expense of replacing the destroyed window glass was not supplanted with any sensation of security. I had a feeling that worse was yet to come, that more punishment was to be meted out to me for my ambitions. I lived on in dread of the darkness and what it and the morrow would bring.

I went about my work knowing there was nothing that I could do to prepare myself for the blow or hinder its coming. I did not know what it would be, nor the form it would take. Would it be fire? I had known its terror and its devastation when our home was burned to the ground with loss of all of our possessions. Explosion, perhaps? A shot in the dark? Or would it be an undreamed-of exercise in cruelty that would lay waste to me or to my business, perhaps to both?

Once in deep perplexity, I walked out to the street in front of the barber shop and looked up through the branches of the trees to the cross that stood facing straight and true to the north and to the south at the summit of the steeple that rose far above the roof of the sanctuary of the Davidson College Presbyterian Church, where songs were sung and prayers said. I had looked upward to this cross before. This time, I looked at it with a queer feeling inside me. The worshipers who prayed beneath it had in no manner come to my aid to stop the meanness that was practiced against me. It was as if I were not there. Or as if the cross were not there. Or as if neither I nor the cross were there. It was a lonely feeling, fraught with disturbing thought. I was outside the protection of that congregation. I was outside the protection of the organizations of society.

George Washington's Birthday, 1968, marked the second
anniversary of the barber shop in my own building at Main
and Depot Streets. Since I had acquired this building with all
of its many advantages over the other place and moved the
barber shop into it, I had had nothing but trouble. And instead
of my business getting better as one might expect it to do, it
had gone into a steady decline.

The window breakage had stopped; now, I dared to hope
that the memory of it would soon be gone from the public
awareness, so that no feeling of possible danger would lurk in
the minds of patrons. This I thought might restore the public
confidence, and my business would thrive again.

With the departure of winter and the coming of the green
grass of spring, my hopes mounted with the brighter days.
Gone were the drab, bleak and barren days of winter. The
leaves began to grow, birds fluttered here and there, and squirrels scampered up the oak trees, one after the other in the
exuberance of joyful living.

Maybe, I thought, the days of my winter, when mean and
evil things had hidden themselves in the dark as if they were
ashamed to be seen, maybe they were gone with the coming of
spring.

But even in this quietness, totally unknown to me, forces
were marshaling themselves for a mighty outpouring of hate
and invective against me. In secret, the stage was being set to
punish and to scorn me for the existence of a social practice
that had held me in its vicious tentacles and heaped injustices
and deprivations upon my head for the whole of my life, and
for all of the generations of my Negro forebears. The seeds
of hatred against me were about to burst forth into hellish
flower.

In my innocence of any knowledge of these preparations
being made to pounce suddenly and devastatingly upon me, I

had begun to sleep easier. At last I could awaken in the night without a start and a jerk of apprehension. It was an illusion quickly dispelled, for I was about to be dropped precipitously and without warning into a cauldron boiling with hate and danger to me, and which was to be the destruction to my business.

This plot was being laid in secret on the campus of Davidson College, an affiliate of the Southern Presbyterian Church. And when it was ready and honed to perfection, it would be hurled against me in sudden fury by members of the student body, faculty, and administrative staff. It was an aggregation that could total more than a thousand men, and to this was to be added that considerable part of the Negro population of the town who were to find themselves drawn into it. Outsiders would come to join in the fray once it had begun.

In my innocence I sat on Tuesday afternoon, April 2, in the rear of the barber shop looking straight out the front to the street when two Negro men whose names I knew entered the door and advanced directly towards me. At first sight of them, I wondered at their coming into the barber shop, what their business would be there. Since it was well settled that Negroes and white people were not served in the same barber shops, it was unusual for Negroes to enter the shop unless they had a personal reason for seeing someone there.

I had previously had no relationship of any kind with these two, and I wondered at the purposefulness of their manner and stride as they walked the length of the shop towards me. They were dressed up, too, in their dark suits and white shirts, complete with neckties. This was an unusual circumstance, because they were usually dressed in work clothes, consisting of rough trousers and colored shirts, since they were ordinary workmen at common labor, one at Davidson College, the other in local industry. All of this flashed through my mind as they approached me, because everything about them was unusual on this weekday, even to the way they walked, side by side, erect and briskly. I wondered if there had been a funeral. They were dressed for a special occasion. Little did I know that they were the "Judas goats" sent on a mission of betrayal and entrapment.

When they were directly in front of where I sat and very near, they came to a halt, still side by side. Then one of them addressed me, saying that they wanted to get their hair cut.

This was a request that I had not previously been confronted with. Since my earliest youth I and everyone I knew and all others around me had known only that white and Negro people did not patronize the same barber shops. In an instant, I thought there was more to this than was apparent in their appearance and request. But whatever their reason for asking for service could be, I was taken completely by surprise and found myself searching for a courteous way to tell them what they already knew, that custom and the laws of North Carolina forbade what they were asking me to do. My thoughts were racing.

Then I said that I was sorry, but I could not let their hair be cut in the shop. The one who had remained silent asked, "Why?" The one-word question and the manner in which it was spoken irritated me, but I answered quietly that it was not necessary for me to explain to him a thing that he already knew as well as I did. Then he made a remark to the effect that all of that had nothing to do with why I was refusing to cut their hair. He seemed disposed to argue about it, when the other one quieted him with a gesture and said, "Let's go." With that, they turned and left the shop. They had done what they had been engaged to do.

It was possibly less than ten minutes after the two Negro men left the shop, and well before I had gotten over my surprise and bewilderment at their request for barber service, when three tall young white men entered and made their way to where I sat. I recognized them immediately as Davidson College students. They introduced themselves by name and said they had heard that I had a few minutes before refused to cut the hair of two Negro men. They wanted to know why I made it a policy not to serve Negroes in my barber shop.

Such a question coming from three young white men who were students in a college in a Southern state and presumably Southerners themselves seemed the height of absurdity, since it was true that separation of the Negro and white races was at the insistence of white people and enforced by laws of their making.

I tried as best I could to say that my reason was the existing custom that had been in existence as long as I could remember, and that I could not hope to change this custom. And, furthermore, if I opened the doors of the barber shop to Negroes generally, I was fearful that it would ruin my business, because I felt that my white patrons, upon whom I depended for the survival of my business, would no longer patronize the shop.

Here was a case of my trying to put into words a situation that was well and perfectly understood by these three white men.

Instead of displaying any understanding of what I was saying to them, they assumed the attitude that it was my action and mine alone that was responsible for a state of affairs that would not permit Negroes to get haircuts in a white barber shop. There was no willingness to hear that I was caught up in this custom, which was not of my making, and that I had to conduct my business within this framework. It was of no use when I tried to explain that patronizing the barber shop was a voluntary matter on the part of customers, and that I had no way of getting their business except by conforming to their wishes.

When these young men were gone, I had the feeling that they had come with their minds fully made up to a purpose, and that they were not to be deterred from it.

I had not long to wait for the unfolding of the next episode in their plan. And plan it had to be, for it was not possible to execute the next step without advance preparation.

CHAPTER TWENTY-THREE

Hell Breaks Loose

In a matter of minutes after these three college students stalked out, all hell broke loose. On the sidewalk in front of my business as if by magic, a considerable number of college students appeared milling around and bearing signs and placards denouncing me and the policy of the barber shop for what they termed my "discrimination against Negroes."

The whole of this plan to attack me must have been worked out in detail before the trap was sprung by sending in the two Negro men to ask for service in the barber shop. There is no other explanation, because only a few minutes had passed between the time when the two Negro men came in and the appearance in front of my business of a crowd of students bearing printed and mounted signs denouncing me. All of this couldn't happen in an instant. It required time to hand-print the placards and signs. And the bearers of these objects of denunciation had to be obtained and assembled at a close-by location and kept out of sight until the time was ready to launch their assault on me. All of this cannot be done in a matter of a few minutes. Much craftiness went into the formulation of this plan.

With all of the advance preparation that had to be done, and their avowed morality of purpose, not one word of this matter had previously been mentioned to me. As far as I was concerned, it was kept in strictest secrecy. It seemed to me that honorable people, about an honorable pursuit, would not find it in their conscience and disposition to act in secret to mount an attack of such magnitude and far-reaching consequences against an innocent person, especially one who was himself struggling under the burden they claimed they wanted to correct. Such actions bring into serious question the stated incentives behind them.

The circumstance that invites close scrutiny and offers a speculative commentary on motives is the fact that I, as owner of the business, was never at any time prior to the execution of this planned attack on me consulted in any way about the policy of segregation in my business. Had I been a white man, I am sure the situation would have been less arbitrary. I did not originate the practice of segregation of the races. I had been forced to live under its rule for more than sixty years. But these young white men behaved as if I had been its founder from the beginning, and that but for me the whole evil thing would disappear from the earth. They moved against me as if I, and I alone, was the last vestige holding together this prejudiced world which they had so lately come to denounce. Their fathers and their grandfathers and all the generations before them were absolved of guilt, and all of this shame and scorn they heaped upon me.

And so they milled about on the sidewalk in front of my place of business, carrying high their black-lettered signs, denouncing me for segregation and discrimination against Negroes. More and more of them came until it seemed that I was at the center of a mounting mass of hatred.

I was bewildered by the suddenness of it and by its intensity. I felt I had done nothing to merit such a display of hate and scorn against me.

The cross at the very top of the steeple on the church directly across the street might have thrown its shadow on this frenzied activity had the morning sunlight not passed to afternoon.

The police came on the scene to disperse the crowd that by now was hindering the movement of cars in the street and blocked the sidewalk in front of my place of business. This action on the part of the police was met with indignation by the students, who seemed to think they had a right to do as they pleased, without regard to others. At length, most of them were dispersed, but there appeared almost immediately a group passing out printed leaflets urging a boycott of my barber shop. The following is a copy of the text of the leaflets:

> This afternoon, two Negro men from the Negro community in Davidson entered Ralph Johnson's barber shop to get a haircut. They were refused service. This is not a new situation. This has happened before. It is Mr. Johnson's policy to cut the hair of only those Negroes who are also students here at Davidson.
>
> We feel that it is time for this situation to come to an end. We feel that it is unfair, unjust, and immoral. We simply feel that a community barber shop should be open to all the members of the community. However, because barber shops are not covered under the Civil Rights Act, we have no recourse through the courts. We have decided to approach you, the students, to ask you not to get a haircut at Mr. Johnson's until he gives written commitment

that he will cut anybody's hair whether they are white or black and whether they live in a dormitory or in the community. Because Mr. Johnson's primary support comes from the students, if the students refuse to give him their patronage, it will be a strong factor influencing him to change his policy.

So please show him by your absence that you don't like the policy. Two or three students cannot convince him. Together all of us can. We ask you to do your part.

Joe Dial	Bill Schmickle
Roger Buttweilder	Paul Schneider
Nat Hayward	Ken Tarleton
Fred James	Ashton Trice
Bobby Lane	Cary White
Mike Norris	Ted Winter.
Robert Pyeatt	

All of this was a stunning blow to me. It had come as a violent storm out of a clear and tranquil sky. All I could do was stand in confusion and look through my windows, still taped with the burglar alarm to warn me of glass breakage, at this latest meanness that had been unleashed against me. The milling about and sign carrying in front of the barber shop continued until it was time to close the business for the day.

I went home in such utter confusion that I hardly knew what to do at all. I thought this attack on me a most unjust thing. I was not responsible for the conditions under which I had been forced by law and custom to operate my business for more than forty years.

My first consideration was how I could keep the barber shop from being torn to pieces by all this tumult about it. I had worked long and hard and under difficult conditions for nearly half a century to establish it. I didn't want to see it destroyed. It was a night without sleep. I hoped that the next day might bring an end to the demonstrations against me. Perhaps the officials at the college would take hold and bring the students under control.

In passing, it may be stated here that, a number of years before, a group from the college had contacted all places of public accommodation in the town and requested that services be extended to one or two black African students who were expected to attend the school. Since these were foreign exchange students, it had been agreed by the business people that this concession could be made. This was before the Civil Rights Act was passed.

Later when American Negroes were admitted to the college, after the Civil Rights Act, the barber shops continued the practice of serving all college students, although we were not covered by the Civil Rights Act. This had been discussed with our white customers before the practice was initiated and most of them were agreeable to this limited arrangement, since they were students at the college. But even this concession was frowned upon by some.

As for my policy of cutting the hair of only the Negroes who were also students at the college, this was a concession made by me and the one other barber shop owner in town, Hood Norton, also a Negro man, to cut the hair of all Davidson College students, regardless of race.

There were possibly four or five dark-skinned Orientals among the students, and we had been cutting their hair. But the prejudice against Negroes was such that we were afraid to admit them, even the ones in the student body, without first consulting a large number of our white customers. Our word-of-mouth survey indicated that we could serve the very limited number of Negro students without too much adverse effect on our business. However, this acceptance was based upon the fact that they were Davidson College students, and presumably of a "status" other than the general Negro population. This was a distinct exception to the rule.

Even so, we found ourselves continually explaining to some of our white customers the circumstances under which these few Negroes were served in the shops. At the time of the attack on me, there were five Negro students, in the total student body of more than a thousand men at Davidson College. And the patronage of these five was divided between two barber shops. This was quite different from a general admission of Negro patrons to the barber shops.

It must be remembered that the barber shop was not operated exclusively for the people at Davidson College. Nor did they have ownership of it or in it. Our patrons were scattered over a wide rural area outside the town of Davidson, and consideration had to be given to the preference of these people, whether we were in agreement with them or not. Without the patronage of these people, the barber shop could not survive. These were twelve-months-a-year patrons, and the volume of their business was the major support of the shop.

During that fretful night, I examined closely and at length another one of the printed leaflets the students had passed out. The opening paragraph read as follows:

> This afternoon, two Negro men from the Negro community in Davidson entered Ralph Johnson's barber shop to get a haircut. They were refused service. This is not a new situation, This has happened before. It is Johnson's policy to cut the hair of only those Negroes who are students here at Davidson.

I was struck immediately by the deceitful duplicity of the opening sentence. It stated simply and innocently that two Negro men had entered the barber shop to get a haircut. No mention was made of the fact that the students had induced them to do so, nor that they had set up a whole plan of action against me which was a planned creation of a new situation. The general policy throughout the South was well established that Negroes did not go into white barber shops and ask for service.

> We feel that it is time for this situation to come to an end. We feel that it is unfair, unjust, and immoral. We simply feel that a community barber shop should be open to all the members of the community.

The opening sentence in this paragraph expressed a sentiment that had been in the hearts of Negro people for three hundred years, not just about haircuts, but about the whole Negro situation in America. It had distressed me all of my life, but it was a reality I had to live with. This was not something that I could change. It was instituted and maintained by white people, and I felt deeply wronged that the white students at Davidson College were now shifting the blame for its existence to me, when I had been all my life subjected to its humiliations and deprivations. I had not ever gotten my own hair cut during business hours in the barber shop that I owned and operated because I knew that my doing so would be considered inappropriate by so many of my customers, and would cause me to lose their patronage.

As to whether or not the system of segregation is "unfair, unjust, and immoral," I leave to the consideration of the reader. But since an issue was raised about the three words above, I wonder if these bright young men had considered whether it was unfair, unjust and immoral for them to secretly arrange an attack upon me and my business for a condition that had been imposed upon me by their elders and had been severely maintained by all the pressures of a white-controlled

society. It was indeed a strange morality that excused them
from culpability in a sneak attack upon an innocent victim of
the very wrongs that they, in an extremely odd quirk of reasoning, now accused me of perpetrating on Negro people.

As to the expressed sentiment that a "community barber
shop should be open to all the members of the community,"
my curiosity was aroused as to what these white students had
done in their home communities about segregation that existed
in the barber shops, practically all of which were operated by
white barbers. This question was answered for me a few days
later when I was told that this was asked of one of the student
leaders of the picketing. He is said to have replied that he
would not have engaged in such an activity at home for fear of
being run out of town.

This answer indicated that he had a very keen awareness of
"possible danger" to himself, and that he would have behaved
in a manner to insure his own safety. Apparently, he had no
regard for the very precarious position that his actions, singly
and in concert with his fellow students, had brought into my
life.

> However, because barber shops are not covered under
> the Civil Rights Act, we have no recourse through the
> courts.

It is revealing that they had acquainted themselves with the
fact that barber shops were not covered by the Civil Rights
Act, and that they had no recourse through the courts. If they
had made these inquiries and acquainted themselves with these
facts, why had they circumvented me? Why had they not come
directly to me and at least done me the courtesy of a preliminary talk or discussion of the matter before launching an attack
on me? I was the owner of the business and the one to take
the consequences, financial and otherwise, of any decision that
I made with reference to it. I was easily accessible. But, no, not

ever a whisper of it was brought to my attention.

Then the long, arrogant and insolent sentence that ground into my guts:

> We have decided to approach you, the students, to ask you not to get a haircut at Mr. Johnson's until he gives written commitment that he will cut anybody's hair whether they are white or black and whether they live in a dormitory or in the community.

I considered it an insult of the highest order that anyone would have the brash arrogance to make a demand of me that I give my written commitment to them to operate my business according to their dictates and without regard to my own wishes or necessity in the matter. I was not even required under the law to give "written commitment" concerning the operation of my business before certification for its operation was granted. I was certain that I would not give such a commitment to any group of insolent zealots without any authority whatsoever over me or my business. It was unthinkable to me that I give such a "commitment," regardless of what might happen.

> Because Mr. Johnson's primary support comes from students, if the students refuse to give him their patronage, it will be a strong factor in influencing him to change his policy.

The students from Davidson College did constitute a considerable part of the business in the barber shop during that time of the year when college was in session. But this was not my "primary support" as stated. This was an arrogant but mistaken assumption based, perhaps, upon the fact that most of the students were patrons of my barber shop, and on their desire to be all-important. But it was also true that mine was recognized as the predominant barber business in the whole area, and that I not only had most of the student business, but that of the community and the surrounding region that extended for many miles, as well as a considerable patronage from nearby towns.

It was this widely dispersed patronage that allowed me to provide a good living for half a dozen black men and their families, and that kept me free from domination by the people from the college.

These from beyond the college community were also my main support, because my business operated twelve months a year. The college was in session only about eight months during the year considering the summer vacation period and holidays during the school year. Had it not been for this twelve-month business, I could not have maintained the barber shop. I had to have business all the year to give employment to my barbers and to bear the other expenses incidental to the operation of the business, not to mention my own requirements.

These were the factors that I had to consider in making decisions concerning the policy of the barber shop. I did not make policy capriciously, or according to my own whim. Such decisions were made in answer to what I had come to know as the demands of the customers who supported the business and made it possible.

The last short paragraph in the leaflet was devoted to urging the students not to patronize my barber shop. Then the names of thirteen students were printed at the bottom of the page, as if they were the signers of the leaflet. All of this was given above.

The thoughts as I have set them out rambled through my

troubled mind throughout that night. Then the new day was dawning. I wondered anxiously what it would bring. This was Wednesday, the day after the picketing began. The barber shop, along with other businesses in the town, closed on that afternoon each week to give a half-day holiday to the people occupied in these pursuits that required a six-day work week. I hoped this day would also bring the administrative staff and faculty members at the college to bear on the students and get them under control.

I knew that the president of the college, Dr. D. Grier Martin, was incapacitated by an illness that affected his ability to function in his office. I understood that the dean of faculty, Dr. Frontis Johnston, had been named acting president, and I hoped that he, along with the dean of students, Dr. Richard C. Burts, Jr., and faculty members, would act to restrain the students and let me run my business in peace.

As the morning wore on and no more students appeared marching and bearing placards in front of the barber shop, I dared to hope that the demonstration had come to an end, although there were some students milling about on the sidewalk.

Then I learned that the police had told them the afternoon before that they could not march or parade in front of my place of business, or on the street, without a permit from the town. The students were that morning trying to arrange for a permit.

The two large daily newspapers in Charlotte, twenty miles away, had called me for a statement the night before, as did the two major radio and television stations. I felt that the students had alerted them to their activity at the barber shop and were seeking all the publicity they could get. I maintained a strict "no comment" to all their questions. But the next day, Wednesday, the story was on the air and in the papers.

The Charlotte Observer carried this headline and article:

DAVIDSON BARBER SHOP PICKETED

White Davidson College students Tuesday picketed a Negro barber, saying that he would not cut Negroes' hair.

The students picketed and distributed leaflets asking other students to boycott the barber shop until they were asked to move by police.

The students then disbanded, determined to ask for a "parade permit," and left one of their number behind to continue handing out leaflets.

According to Robert Pyeatt, associate editor of the campus newspaper, *The Davidsonian,* Ralph Johnson, owner of Johnson's Barber Shop on Main Street, will only cut Negroes' hair if they are students at the 131 year old school.

There are five Negroes among Davidson's 1008 students.

Students arranged the picket by asking two Negro residents of Davidson to enter the barber shop about 4:15 p.m., according to Pyeatt.

When they were refused service, Pyeatt said, the picketing began.

Pyeatt said that the barber shop, which employs about five barbers, was too small to come under the 1964 federal law prohibiting racial discrimination in public accommodations.

There is one other barber shop in town, Pyeatt said, also owned by a Negro man and also under the same policy.

The leaflets asked all students to "please show him (Johnson) by your absence that you don't like the policy."

Estimates on the number of pickets ranged from five to twelve, but it was reported that the pickets plan to remain "until the policy is changed."

The picket comes on the heels of an apparent growing dissatisfaction among white Davidson students with what they consider to be discrimination toward Negroes.

A recent editorial in *The Davidsonian* charged that Negro students "face extinction because of admissions policy."

H. Edmunds White, director of admissions, emphatically had denied that admissions policy discriminates against Negroes, but rather concentrates on "quality." A few Davidson students have asked that the Presbyterian-related college make more effort to lend academic help to those who come from poor public school backgrounds.

Robert Hooker, editor of *The Davidsonian,* said recently that Davidson students rarely demonstrated their concern for minority causes.

"You only hear about that sort of thing in Chapel Hill in this state," Hooker said.

In this article, two statements that were attributed to Robert Pyeatt, associate editor of *The Davidsonian,* the campus newspaper, were of special interest to me.

First was the admission that "students arranged the picket by asking two Negro residents of Davidson to enter the barber shop about 4:15 p.m., according to Pyeatt."

This I considered as positive proof that the students had carefully constructed their plan of action against me before launching their attack just as I thought they had because of the fast moving sequence of events. It was also plain as day to me that they intended a sneak attack by reason of the fact that none of them had consulted me about a change in my policy towards Negro patrons, the policy dictated by law.

The second quote was in black print: "There is one other barber shop in town, Pyeatt said, also owned by a Negro man and also under the same policy."

This was the first time I had heard any mention made of

"that other barber shop," which was located just forty steps, by actual count, away from my place of business and on the same street. The students knew that shop was being operated under exactly the same rules regarding segregation of the races as mine was. If these people at Davidson College were interested in abolishing segregation, why had they not attacked that shop, also? There was much food for thought in that question. Why discriminate against me? I was unable to erase it from my mind. I would wait with interest to see what developed in reference to this.

The Charlotte News, a large circulation afternoon paper, carried this headline and article:

DAVIDSON BARBER SHOP IS TARGET OF RACIAL PROTEST

Davidson—Davidson College students are protesting the racial policies of a barber shop here that refuses to cut the hair of Negro townspeople.

Johnson's Barber Shop, owned by Ralph Johnson, is the target. Johnson and his barbers are Negroes.

A white student group picketed the barber shop on Main St. yesterday after two Negro townsmen were refused service there.

Robert Pyeatt, associate editor of the school paper, *The Davidsonian,* said Johnson will serve Negroes only if they are Davidson College students. There are five Negroes enrolled.

The pickets urged students not to patronize the shop until the policy is changed. Johnson could not be reached for comment today.

The pickets were back in front of the shop today.

A large daily paper of heavy circulation in Winston-Salem, seventy-five miles away, carried the following:

STUDENTS PICKET DAVIDSON SHOP

Davidson (UPI)— About 50 white students at Davidson College picketed a Negro-owned and operated barber shop here Tuesday because they said it refused to serve Negro townspeople.

The students complained that the only Negroes accepted as customers by Johnson's Barber Shop are the five who are Davidson students.

Johnson's is the main barber shop serving students. The six barbers working in the shop are Negroes. So is the owner, Ralph Johnson.

Picketing started about 4:15 p.m., shortly after two Negro residents of Davidson were refused service. Police told the pickets they would have to leave because they did not have a permit. After that, the students passed out leaflets urging a boycott of the shop.

CHAPTER TWENTY-FOUR

Pressures
Mount

Mayor Jackson, my old adversary in the matter of the apartment buildings, was the town's officer to whom the students made their request for a parade permit. I understood later that on this occasion Mayor Jackson was my staunch ally and supporter, that he tried to talk the students out of pursuing their objective. But they persisted, and the permit was issued. I was told that Mayor Jackson even called on Dr. Frontis Johnston, acting president of the college, and tried to get him to use the influence of his office to stop the students. He, apparently, did not get a favorable reply to his request.

At any rate, by the noon closing time of that Wednesday morning, nothing much was accomplished affecting the picketing of my place of business. The atmosphere was a charged one, however, with milling about and sullen glances into the barber shop as the morning approached noontime.

That afternoon I received a letter dated April 2, 1968, the same afternoon the picketing started. It was written on Davidson College stationery and contained the printed legend "Department

of Philosophy" in the upper left-hand corner of the sheet. It
read as follows:

> Mr. Ralph W. Johnson
> Johnson's Barber Shop
> Main Street
> Davidson, N.C.
>
> Mr. Johnson:
>
> I am sure you are aware a group of students from
> Davidson College have stated that it is the policy of your
> barber shop to refuse to cut the hair of local non-student
> Negroes during your regular business hours; these same
> students have requested that I, as a faculty member of
> Davidson College, not patronize your shop until you have
> publicly repudiated, in writing, this discriminatory policy.
> This letter is to inform you that I am wholly in sympathy
> with the sentiments of these students. I shall refrain from
> patronizing your shop until your policy has been changed.
>
>   Sincerely,
>
>   Raymond Martin

It appeared to me that, if the writer of this letter was old
enough and had received sufficient education to be a faculty
member at Davidson College, then he should have known
beyond the shadow of any doubt that I, a Negro, was locked in
the mores and practices that had been imposed upon me by his
own forebears. Surely he was not trying to say to me that he
had not known of segregation before this time.

I thought the part of a sentence that read "...until you have
publicly repudiated in writing this discriminatory policy" was
particularly disgusting and arrogantly insolent. Who was he to

lay down to me some rule that required me publicly to repudi-
ate anything in writing? I was not the one who had brought
segregation into being. It was his people, white people, who
had forced it on me. Now, it seemed to me, he was holding me
responsible for its existence, as if it had been nowhere except
in my barber shop, and that all I had to do was to change the
policy that I had been forced to operate under for all these
years and the attitudes of the whole region regarding separation of the races would vanish. I knew the general knowledge
was, and he should have known, that admitting Negro patrons
to the barber shop would bring serious repercussions from the
white patronage of the shop.

Wednesday night brought renewed insistence from the news
media for a statement from me. In fairness to my own position, and because I didn't know anything better to do, I gave
them a statement.

Thursday morning *The Charlotte Observer,* a widely circulated
morning newspaper, ran the following article.

LET STUDENT PICKETS HELP POOR,
NEGRO BARBER SAYS

A Negro barber had some scathing remarks Wednesday for white Davidson College students picketing his
shop, suggesting that their efforts would be better directed
toward helping the poor.

Ralph W. Johnson, who is being picketed because he
will not cut the hair of Negro residents, asked:

"Do you know of any barber shop where they cut the
hair of both races?"

(A member of the Charlotte chapter of the all-white
Associated Master Barbers of America, informed of
Johnson's comment replied: "Gosh, I don't know of a
one.")

Johnson said, "I don't know why these infants are singling me out to bear the burden of society's prejudices

and practices."

Students, who began their picketing and called for a boycott Tuesday, got a parade permit Wednesday from Davidson Mayor F. L. Jackson.

The students were asked Tuesday by police to leave the Main Street sidewalk in front of Johnson's seven-chair shop because they didn't have a permit. They left behind a student handing out leaflets calling for a townwide boycott.

The students charge that Johnson will only cut the hair of Negro students at Davidson College, but not town residents. Five of the 1,008 students at Davidson are Negroes.

Johnson charged that "these prejudices (against Negroes) were here before I came on the scene...

"I understand that one of these boys is from Mississippi and another from Arkansas. It seems to me they could find a few things to work on where they came from.

"There are many poor Negro families in Davidson," Johnson said, "but I don't see the students going out to sacrifice themselves.

"Why don't they volunteer to go to Vietnam?"

Johnson, 63, saying that he had worked hard to make his shop a success, asked: "Who's going to make restitution if this costs me my business?"

Johnson described the picketing as "most unfair" and added: "I noticed that when it started to rain they stood under my awning."

This Thursday morning, I was full of hope that by now the college authorities had taken the students in hand and brought them under the disciplinary rules of the school. But shortly after the shop opened for business, the pickets began assembling, and I knew that they were not, at least not yet, under the restraining influence of the college. In back of my mind was the thought that the students would be brought under the rules of behavior of the college, and so disperse and not interfere with the operation of my business.

The first pickets of the day seemed completely organized, with the leaders putting them in place and starting them on their march back and forth in front of the barber shop. More and more students came, and those not marching with placards stood on the sidewalk until persons about ordinary pursuits of the day could hardly pass. These students were mostly of the long hair variety, some with beards, and of slovenly dress. Their presence and activity attracted people from the community who came to stand and watch.

It was then that the community began to express its disapproval in looks and comments. Traffic in the street increased as motorists rode slowly by and called insults and made disparaging remarks to the assembled students.

The students had devised a system whereby the pickets were relieved at intervals and others would take their places in the line. Fresh pickets were continually being supplied from the sidelines, where others milled about.

Dr. W. G. Workman, professor of psychology and an ordained minister in the Presbyterian Church, that morning paid me the first of his several visits pertaining to the picketing.

A native of Georgia, Dr. Workman had over a period of some years discussed race relations with me. I had been interested in one student-day incident in his particular life which he had related to me, that had to do with his own prejudice and his difficulty of overcoming it.

When this man entered and indicated that he wanted to talk to me concerning the problem of integration in the barber shop, I had a feeling that here was a man who would understand the situation that confronted me, that he understood the deeply ingrained attitudes of the white public with which I had to deal. I felt, furthermore, that he was probably a person from the college with whom I could reason and explain my dilemma with the hope of putting an end to the demonstration at my door.

In a very short time, I was to understand that he was not there to hear anything I had to say. Rather, he had come to urge me to integrate the barber shop in accordance with the students' demands. He seemed to disregard me, not even to hear me, when I tried to explain the thing that should have been very obvious to him, namely, that the extensive community of white people which I served would not accept or support with their patronage a barber shop that attempted to mix white and Negro customers in the business. He was well aware of the concerted resistance to integration in the public schools in our own county (Mecklenburg).

I was soon convinced that Dr. Workman was there for the sole purpose of breaking down my resistance to the students' demands. I was later to wonder if his role had been determined in the planning stage, because he was a psychologist and so assumed better able to break down my resistance.

One thing clearly evident was that these people regarded themselves as having the rightful place to control my business, that they, by some unknown authority, had a right to dictate how it was to be operated. This was implicit in their behavior and in Dr. Workman's urging that I comply with their wishes. Back of all this seemed to be an overweening conviction that the barber shop was operated solely for them, and that it was only through their patronage that it existed at all, and that I was behaving like an unruly manager who had somehow gotten control of their property.

Dr. Workman had not done me the courtesy of asking my opinion about integrating the shop before the picketing began. But he was now on hand to insist on my doing so. I was very disappointed in him that day, and in other days to follow during this episode. I thought he should have known better.

At mid-morning the congestion in front of my place of

business was so dense that customers could hardly get in the door. Then the Mecklenburg County Police arrived under the direction of Captain Wall.

At first, the officers stood at the edge of the crowd and assessed the situation, then they moved in and ordered the milling crowd of students on the sidewalk to move on. They laid down the rules under which they could march or parade in front of my place of business. The students seemed resentful at this exercise of authority over them, but they conformed to the orders of the police by limiting the number of pickets and the distance between each one. Most of the others then went to the campus just on the other side of Main Street.

They were foiled in their apparent attempt to keep customers from the barber shop by crowding the sidewalk and the doorway. Meantime a student photographer became active on the other side of the street. As customers entered or left the shop, particularly if they were students or others connected with the college, he raised his large-lensed camera to his eye in a gesture of taking pictures of those persons. It was clearly done as an act of intimidation against the persons being photographed, a way of identifying them as patrons of the shop and thus subjecting them to "exposure" or criticism from the ones who had arrogated to themselves the right to place my business under siege.

This assumption was shown to be correct later when the student newspaper, *The Davidsonian,* came out with a picture of football coach Homer Smith prominently displayed on the front page. He was emerging from the barber shop door. The caption at the bottom of this picture stated:

NO MAN' S LAND - Homer Smith emerges with a new trim.
(Staff Photo by Robinson).

Later that day, Thursday, Dr. Richard Burts, dean of students, came to the front of the barber shop and stood with me on the sidewalk and observed the pickets. The next day, Friday, April 5th, *The Davidsonian* had this picture on its front page, with the caption:

DEMONSTRATIONS CONTINUE - Peter Hobbie car-
ries placard as Johnson and Dean Burts observe.
(Staff Photo by George Robinson)

I thought the arrival of Dean Burts on the scene would certainly have some bearing, either immediately or later, on the conduct of the students, and that now that they were under official scrutiny they would be brought under control by the college.

This long hard day for me wore on, with the students marching and carrying their denunciatory placards, and greater numbers of people being attracted to the scene as word spread throughout the region by radio and television news announcements and by published accounts in the Charlotte newspapers. The barber shop was known over a wide area, and what was happening there was of interest to many people of the region.

Early in the afternoon, television cameras from the major TV stations in Charlotte were on the scene grinding out their film to be broadcast later in the day. As a part of this coverage, cameras and sound equipment were moved from the street into the barber shop and set up for an interview with me. This, too, was put on the air.

And all the time the pickets kept up their marching and carrying their placards. Crowds of people gathered about, and the police came and dispersed them from time to time.

One thing particularly noticeable was the revulsion of the motorists who passed in the street and others who congregated from the non-college community. There was a great deal of name-calling and unfavorable comment directed at the students, the white community's reaction to the idea of integrating the barber shop.

I thought if the students had called for and been responsible for the wide news coverage that was being brought to bear here, as I believed they were, then they must have been disturbed at the public reaction to their picketing and the purpose of it. For as the news spread over the region of their activities at the barber shop, more people who disapproved of them were attracted to the scene.

The students' sensitivity to this rising tide of resentment and disapproval of their movement was becoming noticeable in their demeanor. They were no longer so jaunty and cocksure as they had been earlier in the day. They were removing the shabbily dressed, bearded and long-haired demonstrators from the picket lines and replacing them with students with shorter hair and clean faces. As the day grew older, a certain grimness seemed to invade their ranks. The holiday spirit and self-assurance were not as evident as in the morning.

The Charlotte News, the large circulation afternoon newspaper, had this to say that afternoon:

THE BARBER IS SYMPATHETIC

Davidson - A Negro barber here today admitted he is "in sympathy" with pickets demanding that he fully integrate his shop but said such a move "would ruin my business."

Ralph W. Johnson, an articulate 63-year-old who has owned his Davidson barber shop for 40 years, said integration of barber shops in the South "is just something that isn't done."

Davidson College students, mostly whites, have picketed Johnson's shop since Tuesday because its seven barbers, all Negroes, refuse to cut hair of Negroes who are not college students.

"We do business with (white) people from all over this area, and they wouldn't support this," Johnson said. "I've spent a lifetime building up this business.

"I think it ought to be that everything would be open to all people. But then we have attitudes to deal with, and I didn't create the attitudes. I don't think I should have to bear the brunt of them."

Nat Heyward, a leader of the pickets, said the protest will continue "indefinitely" and might be extended to Davidson's only other full-time barber shop, also owned by a Negro. Hood Norton, owner of the second shop, refused to comment.

Heyward, a Davidson College senior in psychology from Dunedin, Fla., said the protest "grew out of response from the Negro community."

"Johnson says he bases his policy on public consensus, and we're trying to show him there is a section of his public that does not agree with his policy," Heyward said.

Johnson and Heyward each claim that the majority of the college students and faculty are on his side of the argument.

But Heyward said he was "unsure" about the strength of backing from Davidson residents not affiliated with the college.

A parade permit issued by the mayor of Davidson limits the number of actual pickets to 10 at any one time, but about 150 students, merchants and shoppers stood nearby watching the protest this morning.

Although Heyward has a clean-cut appearance, some of the pickets were bearded and sloppily attired— a factor that obviously disturbed a number of townspeople who shouted taunts questioning the pickets' political lean-

Johnson said he could not yet determine whether the protest was causing a drop-off in his business.

He said Davidson has a third barber shop, exclusively for Negroes, that is staffed evenings by some barbers employed days in the two other shops.

However, he said he does not participate in the night work.

Two statements in this article need comment: the heading and first sentence of this article.

THE BARBER IS SYMPATHETIC

A Negro barber here today admitted he is in sympathy with pickets demanding that he fully integrate his shop...

certainly did not represent my sentiments in regard to the pickets and their activities in front of the barber shop. I might have expressed a sympathetic attitude towards the idea of equality of treatment of all people, but there was certainly no sympathy on my part for the group marching in front of my door, nor for their demand that I fully integrate the barber shop. Had the climate been such in the region which I served that integration seemed feasible and acceptable or desirable from a business standpoint, then I should long ago have made it a part of my business practice, had it been possible to do so under North Carolina law. My personal sentiment did not necessarily dictate my business policy. And as far as I could reason, those marching to and fro bearing placards absolutely had no right to insist in such a manner that their wishes be carried out in my business.

"Nat Heyward, a leader of the pickets, (continued the article) said the protest will continue 'indefinitely' and might be extended to Davidson's only other full-time barber shop, also owned by a Negro. Hood Norton, owner of the second shop, refused to comment."

In this paragraph, reference was made to "the only other full-time barber shop, also owned by a Negro." This was a subject that was exciting considerable comment in the community. Why had I been singled out for attack when another barber shop only forty steps away from my place of business, on the same street, and operating under the same policy of segregation, went unnoticed by these protesters bearing placards denouncing me for not serving Negroes?

If these people from Davidson College were so morally opposed to discrimination, why were they discriminating against me in so flagrant a manner? If they were so bent on abolishing segregation, as they vowed they were, why did they not attack it wherever it existed, instead of singling out one place and ignoring the other?

Two or three Negroes joined the students in the afternoon, and they, too, carried placards in the line of marching pickets. The pickets and their followers and helpers stayed until the barber shop was closed for the day.

The announcement that night of the slaying of Dr. Martin Luther King, Jr., signaled episodes of great emotional response in the country, especially among Negroes. I knew that since the picketing at the barber shop was in progress regarding racial segregation, we of our household in the Negro community where we lived were in a precarious situation, one fraught with potential danger to us. Noise in the street and in the neighborhood around us brought with it the frenzy and the agitated anger of an aroused and greatly disturbed people, many unreasoning and dangerous. Once a pellet of some sort struck the front of our house, penetrating the screen and a window pane. We kept to the inside.

Later that night, the police called to tell me that a plate glass window had been broken at the barber shop.

The next day, Friday, I went to work with a great dread of what the day would bring. I knew that on this day, the day after

Martin Luther King was killed, the environment would be charged heavily with emotion and anger. And that much of it would be directed at me as the object of a protest movement.

Shortly after the barber shop opened for business that morning, a group of students arrived at the front of the building and pickets took up their positions in a marching line. I sensed that the day would indeed be a full one.

The morning mail brought two pertinent letters. Both of these letters were somewhat of a shock to me. Written on stationery bearing the printed letterhead "Davidson College" and in the upper left-hand corner the legend "Office of the Dean of Students," one letter read:

Dear Mr. Johnson:

At its regular meeting on April 3, 1968, the Student Life Committee passed the following motion:
The Student Life Committee supports the boycott of Johnson's Barber Shop so long as it continues its policy of racial segregation.
This action conforms with the policy of the College and expresses the hope that businesses within the community will make their services available to customers regardless of their race.

Sincerely,
Richard C. Burts,
Chairman.

The signature at the end of this letter was that of the dean of students at Davidson College. The last paragraph in this letter which began, "This action conforms with the policy of the College..." was of special interest to me, because it indicated that the administrative officers of the college not only had no intention of restraining the students' activities, but, in addition to this, they were lending their support to them. This was incomprehensible to me.

The second letter of that morning was also written on the printed stationery of Davidson College. It bore the legend "Department of Economics" and read as follows:

Dear Mr. Johnson:

I am writing to inform you that I support the members of the Davidson black community and some Davidson College students to integrate fully the barber shops in Davidson and that I will not patronize any shop in Davidson until the shop integrates fully.

There may be legal and economic arguments against integrating the barber shops, but there are moral and ethical arguments in support of the action that, in my opinion, greatly outweigh the legal and economic arguments. I personally do not believe that any economic harm will come to your business if you integrate. I know of no business that has had to close because of having integrated. I know that if you do integrate, you will gain the respect and admiration of all decent and thoughtful members of the Davidson community and, more important, your self-respect and self-esteem will be greatly increased, because you will know that you have done what is right and just and honorable.

I urge you, as a friend, to take the lead and initiative in opening your doors during regular business hours to all customers, regardless of race, sex, religion, or politics.

Yours faithfully,
E.F. Patterson,
Professor.

My first reaction to this letter was that it breathed the spirit of "Let's you and them go out and fight." Here was a man who, as far as I could remember, had never been a customer in my barber shop, and who I had reason to believe was a patron of the other shop. Yet he was now giving me high moral preachments about gaining the "respect and admiration of all decent and thoughtful members of the Davidson community."

The statement in this letter that "I personally do not believe that any economic harm will come to your business if you integrate" seemed, indeed, a too slender reed of unsupported confidence for me to gamble away the nearly fifty years of hard work and sacrifice it had taken for me to build my business.

This man, secure in his well-paid, tenured position as a professor of economics at Davidson College, with ample retirement benefits provided, had the audacity to implore me to take a course of action in my business that I felt would have a crucial impact on its value as a business and upon my own earning potential.

He had nothing to lose but the little time it had taken to write the letter. The sheet of paper bore the letterhead of Davidson College and was presumably free of cost to him. As for the stamp for the mailing? Well, who knows, maybe he had that much invested in this great experimental social enterprise. Did he not know that I had great pressures of many kinds upon me? I had no patience with his reasoning.

Then I looked out the window and saw Dr. Patterson, the writer of this letter, in the line of marching pickets in front of my place of business. He was marching and carrying a placard in front of my barber shop, not the one a few paces down the street where he got his own hair cut and which was operating under the same rule as I was with reference to Negro patrons.

I went out the side door of the barber shop and called to Dr. Patterson. When he left the picket line and came to where I was standing, I pointed out my broken plate glass window and engaged him in conversation concerning the breakage and other damaging aspects of their attack on my business. During our short talk I alluded again to the broken window and the considerable cost of replacing it and asked if he or they were going to pay for this damage to my property.

He interrupted me to say "no" and continued with a statement to the effect that all of this that I was saying was of no consequence in the light of the great principle involved. He added, "Someone must pay the cost." This I thought a particularly crass and uncaring outlook and expression on a situation that he was helping to create for me by his presence in a line of pickets parading in front of my business.

Anger welled up in me and I exploded, "You are nothing but an unprincipled scoundrel." When he gave no answer to this, I turned and went back into the barber shop. He returned to the picket line, where he resumed carrying a placard.

I could sense that pressures and tenseness were rapidly building up after the slaying of Dr. Martin Luther King, the evening before. More students and people from the college were congregated on the sidewalk. And across the street on the campus more of them had gathered on the grass. The line of pickets lengthened so as to extend around the corner and down Depot Street. They had heretofore marched only on Main Street directly in front of the barber shop. Negroes were joining the pickets in increasing numbers. They were for the most part a sullen lot and hostile.

I was in conversation again that morning with Dr. W.G. Workman, who expressed his regrets at my broken window and urged me again to accede to the students' demands that I desegregate the barber shop.

Soon Dr. John C. Bailey, another professor at the college who had for a number of years been dean of students, entered the building and came directly to where I was standing in about the center of the barber shop. I had known this man for more than thirty years and had a friendly relationship with him over this span of time, during which he was a customer in the barber shop. It was immediately apparent that he was under considerable emotional stress, a condition which I had only

once before observed in this ordinarily pleasant and unper-
turbed man. We spoke some words of greeting, then he paused
as if to bring his voice under control before he continued.
Even so, there was a quiver in his voice when he said: "Ralph,
we white people have been mean to you colored people for a
long time. I want you to open your door here and cut their hair
like anybody else."

This man, a native of South Carolina, had for some years
headed the public schools in Davidson (which included the
separate white and Negro schools), and I knew he was familiar
with the racial attitudes of the region. Yet he could tell me in
all earnestness to alter my business practices without apparent
regard or awareness to the risk such a course of action involved for me.

This man was caught up in the heavy emotions of the day,
and he had responded by coming to me with his suggestion as
if that one act of desegregating the barber shop could or
would erase the whole of racial injustice. I was utterly amazed
at such unrealistic thinking.

It seemed to me that the people from the college who were
urging me to desegregate the barber shop had suddenly
blinded themselves to the continuing reality of racial prejudice.
They assumed the attitude that, because they had reached some
conclusion on a matter, no matter how recent or shallow, it was
impossible for others to hold a contrary or an opposite view.
This had nothing to do with the reality of the situation, and I
was in serious doubt about the sincerity of their own newly
expressed sentiments.

I was also acutely aware of the strong tide of opposition to
them and their movement in the whole surrounding region.
And another thing, the overwhelming sentiment of the region
was not in agreement that Dr. Martin Luther King was a
benefactor of mankind. Many of the white people regarded

him as a trouble-making rabble-rouser and a jailbird who had
no respect for the law. Instead of being depressed or saddened
at his death, there was much satisfaction over it. The anger and
great sense of loss felt by Negroes was far exceeded by sentiments of "good-riddance" in the white community at large.

These vastly different opinions were in ideological conflict
in front of my barber shop door as the college group and
Negroes marched and carried their placards, and the community and regional white population gave greater and louder and
increasingly hostile utterance to their emotions. Traffic in the
street was greatly increased, and when cars came to a halt in
front of my door at the corner stoplight, occupants hurled
abusive epithets and threats at the marching pickets.

I felt with sadness that I and my place of business had
unjustly been made the focal point of great contention and
agitation by the people from Davidson College who were
marching and carrying their denunciatory placards in front of
my business. None of the background of this strife was of my
doing. Yet I felt a certainty that the end of this would be the
exacting of another great price from me personally.

I resented the actions of these people who had caused me
to be placed in this situation and who were relentlessly marching to and fro, with relays of pickets standing in readiness
across the street on the campus. Some out-of-towners, too,
were being added to the ranks. A group in a small car bearing
an out-of-state license were particularly weird in their appearance. One man with a great mass of hair on his head and face
was squat and of heavy, muscular build. He swaggered when
he walked. If he was white, his complexion was dark. If he was
Negro, his complexion was light. A swarthy woman companion was dressed in a long vari-colored dress in large floral
patterns. The man joined the line of marching pickets for a
while. He seemed particularly purposeful as he strode back

forth bearing a placard. I thought of him as a roving revolutionary who somehow heard of a protest and came to lend his weight to it.

I owned a good yet fairly compact tape recorder with volume playback sufficient to be heard and understood at some distance. That day after lunch I made an impromptu voice recording on this instrument. I give here the complete text of this recording:

> I am Ralph Johnson speaking. I have spent forty years of my life in building up this business. I have worked hard, I have worked with my body sick and aching over these years to build up this business, to serve the patrons in this community. I think that I have some rights in saying how it should be used.
>
> These people who are marching in front of my place of business in protest against discrimination as they call it, have nothing to lose except the little bit of time that each one puts in. They are taking shifts at coming a few minutes at a time and walking in this line here to protest and to create ill-will in this community.
>
> I have suffered damage already to one of my windows which has been broken, and when I asked Dr. Patterson, who is parading in this group of protesters, if he or they would be responsible for the replacement of my window, he said, "No," that this is the cost that must be paid. By which they mean that it is the cost that I, Ralph Johnson, must pay for their sociological experiment here. They are assuming no responsibility for damage which they have caused me.
>
> They have hurt the value of my property immeasurably. They have offered no restitution for this. They continue to march in front of my place. I ask

the public, who will bear this expense? Am I— am
I, Ralph Johnson— required to bear this because
some people here in the name of idealism want to
come before my place and march and march and
march and cause me destruction to my property, and
cause me ill-will in this community, and they do
nothing to repair it?

Will they be as diligent to watch over my property at night and so see that it is kept from damage
as they are to walk in front of it and create the climate in this community which will cause damage
to me and to other people? I think that these are
very irresponsible people who take the attitude that
they may appropriate to their own use properties
which do not belong to them.

If I were to go out and appropriate to my use, let
us say, someone's automobile, and drive it off and
use it for my own purposes, then I could be indicted
for stealing a car which did not belong to me. These
people here have arrogated to themselves the right
to come here and appropriate the property which I
have accumulated in my business to their own self-
ish interests and to dissipate it at their will, without
any responsibility on their part. They are willing to
make experiments, if someone else will pay the cost.
Am I, Ralph Johnson, going to be the one who is
required to pay this cost? I regard this as an act of
piracy which is being carried on in front of my place
of business, since these people are taking for their
own use property which belongs to me.

They have arrogated to themselves the right to
fling it up into the air for the wind to blow it away,
a thing that I have given forty years of my life to
accumulate, and they take no responsibility. They
say they are doing something in the community to
benefit the Negro people. I notice that they do not
go into areas where Negroes are poor and sacrifice
themselves for aid and assistance.

I notice in Smithville they are in need of help there to build toilets for people who do not have them — old and sick people. These able-bodied people who walk this picket line could take turns and dig those pits and erect those privies if they were interested in doing something for the good of the people.

Already, a window has been broken from my place since this began. These windows are very expensive and yet these people here who are walking in front of my place say they bear no responsibility for this loss, that this is something that must be borne. By which they mean it must be borne by me. But, as for themselves, they have no responsibility. All they do is walk to and fro and tear down and create ill-will here for me in this community. None of them have offered to make restitution to me for the damage which has been caused me. None of them, none of them, not one has said that I am sorry for your loss here. None of them have come forward with the money to replace the damage which is done to my place.

The value of my property has been reduced as a result of their activities, and they have not offered to replace it. A window has been broken, they have not offered to replace it either. They say that this is a cost that must be borne by someone outside themselves, because they do not assume the responsibility for damage which is done.

They do, however, assume responsibility for what they call community improvement here, to label me as a blackguard and a scoundrel, my name being cast all over the world as someone who is mean and despicable because of their activities. They are not assuming any responsibility for all of this either financially, morally, or otherwise. Yet they walk to and fro before my business. What damage will they cause me? What damage will they cause

me in the future? They are not paying for anything.
They have appropriated, they have stolen, they have
stolen my goods, they have stolen my goods in the
name of their own virtue.

I have given here a verbatim account of this voice recording.
A portion of it was a few days later brought into question in a
letter from Dr. Patterson.

My tape recorder could be operated either on house current
or batteries, and this recording was made sitting in my car at
the back of the barber shop building immediately after I
returned from lunch and not more than four or five hours after
I had spoken with Dr. Patterson. It was totally unrehearsed, but
made and used in the immediate environment of the marching
pickets and a tense atmosphere.

Repeated reference to the broken window was because I was
convinced that this was directly related to the activity of the
pickets. I had had many windows broken before and was thoroughly familiar with the cost of replacing plate glass windows.
But that was in the past now, and this breakage seemed to me
the direct result of the new agitation about my place of business.

This tape was played at near full volume on the sidewalk just
in front of the door of the barber shop. It attracted much
attention, and I was aware that the pickets were affected by it.
It was played at intervals during all of the rest of the time
when the picketing continued.

During the afternoon, an increasing number of people were
attracted to the scene. More Negroes joined the picket line and
stood about in the gathering on the sidewalk and on the campus across the street. Their attitude was one of hostility, as if I
had perpetrated some great wrong against them. Traffic in the

street continued to increase as more cars drove slowly by or stopped at the stoplight there. These cars were for the most part occupied by white men of stern visage who glared coldly at the pickets and called insults at them.

My barbers were noticeably affected by the tumult on the outside. The ones who worked near the front of the building began to express anxiety for their safety as more Negroes assembled. The news of the killing of Dr. King had brought many more than the usual number of Negroes out into the street and centered their attention on my place of business.

My barber shop had, indeed, become a center of contention and striving emotion. There was tenseness everywhere. Customers to the shop belligerently pushed their way by the pickets and into the door for barber service. And I, in this mountain of trouble that had been caused me by the people at Davidson College, was caught helplessly in a whirlwind of hate.

A Negro friend brought me a pistol and bullets for my protection at the barber shop and at home and offered to stand armed guard over my place of business at night.

A white man who occupied a prominent position in the town urged that I, my sister and my mother leave our home and come stay with him and his family in their home where we would be safe as long as the dangerous condition existed. He assured me that he was joined in this invitation by his very gracious wife. I was deeply touched by this kind offer of refuge in his home. But I thought it better that we continue to live at our house and not leave it vacant. Too, our presence in his home would have been unusually disruptive for our mother, now past eighty-four years old and troubled with the infirmities of age. She was greatly affected by radio and television accounts of events at the barber shop and the picketing and the milling crowd around it. She was extremely fearful of our

danger, especially of the danger to me at the barber shop and
in the streets. Her condition was to add greatly to the strain
and stress at this time, because she continued to need one of
us with her throughout the night. My sister and I took turns
of a few hours each during the nights sitting up with her,
except at those times when it was necessary for both of us to
be with her. This nightly routine was to continue almost without interruption for the next two months.

A little after four o'clock that Friday afternoon, Dr. Dan
Rhodes, professor of Bible at Davidson College, and Mr. H. B.
Naramore, a Northern man who had come to live in Davidson
a few years before when he relocated his industrial plant here
and who was also a member of the Davidson Town Board,
came to talk with me. These men were not customers in my
barber shop, and I had some curiosity about their mission.

At the time of day of the visit there was no place inside the
barber shop where we could talk without the possibility of
interruption, so I suggested that we sit in my car parked just in
back of the building. They accompanied me there, and when
we were seated they said they had come to me with a proposal
that they didn't think I would accept, but that they were going
to ask me anyway. This, I thought, was an extremely odd
approach, but I responded that I was willing to listen to what
they had to say.

They said that in view of the considerable agitation at my
barber shop, they had gone to Hood Norton, the owner of the
barber shop just down the street from my place, and that he
had agreed to their proposal that he close his shop all the next
day, Saturday, if I would agree to close mine. They thought this
would be in the interest of reducing the tensions that had
developed as well as possibly averting other undesirable situations that might come to pass.

Before I could answer, they repeated that they didn't think I would accept these terms. I was at a loss to understand why they would come to me with a proposal and at the same time say they didn't think I would accept it. Was this statement supposed to exert some psychological influence on me to do as they had asked? Were they saying in effect that they had expected me to be uncooperative and stubborn? (This last statement was something of the attitude of the group at Davidson College who were trying to dictate the operating policy of my barber shop.) Or were they so conscious of the unreasonableness of their proposal that they were being half apologetic for making it?

Both of these men were customers at Hood Norton's barber shop, and I wondered why they had seen fit to concoct a plan for me to close my business on Saturday, our busiest day of the week, unless it was because Dr. Rhodes was concerned for the safety of the pickets from Davidson College. I felt certain the concern for me was less, since neither of them had bothered to consult me before going to someone else and making arrangements for me to close my business for the day.

I wondered why they had not taken the students back to the college where they belonged, instead of asking me to close my business. They were the ones who were creating the problem. I was only trying as best I could to run my business and serve my customers. They made no mention of compensating me for business lost, or for paying my barbers who would have been idled by such a course of action.

And why had they gone to my uncle, Hood Norton, owner of the barber shop just forty steps away from my business, a man estranged from me, a business rival who had not spoken to me for more than a dozen years, and concluded with him an agreement to close his barber shop on the busiest day of the week, Saturday, if I would close mine?

I reasoned for a certainty that Hood Norton had not entered into such an agreement for the purpose of cooperating with me, nor for any reason that he considered to my advantage. Speculation was rife as to why his barber shop was not being picketed. The practices were identical in the two shops in regards to Negro patrons, yet his shop was not attacked, and some of his patrons had been marching in the line of pickets in front of my shop.

These questions and more raced through my mind during the few minutes of our conversation. These men made no mention whatever of trying to get the people from Davidson College away from my door with their picketing and other activities.

I refused to comply with this very unusual and, to me, unreasonable request and went back inside to work. Meanwhile, the picketing and milling about in the street outside continued with gathering strength, particularly so with more Negroes present.

At closing time, 5:30 in the afternoon, my barbers gathered about and expressed their concern about working the next day, for fear of being attacked during the day by some of the hostile Negroes. I had observed the last few days that at least two or three of my barbers had been in conversation more than once with some of the student leaders of the picketing. I became aware that a part of their concern was rooted in the fact that they had been convinced that the barber shop ought to be desegregated, that it was the "right" thing to do. I knew, too, that they were under considerable pressure from their Negro friends who all of a sudden regarded as an affront to them the long established practice of barber shops not to serve both white and Negro patrons.

Somehow, all of them, together with the people from the College, were taking the position that I was responsible for the whole thing, that all that was necessary for the eradication of the condition was for me to make the "correct" decision and open the doors of my place of business to Negroes generally. No one seemed to be aware of the tremendous social pressures that had been responsible for the practice in the beginning and that still existed. It was as if I, by some magic, could drive out of the hearts and minds of the overwhelming majority of white people their demand for separation of the races.

I knew, as my barbers left that evening, that they were another facet of the irresolvable problem that confronted me.

CHAPTER TWENTY-FIVE

Assassination

The pistol my friend had brought me that day was cold and repulsive to my touch and inclinations as I put it in my pocket when I was ready to go home for the night. But its potential for deadly violence was reassuring as I went out into a world that had assumed vast new proportions of ill-will and hatred. It was as if the simple act of getting a haircut at Johnson's Barber Shop had become the ultimate solution to age-old habits of mind.

This was the 5th of April, 1968, the night after Dr. Martin Luther King was slain in Memphis, Tennessee. Millions of Negroes throughout the nation were on the loose, venting hatred and spewing violence. In our community, I felt I was the focal point upon which my fellow Negroes centered their hatred and hostility. I was, at this moment, the symbol of resistance to what had now become their demand. Throughout the night they passed back and forth in the street by our house and their angry threats could be heard on the inside. My sister and I were up most of that night with Mama. The next morning they admonished me to search the car carefully before entering it or trying to start it.

Saturday had dawned with clear skies. I had hoped it would rain all day and thus keep away the pickets and others bent on making trouble for me. But it was clear and warm throughout the day, a fine day for being outside. This was to contribute to the increase of persons milling about in the street in front of my place of business. It was also to contribute to the number of persons in the street who were hostile to the purposeful movements of the people from Davidson College and the Negroes who had joined with them.

Since the death of Martin Luther King, the news had been filled with accounts of destructive riots, burning and other acts of recrimination by Negroes all over the country especially in the big cities. A great many white people were concerned and fearful because of these mass disturbances and strongly disapproved of them. Locally, their attention centered on the activity around my barber shop as an incident that was part of the turmoil and strife following or accompanying Dr. King's assassination.

The picketing from the first had been the object of region-wide disapproval by many white people. Now a new dimension had been added to excite their anger and strong disapproval. The picketing activity was seen as and equated with the Negro disorders rampant all over the nation. This trend of mind heightened scorn and anger towards the white students and faculty members of Davidson College who were mounting the attack on my place of business. The strong regional censure of the activities at my door had now become more widespread and intense as increasing numbers of people in the area knew about it from radio, TV, and newspapers, not to mention the considerable impact of sentiments passed between individuals by word of mouth.

From the very beginning of that Saturday morning, there was a decided change in the student pickets, as if there had been communicated to them a greater awareness of the ever mounting tide of anger and hostility towards them by the white population of the surrounding area. They had removed from their ranks most of the longhaired, bearded, and sloppily attired students the day before in answer to the continued abusive references to them by people attracted to the spot. But now there was an infusion of a ragtag element of Negroes into their fold. I sensed the pickets were not proud of this addition to their number, although they were avowedly striving for complete Negro integration in all activities and services in the community. The placards they were carrying said so, and yet...

We were especially busy in the barber shop that day. Saturday was the day when most working people were off from their jobs. Customers from the outlying areas of the region had heard of the picketing and agitation at the barber shop, and they came to see and lend their voices and presence against the activities of the people from the college. Many of these customers pushed and shoved their way belligerently through the line of pickets on the sidewalk and entered the barber shop with anger showing in their faces. Many people of the town and surrounding region were there that day to give voice to their sentiments in the matter. They were unmistakably not in favor of integrating the barber shop and said and acted so.

A striking thing, however, about the behavior of these people was that, while most of them let it be known that they were against the integration of the shop and voiced their disgust and scorn of the pickets, they had one characteristic in common that had not been displayed by the originators of the strife. All of them respected my ownership of the business and my right to make decisions with reference to its operation. These people were the real backbone of the barber shop's support through the years. A few told me that, regardless of what I decided to do about integration, they would continue to patronize the shop. I was very favorably impressed by this expression of their sentiments regarding the issue, and at the same time their courtesy in granting me the right to run my business as I saw it necessary or desirable to do, although I felt deep down that a great many of them would not continue their patronage of the shop if it were integrated. This was a wide departure from the demanding arrogance of the college crowd and their cohorts from the Negro community.

I noted that the Mecklenburg County Police were keeping watch over the situation as they came and went from time to time. At the very beginning of the picketing, when the officers first arrived, I got the impression that the pickets thought with satisfaction that they were there solely to protect them in their haughty conduct as privileged beings outside the regulations imposed on ordinary people. But, as their activities continued, I sensed that the pickets were not so sure that the officers had just their welfare in their concern. By this Saturday noon, much of their cocksureness had been drained out of them. They cast anxious glances at one another when they were confronted with so many men charging through their lines with the evident aim of knocking them aside if they interfered or got in the way.

I thought that Dr. Rhodes and Mr. Naramore had surely become sensitive to the fast growing mood of the community against the pickets when they came to me the evening before and asked me to close my business the next day. There had perhaps been great concern in their minds because of the exposure of college students to the anger of the white people of the region. If they had any concern for the predicament in which I had been placed by these same pickets and demonstrators, it was not expressed to me.

More Negroes joined the pickets during the afternoon.

Some of them were women, and it was reported that one
Negro woman was drunk and lying on the church lawn across
the street among some other Negroes and students. This
presence of Negroes among them seemed to disturb the white
pickets from the college. It had the effect of equating their
activities with Negro disorders and rioting that were causing
great concern all over the country. Community and regional
white people were taking a dim view of the picketing and
demonstrations promoted and led by this group of students
and faculty. The risk of hurtful violence was increasing.

At mid-afternoon tension was very thick as Negroes and
students gathered on the campus directly across the street.
Town and regional citizenry congregated on the sidewalk or
drove slowly by in cars and small trucks. There was a general
feeling of high tension in the air. But constant evidence of law
enforcement kept the situation just under the point of boiling
over.

At six o'clock, closing time on Saturdays, my barbers finished their work and caught up their hats and coats and fled
out the side door and away from the building. I was left alone
inside to count up the proceeds of the business for the day
and attend to necessary bookkeeping. Darkness was fast coming on and the pickets were still marching at the front door.
They would not leave the premises until the barber shop was
closed.

Presently a police officer called urgently for me to draw the
drapes and turn out the lights in the barber shop. I went to the
front of the building and saw that some sort of a melee was in
progress across the street. The officer called again to me to
draw the drapes and turn out the lights. Drawing the drapes
indicated that the shop was closed for business, and the pickets
quickly dispersed and most of them left the scene. I learned
later that a car filled with men had stopped and that some of

them had threatened the students with knives, and there was a feeling that they had other weapons. The police had gotten there in time and stopped the affair before it was much out of hand.

When I had finished with what I had to do inside and was ready to leave the building, it seemed that most of the crowd had gone. But I had hardly stepped to the sidewalk when I was approached from the shadows by a group of students and Negroes. They said they just wanted to talk to me, and, since I was pretty much surrounded by them before I was aware of their presence, there was nothing much else I could do but talk to them.

I was apprehensive about this, but they showed no disposition to attack me, although there was some vehemence in their manner of speech. I proceeded to talk to them, mostly to answer their questions as to why I was refusing to integrate the barber shop. The little knot of students and Negroes—there were some Negro women and girls present—grew progressively larger, and in a short while I found myself with my back to the brick wall at the corner of the building surrounded by a sizable crowd; some of the language was becoming shrill.

One student whom I knew had come forward and was standing almost directly in front of me. He appeared to be taking my part. As his was the only fairly conciliatory voice in the crowd, I felt a degree of comfort in his presence there. Then one of the town's businessmen and a friend of mine pressed through the crowd with deep concern showing on his face. He asked if I were all right. I answered that I thought I was. But apparently he thought otherwise because he left hastily, and very shortly the Mecklenburg County Police arrived in some force.

I must confess I was glad to see them. They came in a businesslike manner and ordered the crowd to disperse. Some

were slow to move, and the officers made their way into the
crowd and took hold of the student standing in front of me.
He was hustled to a waiting police car which sped away with
him. The others milled about some and moved away slowly.
Then I was free to go home. This had been a very long and
trying day, and I was very, very tired.

That night was one of terror all over most of America as
bands of Negroes burned and looted and killed in the aftermath of the slaying of Dr. Martin Luther King, Jr. We felt
unsafe and very distressed in our home in the Negro neighborhood. We took what precautions we could think of and kept
indoors. It was some comfort to know that I had a pistol at
hand. We were truly Negroes set apart that night.

The day had convinced me beyond any doubt that the
strongly differing and contending factions in the community
centered their emotional conflict on me. Every faction was
sincere, devotedly sincere and immovable in its conviction, and
I was in the middle of all these firmly fixed sincerities that
were tearing my business apart and rendering my property, my
life's work, worthless. I had not asked to be in such an unfavorable situation, and, if I were permitted a preference in the
matter, the whole thing would vanish from my view as a nightmare suffered in fitful sleep.

I not only had no desire to be involved in this strife and
contention, I had no choice in the matter. I had not so much as
been consulted about it. It had been conceived in secrecy from
me and thrust over and upon me, and wound about me and so
overwhelmed me that I had the feeling of being bound hand
and foot and thrown by fiends into deep and black and
swampy waters.

From my talk with the students and Negroes in front of the
barber shop that night, I was able to arrive at one conclusion:
that I was confronted in my problem with a coalition of

ignorant blacks and half-educated fools. If any of them had
the smallest understanding of the problem that confronted me,
it was not apparent in anything they had to say. The startling
thing was that in their thinking, if one can call it that, there was
such unanimity that the mouthing from one group could not be
distinguished from the other in its unreasoning arrogance.

On Sunday morning, I awakened with the thought that I
wanted to talk to Mr. Naramore, the industrial plant owner
who had come with college professor Dr. Dan Rhodes on
Friday to ask me to close my place of business on Saturday. I
felt that Mr. Naramore had joined in this proposal at Dr.
Rhode's suggestion or request, and that, as a businessman, he
had a better understanding of the problem that I had to deal
with than any of the college people had exhibited or cared
about.

In answer to my telephone call, Mr. Naramore very gra-
ciously invited me to come to his home that morning, saying
that he would forego church services and devote the time to
me. I had thought that through his influence with Dr. Rhodes I
might be able to penetrate the adamant stand of the college
people and at least to some extent mitigate the hardship that
was being imposed on me.

We spent the better part of an hour discussing the difficulties that were facing me. During this time I gave him the
background, enumerating the highs and lows of my struggle to
achieve a business career. He listened very respectfully to what
I had to say and exhibited insight into my background by
relating some incidents in his personal history. I made no
request that he intercede with anyone in my behalf. I only
hoped that by his understanding of my predicament and some
of the unusual circumstances surrounding my situation, he
might see fit for his influence to be felt in my interest.

Then I went home and tried to sleep, waiting for what the
next day would bring.

Monday morning's weather gave every promise of another beautiful, warm spring day. Ordinarily it would have been a joy to look forward to. I went to work that day with heavy memories of the week before, and the beginning of this week offered no expectation of anything better in the immediate future. The pickets assembled shortly after I opened the shop for business and began their by now familiar line of march along the sidewalk in front of the barber shop. But on this day, it was immediately apparent that the jauntiness of the earlier days of picketing was completely gone out of their step as they tramped to and fro. There was more of a dogged, somber look on their faces. They were there in some force, with spares standing by, but the enthusiasm of earlier days seemed lacking.

That morning on my way to the barber shop from the post office, which was a few paces distance along North Main Street, I encountered Dr. Workman. Near the corner as we were about to cross Depot Street, he pressed an ordinary letter-sized envelope into my hands. The envelope was bulging somewhat with coins, and Dr. Workman told me that the students were going to pay for my window that had been broken out a few nights before, indicating that more money would be forthcoming at a later time for this. I carried the envelope into the shop and thrust it into a desk drawer without counting its contents. I knew within reason that the amount it contained was a mere pittance compared to the cost of my broken window. I was disgusted with this handful of small change. I was not begging them for anything. I felt insulted.

I was to learn later in the day that the arrest of the student on Saturday night had gone through the Davidson College campus like a strong electric shock. This was a stunning and wholly unexpected development. Lewis Homer, the student arrested, was a football player and very popular on the campus.

The people at the college were in shocked and indignant that the police would lay hands on one of theirs, let alone throw him in jail and hold him under a $250 bond on a charge of disorderly conduct. I believe they had convinced themselves in their arrogance that they were, or should be, free agents and not bound by any restraints other than their own will. Events over the weekend had rudely awakened them to the strong disapproval of the people of the area for their activities.

This Monday, the 8th of April, 1968, was the fourth day after Dr. Martin Luther King had been killed in Memphis, Tennessee, and the day before he was to be buried in Atlanta. In these few days, the whole of America had witnessed unprecedented rioting and disorders by Negroes as they unleashed fury and hate in the aftermath of Dr. King's murder. Negroes, too unschooled and ignorant to understand the issues involved or the depth of consequences, seized on this event as a time to vent their long pent-up hatreds and frustrations by acts of senseless violence. Troops were called out in the nation's capital and other major cities across the country to quell the disorders. The seething ferment of the larger cities was taken up by Negroes in small towns, and there was a general uneasiness about the explosive possibilities inherent in the mass hatreds that had been aroused and unleashed in the Negro settlements.

Our little town was no exception to the rule in high emotional response. The one distinguishing factor here in Davidson was that I was the central symbol of resistance to Negro demands and progress by my refusal to cut their hair in Johnson's Barber Shop. It made no difference that there was another barber shop nearby with the same position as mine, the sentiment of this vast hatred and potential danger was focused sharply on me, as if I were the one who had brought into being and was maintaining the whole structure of racial

discrimination. Forgotten was the fact that I , too, was a Negro,
and had been for all of my life subjected to the same restraints
that were imposed on other Negroes. They could only project
their hatred onto me. I was keenly aware of the danger that
surrounded me personally, and of the possibility of the destruction of my property.

It follows then that I was intensely conscious of the growing number of Negroes who joined the pickets and milled
about outside the barber shop. They were hostile, and I noticed
strangers in their ranks. So far none of the pickets, nor any of
their followers, had entered the door. All of them kept to the
outside, and no disorders had been brought to the inside of the
barber shop. But about four o'clock that afternoon, a big-
bodied, strong-looking young Negro man whom I had seen
earlier in the line of pickets burst into the door and lighted
either a match or a cigarette lighter and held it above his head,
waving the flame slowly around in a gesture that indicated the
danger of fire to my place of business.

His sudden entry and actions inside the barber shop
brought instant attention to him from the inside and outside of
the building. Necks were craned on the outside to see through
the glass window, and a deathly quiet fell over the inside.

I was standing at the very back of the shop with my but-
tocks resting lightly on the top of a low-standing metal filing
cabinet when he entered. In the top drawer of the file was the
pistol my friend had given me for my protection. After this
insolent person made his threatening gesture with the flame, he
started walking slowly in my direction. Crouching as he walked,
he did not speak but fastened his eyes intently on my face as
he advanced nearer and nearer.

My position was about forty feet from the front of the
building. When he reached the point halfway between us, I slid
open the drawer where the pistol lay and let my hand take hold

of it. Neither of us spoke a word but we were looking steadily
into each other's eyes as he came forward. Every eye was on
the tense drama being enacted here, and everything was deathly
quiet, without and within. When he was a dozen feet away, my
grip tightened on the weapon in preparation for drawing it
quickly into use. He stopped where he was, stood a moment as
if in indecision, then turned and went out the door.

This confrontation brought all of us into a stern awakening
to what might happen here, and presently the crowd began to
disperse. By closing time there were mostly just the student
pickets and a few others about.

My barbers and I had a lengthy talk during which they told
me of their grave concern with events as they were developing
for them. One young man said he had been threatened by a
group of blacks because he worked in my shop. Others said
they were the increasing targets of denunciation among their
friends and other Negroes because of their employment in the
shop. I detected in them a strong desire to relate to the outside
Negroes. Gone was any recollection of the advantages and the
vastly improved conditions that had been brought into their
lives. There was expression of fears of possible attack on the
outside, or even during working hours in the barber shop.

In addition to this, I was certain that some of them had
come heavily under the influence of the college activists and
were committed to doing whatever they could to bring about
integration in the barber shop. This was not a too surprising
development in view of the prevailing attitude of most local
Negroes that whatever was said at the college had of necessity
to be obeyed. They were so much under this domination that
they were unable to understand that the white people of the
region were not under this coercive influence and would,
therefore, make their decision as to whether they patronized
Johnson's Barber Shop independently of the dictates of any

faction at Davidson College. This was the situation that was paramount in my consideration at the end of our talk. I was convinced that a new dimension of possible deep significance had been added to my troubles.

The next day, Tuesday, April 9th, was the day when Dr. Martin Luther King would be buried in Atlanta. If past events were an indication of what the future might hold, prospects of vast pillage, destruction and hate could be expected in its wake. I spent the night in uneasiness and dread.

Morning brought a surprise. At opening time for the barber shop, no pickets were on the scene, and not even the usual knot of student standbys. Nine o'clock went by, then ten o'clock, and still no demonstrators.

Then I heard that the picketing had been called off, but that the boycott was still in effect. The quiet of this Tuesday morning was almost unbelievable. Since the last Tuesday afternoon a week ago, I had been in a continual nightmare. Now as suddenly as it had begun, the tumult at my door was gone. It had vanished as it had begun without my having any prior indication. In neither instance was I informed or consulted.

At mid-afternoon, I walked out onto the sidewalk into the spring sunshine and caught myself looking up through the small green leaves on the trees that grew on the campus, to catch a fleeting glimpse of the cross that faced north and south and stood atop the spire of the massive church that sprawled just across the street. It was there, and it glistened white and pure in the sunlight.

Then I was flooded with a conviction that I had been lynched and my life destroyed by zealots, who, in trying to expiate their own guilt resulting from their long practiced racial abuses, had only added another shameful episode of abuse to it. They had made me a scapegoat for their own offenses against black mankind. I was at the same time the victim of their age-old wrongs and now the object of their wrath because they had done these wrongs. This to me was a contrary and a contradictory morality, to flay another person because the one delivering the lash was ashamed and laden with guilt for having previously and over a long period of time mistreated and abused the one under attack. They had punished me as a Negro over these many years; now they came in force for revenge because they had punished me.

They were saying in effect that I was the one responsible for discrimination against Negroes, not themselves. It seemed to me that they were a special kind of fiendish devils who were projecting their own guilt and shame over to me, and that they were laying the lash to me and beating me and destroying what I had so laboriously earned and brought into being in an effort to stamp out the guilt from their own minds. It was fixed in my mind that they had done this to me because I was a Negro, and that in so doing they were continuing the old practice of putting a nigger in his place.

No matter what the outcome of the issue, my business was a shambles. The fact of having raised the issue of admitting Negro patrons to the barber shop and dividing the people into opposing camps had accomplished its ruin in the past seven days.

And I, what must I do? I was a pawn in a wanton game, and I would eventually have to pay the price for all of this. I had brought into being this business of mine almost out of the blood of my body over many years of effort. The people at Davidson College had destroyed it with a ruthless hand of vengeance. They had surrounded me and my mother and sister with hate and danger to our lives. Now they would go their separate and prosperous ways, and leave the wreckage and cost to me to manage alone as best I could. This was the true measure of their boasted morality.

CHAPTER TWENTY-SIX

Study and Fear

I gathered from my barbers that they were now regarded as traitors to the Negro race for their continued employment in my barber shop. I was hopeful that this would recede, now that the picketing had been brought to an end. But it was at that time much too soon to tell.

Then I received the following letter from Dr. E. F. Patterson. The text of his letter is as follows:

Dear Mr. Johnson:

The ancient proverb, "Sticks and stones may break my bones, but words cannot harm me," is true only if the words are true and accurate.

I did not personally hear the statements that you made over a loudspeaker in defense of your position regarding desegregating your barber shop, but I was told that you said, among other things, that "Dr. Patterson said he would not help pay for my broken window." You know, as well as I, Mr. Johnson, that I did not say this to you. I would like to recount the short conversation that took place between us on the morning of April 5, 1968.

First, I would like to explain why I was in the picket line at your barber shop. I was there primarily because I believe strongly in the principle involved and because I wanted to show my appreciation to and support of the Davidson community blacks and the Davidson College students for their courage in bringing the issue to a head in our community. I was there on the particular morning of April 5, 1968, because I wanted to pay tribute, in a small way, to one of the finest and noblest men who ever lived and who had been murdered the night before —the late Dr. Martin Luther King.

Now as to what transpired. We were walking only in front of your shop when you came out of the side door and called to me, saying that you wanted to show me something. I went to where you were standing and you pointed to a hole in the side window of your shop and asked me what I thought about that. I said that I was sorry that it had happened. You began to tell me how hard you had worked to build up your business and how I and the students were destroying it. After a few minutes, I interrupted you and said that I appreciated your position and admired what you had done, but that in the light of the principle involved all of it was irrelevant. You then said, "You are nothing but an unprincipled scoundrel," turned away and went back into your shop.

I want to assure you that I hold no animosity or ill will toward you for anything you said to me or for your use of words that I did not say to promote your cause. I know that you were under considerable mental and emotional strain and stress and one says and does things under these conditions that he would never do or say in calmer moments.

With best wishes to you and a fervent hope that, in memory of Dr. Martin Luther King, you will risk economic loss -- which I think will not occur -- for the sake of justice and will integrate your barber shop, I am,

Yours faithfully,
E.F. Patterson,
Professor.

This was the second of two letters that I received from Dr. Patterson. I want here to examine some passages from this letter. Let us take, for instance: "First, I would like to explain why I was in the picket line at your barber shop. I was there primarily because I wanted to show my appreciation to and support of the Davidson community blacks and the Davidson College students for their courage in bringing the issue to a head in our community."

Here it seemed to me that Dr. Patterson, like all the others from the college who were supporting this attack on me and my business, was taking a steadfast stand that I, and I alone, was the discriminator against Negroes, that the policy in my business was dictated solely upon my own desires, as distinguished from the truth that I was being controlled in my approach to the matter by the prevailing attitudes of the community at large.

As to that part of a sentence which reads, "the Davidson College students for their courage in bringing the issue to a head in our community," I had only the utmost contempt. It most assuredly did not take a great deal of courage on their part to concoct a scheme of attack on me and my business in complete secrecy from me, and without once having done me the courtesy of consulting me before taking action against my business.

There were also conditions of long standing on the Davidson College campus that they had conveniently overlooked regarding the Negro employees there, and which were of far greater importance than service for them in my barber shop. These conditions were not of a superficial nature and must have been known to them, or could have been discovered more easily than arranging a concerted picketing action and boycott against my business.

They had only to turn their attention to the needs of the old
Negro janitors and the Negro women workers at the Davidson
College laundry, many of whom had worked for the college for
thirty or forty years at substandard wages. Now, too old and
sick to work, they were turned loose and were stumbling about
the streets in cast-off clothing and in need of medical and
every other help. I asked myself how it was that these zealots
to improve Negro circumstances in the community would find
a prosperous business owned by a Negro and take the time and
energy to lay plans in secret to attack and destroy it and yet
ignore the deprivation of their very own servants at Davidson
College.

To quote again from Dr. Patterson's letter: "You began to
tell me how hard you had worked to build up your business
and how I and the students were destroying it. After a few
minutes I interrupted you and said that I appreciated your
position and admired what you had done, but that in the light
of the principle involved all of it was irrelevant."

What a startling thing to say. All of the nearly half century I
had spent under the most difficult circumstances, building and
acquiring for myself a means of earning a livelihood, had
suddenly become "irrelevant" and was subject to being thrown
into the air for the winds to blow it away into nothing, so long
as it satisfied a whim of the people from Davidson College to
impose their will on me. As to "the principle involved," it
seemed to me that this statement profaned the word "principle." What principle had been applied to me and my rights in
the prosecution of this affair?

In the next paragraph of his letter, Dr. Patterson quite
magnanimously forgave me for what I had allegedly done to
him. For this great favor, I am properly grateful.

Then he went on to "hope, that in memory of Dr. Martin
Luther King, you will risk economic loss — which I think will

not occur — for the sake of justice and will integrate your barber shop."

In this last, there is evidenced at least a small recognition of the possibility of "economic loss" to me. But then he adds, "which I think will not occur." I shall let this last statement stand alone, as it better illustrated the attitude than I could possibly do.

The thought kept recurring to me that during the whole of this assault on me, this group of people from Davidson College had assumed an attitude that was reproachful in its manner towards me, as people of superior virtue dealing with an obstinate culprit.

As time passed, tensions eased in the street, since there was no picketing now. But the college boycott on my business was being tightened and made more secure. My barbers were restive under this, and I was certain they were coming in greater degree under the influence of the college people and Negro associates and taking sides against me. They were caught up in the frenzy of agitation of the time, and had so far lost their perspective as to think forced intermingling of the races would still any objections to it.

Their friends were talking boldly of the "new day" that had arrived. By force of their wills and wishful thinking, they were driving out of mind any lingering references to racial separation. This I knew to be an idle dream of unthoughtful people, but the reality of the belief in their minds was a factor that I now must reckon with as a threat from another front. The stark fact was that if they refused to work for me, as they were being urged by some to do, I would have to close the business, for it would be impossible to replace them. In the meantime, I could only wait and see.

The student newspaper, *The Davidsonian*, carried an editorial on April 12, 1968, that made a weak and sickly effort at sarcasm. It is as follows:

> The long arm of the fuzz reached into our placid little community last Saturday night, plucked a rather alarmed member of the student body off the street, and deposited him in durance vile, charged with disorderly conduct.
>
> Although he may have found calaboose accommodations more comfortable than his dormitory room, the highly questionable, nay, unbelievable, circumstance of the arrest constitutes a ridiculous reason for him to have to explain for the rest of his life why he was once arrested.
>
> The officers seemed to be hearkening back to Grade B movies' tales of the inequities of Southern Justice. They only lacked cattle prods and bloodhounds.
>
> Riot tension may be a cause but is not a reason for the arrest. Such incidents only increase the probability of riots.
>
> If blind justice, urged on by riot backlash, manages to convict the hapless student, we would have to urge the town of Davidson to secede from Mecklenburg County.

The above account of the arrest of the student on Saturday night before, while it tries to treat the incident with some levity, also incorporates in it what appears to be a shocked realization that students, like others, are subject to the law when it mentions "... the highly questionable, nay, unbelievable, circumstances of the arrest." It also shows concern for his being in a position "to have to explain for the rest of his life why he was once arrested." The writer is sensitive to any inconvenience or hardship caused to one of them, regardless of how small. Whatever their attitude towards me, they had discovered that the massive news media coverage of their activities at the barber shop, which they had been at some exertion to obtain, and with which they had expected to bombard me into submission, had instead served to arouse the community against them.

I was told that the combination of the sudden and unexpected assault on me by the pickets, the extensive news coverage and mass publicity, and the boycott of my business was expected to frighten me into submission by the second day of their concerted action. When it had failed to do so at the end of a week, and they had become the butt of community-wide indignation, they were themselves thrown into confusion and withdrew their visible forces of attack.

But they had set in motion other forces that were rising now to bedevil me. Negroes in the community were in increasing numbers taking up the cudgel. Even small children called insults to me. I felt strongly the necessity to search my car thoroughly in the mornings before entering, to raise the hood and inspect the engine compartment for fear of explosive devices that may have been attached to the ignition component.

I noticed, too, the recent formation of a group of Negroes each morning and afternoon at the corner near my home, which I had to pass going to and from work. They had not previously been accustomed to gather there, and I realized that their purpose was to intimidate me with hostile stares and sullen mutterings when I passed them. When this had gone on for a few days, and the mutterings had become more audible, and the insults more evidently aimed at me, I let my car roll three or four lengths past them one morning. Then I stopped it and gently eased it into reverse and the car started moving backward to them. Some of them on the outer fringes of the group began to move away. When I was back to where they were standing, I stopped the car and just sat there and looked from one to the other of them; then I asked if any of them had said anything meant for me. There were no answers, and some shuffling of feet.

That afternoon there were no people on the corner to project hostile stares and insults in my direction. Nor were they there any other time after that. But I knew the feeling was there against me, and especially virulent among the young ones. There were some of the older Negroes who understood my position well, and they were not inclined to hostility towards me about the barber shop. It was mainly the younger ones who were caught up in the frenzy of the times, and they were the dangerous ones, I felt.

Having failed to bludgeon me into submission by surprise attack and other means, the college people now turned to the town government as an instrumentality through which to gain their ends. Pressures were brought to bear, and on Monday night, April 15, a meeting of the Town Council was convened to hear and act upon proposals for a town public accommodations ordinance.

This meeting was attended almost entirely by Davidson College students and faculty members, with a few outside people who had come to assist them. I was the only Negro present, being the party against whom this agitation was directed. I sat silently while all the talk went on. My old friend, Howard Arbuckle, the town attorney, explained the law--that integration of barber shops was illegal in the state. The outcome was that the Council decided "to refer the question to a study group."

About seven o'clock the next evening, when I was home from work, I received a telephone call from Dr. Workman. The purpose of this call was to invite me to meet with him, and, as I understood it, two other members of the Davidson College faculty, with the object of discussing some plan they had in mind to extend to me financial aid or subsidy if I would integrate the barber shop.

I thought the time far gone when I should have been consulted about the management of my business. I was in no
mood to hear such a proposal, since all I could see in such a
scheme, whatever it might be, was their gaining control of my
business and the right to dictate its operational policies and,
above all, to use me as they saw fit in my own business. Whatever happened now, it was well settled in my mind that I would
not bargain away my business to them under any condition.

I told Dr. Workman that up to that time I had managed my
business myself and that I would continue to do so. I refused
to meet with them.

The Davidsonian, the student newspaper, in its weekly issue, on
Friday, April 19, 1968, under a black headline had this to say:

FACULTY CALLS FOR END TO TOWN'S RACIAL BARS

Barbers Refuse Financial Offer

The faculty passed a student-proposed resolution calling for the integration of "all public facilities in the town
of Davidson" yesterday by a large margin. The resolution
was the result of a Tuesday night meeting of the students
involved in the boycott committee. The students also decided not to resume picketing and voted down a motion to
hold a sit-in.

Earlier Tuesday night several members of the faculty
conferred with barber shop owners Hood Norton and Ralph
Johnson in an effort to solve the integration question by
offering Norton and Johnson financial compensation for
losses they might suffer due to integration of their shops.

However, both refused, though the possibility of economic losses had been used by both Norton and Johnson
as a reason not to integrate, said Dr. Dan Rhodes, one of
the faculty members.

Monday night the Town Council discussed a town public accommodations ordinance. They decided to refer the question to a study group and to follow Charlotte's efforts to pass a public accommodations ordinance.

Members of the boycott committee said they were generally pleased with the faculty's passage of the resolution. Senior Nat Heyward, whose name appeared on the resolution as co-chairman of the student group, said, "I was impressed by the fact that they acted so quickly. I was very much encouraged by their decision to commit themselves to our desire to integrate the barber shops."

Another senior, Roger Duttweiler, said, "I feel real happy about the way things came out. The faculty gave me a lot of confidence; this should cause a betterment of student-faculty relations."

The four-part resolution endorsed the students' desire to integrate Davidson public facilities, urged the Town Council to pass a Public Accomodations ordinance, supported the students' desire to establish an open barbershop if Norton and Johnson would not integrate theirs, and requested that the trustees join the faculty in the resolution.

From the above, it is immediately discernable that the high moral indignation of earlier articles was missing. Could it be that the morality of their own actions had been brought into question? It is noted here also that the students had decided not to resume picketing and had voted down a motion to hold a sit-in. Adverse public reaction to their picketing activity and to other circumstances surrounding the whole of their enterprise, I felt, was persuasive in the decision to conclude their personal exposure.

Of special interest to me was the mention of Hood Norton. It seemed a more than ordinarily odd circumstance of this whole episode that here was a barber shop that was being operated on exactly the same segregated basis as mine, and some of whose patrons from the college had marched in the picket line in front of my business. Yet all of the attack of the Davidson College people was directed against me, while the other shop remained unmolested. Now it appeared from the article's mention that Hood Norton had been "conferred with" and offered "financial compensation" for losses that might be suffered due to integration.

I have no idea what transpired, if anything, between Hood Norton and this group of Davidson College faculty, but for my own part, I never "conferred" with any of them. But I do have the fact firmly fixed in mind that the shop that I owned was the only barber shop picketed, and that I and my barber shop were the only ones subjected to widespread newspaper, radio and television publicity in reference to racial discrimination in the town. This was a fact broadly noted and commented upon in the surrounding area of the state.

The town's weekly newspaper carried this article on Thursday, April 18, 1968:

DAVIDSON CITIZENS STUDY HAIRCUT, OTHER PROBLEMS

Johnson's Barber Shop Remains Under Boycott

On the surface little has changed in the Davidson haircut situation. Johnson's Barber Shop on Main Street continues segregated. The students of Davidson College continue their boycott of the place of business. There were no pickets in front of the shop during the week. The tense pitch of the town last week appears to have eased and serious citizens are meeting and talking about concrete solutions.

Two formal meetings of citizen leaders were held during the past week, one a community meeting at the Davidson Presbyterian Church U.S. (Thursday night) and the other the town board meeting Monday night at the

town hall. Both meetings were well attended by both
white and Negro leaders. At both meetings the community relations problems were openly discussed -- ranging
from haircuts to unsatisfactory housing. But in all a tone
of reasonableness prevailed such that one town board
member said afterward that he felt that a new community interest and era of understanding may have had its
beginning.

The haircut matter was left in the hands of the town's
committee on community relations for further study.

One conclusion reached was that no rights of any individual had been violated in the events surrounding the
picketing and boycott of the barber shop. The barbers
are within their legal rights and the students are within
theirs. A board member summed up: "We are not altogether clear on what can and should be done. We are
searching for the right answers."

One sentence in the last paragraph--"One conclusion
reached was that no rights of any individual had been violated
in the events surrounding the picketing and boycott of the
barber shop"-- made a knot in my belly. I had my own ideas at
whose behest this conclusion was reached and adopted.

And the thought occurred to me that if nobody had a guilty
conscience, why was it <u>necessary</u> to conclude that no rights had
been violated? I had reached a conclusion also: if I had been a
white man, none of this would have happened to me. I cannot
imagine that the people at Davidson College would have
attacked a white barber, operating his shop for white patrons,
and demanded that he serve Negroes.

Some days later, word reached me that there was on display
in the Methodist Church a petition requesting signatures of
members who would continue to patronize my barber shop if
Negroes were admitted to it as patrons.

This was another example of persons taking action in

regard to the management of my business that had not been authorized by me. I had not been consulted in any way about such a petition and had no knowledge whatever that it was to be used. I was not personally acquainted with the pastor of that church, nor was he a customer in my barber shop. A considerable number of the members of the church who lived in the town community were patrons of my shop, but I felt certain none of these people would have been party to posting such a petition without first having my permission to do so.

Later, I learned that by far the greater part of that congregation disapproved of the petition and that it was removed. However, after I learned of its existence, I ran an advertisement in the local paper saying that I was not responsible for it. I never saw a copy of this petition and have no idea how many signatures it received, but I had very definite ideas that the Davidson College segment of the membership was responsible for its being there. It was noticeable, too, that no petition was posted proposing Negro membership for the church.

About this time, I returned to Dr. Workman's hands the envelope containing a little more than eight dollars in small change that he had given to me as part payment for the plate glass window broken out at the barber shop the night of Dr. Martin Luther King's killing. At the time this envelope and its contents were handed to me, Dr. Workman said that the students were going to pay for the broken window and that the balance of the money would be paid shortly.

I had heard no more from him or others in this regard, and I regarded this offering of small change as an insult in view of the great damage these people had caused me.

The boycott of the college people against my place of business was now more than three weeks old, and had effectively cut off practically all of my trade from there, except a very few students and faculty members who had not joined in the movement against me and who were not intimidated by the others.

I was now able to operate my business in relative calm. But it was the calm in the eye of a storm, for the turbulence that surrounded me had not been abated. Exterior evidences of the agitation were gone, such as the picketing and the crowds in front of the barber shop. The factions into which the people had been divided and solidified in their thinking were firmly fixed and whirling around me, each looking to me for the answer.

I thought it very unjust that I should have been placed in such a position by the college people, a position in which, no matter what decision I finally had to make, the cost to me would be heavy, if I could survive at all. For whatever decision I made, it stood out plainly that a considerable portion of my business would be lost. This was a painful realization, especially so because I had been placed in the situation of losing a substantial part of my business by the arbitrary actions of the people collected behind a college front who had not one thing to lose. And I had for so many years made such great sacrifices to gain the patronage my business enjoyed. I was an old man now, very tired and confused. And deeply and irreparably hurt.

Since shortly after the beginning of the picketing and strife at the barber shop, our mother, now eighty-four years old, had been in a condition of fear and agitation that required my sister and me to alternate staying up with her during the nighttime hours. To her, a crowd of hostile white men, carrying placards of denunciation against me, brought great distress to her mind and images of a lynch mob.

The Negro neighborhood in which we lived was alive with hostility towards us. If I had to be out after dark, I was very apprehensive of any car that moved in close behind me or drew alongside my car. This was the sort of tenseness and feeling of imminently impending and ever-present danger under which we lived at our house during this period.

Of great concern to me now was the attitude of my barbers. I knew they were under influence from the college people and heavy pressure from other Negroes who considered them traitors to their race for not serving Negroes in the barber shop. They were living in this reproachful atmosphere and it had shaped and conditioned them.

I finally came to realize that this factor was the one at present most dangerous to my position, and I assessed my situation as realistically as I could in the light of these developments. I took in consideration that loss of the college business would reduce the volume of my business if I did not desegregate, as it was doing under the boycott. If I admitted Negroes as patrons, I would lose a considerable portion of the community business, the backbone of the shop. But if I found myself without barbers, I would be out of business completely. These were my melancholy thoughts as I weighed my precarious situation in an effort to find a way out of the problem with the least possible damage resulting to the business. I could now only try to salvage whatever I could from the wreckage that had been heaped upon me.

I had been adamant in my determination not to yield to the demands to desegregate the business, because I felt that such a course of action would bring financial disaster to the barber shop as a result of lost patronage from the white people of the surrounding area. Now, as events had shaped themselves, I found myself forced to look in this direction as a means of being able to continue in business at all.

Both the Negroes and the people from the college were of a single mind in refusing to deal with or accept the reality that there were many people who would not patronize the barber shop if it were desegregated. They seemed to think that money derived from a large patronage was not needed for the carrying on of the business, and, if I thought in that direction, it was from nothing but greed on my part. To them all that mattered was idealism. (Yet the college professors were continually harping about the inadequacy of their own large salaries.)

But I had a payroll to meet, the expense of operation to bear, and the need to earn a living, not to mention the protection of the considerable investment I had in the business. None of these considerations were of any concern to the Negroes and the people from Davidson College.

All of these adverse circumstances were swallowing me up, and it was becoming increasingly clear to me what I had to do if I were to remain in business. It was now more than four weeks since the attack had been launched against me. During this time, circumstances and conditions had arranged and rearranged themselves around me in such a fast and emotional order that it was extremely difficult for me to think with any satisfactory degree of clarity on the whole of the confused situation.

One thing was certain. Vast changes had erupted in my life and my business and these changes had affected the value of my business property during that short space of time. I had to accept the painful fact that there was no way that I could recover from these recent events that had been forced upon me by people who claimed their intentions were to do good and to do justice to others.

CHAPTER TWENTY-SEVEN

It's Over

Amid the shock of the incredible violence and tragedy of the spring and summer of 1968, it was difficult for the most placid of uninvolved persons to keep his mind clear from the passions that permeated the whole of America. There were tumultuous riots and hate-filled burning and looting by roving bands of angry Negroes.

In the city of Washington, D. C., machine guns were mounted on the steps of the Capitol and soldiers were used to seal off the ghetto while dense smoke from burning buildings settled over the White House itself. Troops were called out to quell the strife and pillage in large cities all over the country. Students were running amuck in colleges and universities and causing untold damages to the consternation of their elders and school administrators. There were murders of prominent persons by dissidents, and disrespect for authority -- any authority-- was rampant and blatant. There were bitterness and anger and hatred at every hand.

The super-charged emotions of the times spread out all

over. The Poor People's March on Washington brought into
focus again the role of the Negro in the tumult and strife. It
was within the framework of this country-wide near mass
hysteria that I found myself under great pressure to make a
decision concerning the desegregation of my barber shop. The
issue had been raised at a time when all the forces seemed to
array themselves against rational thinking or actions.

My barbers were caught up in the backwash of the violent
sentiments for change in racial relations, and were pressuring
me to open the shop to Negro patrons. There was little else I
could do now in the way of resisting desegregation, since
without the help of my barbers I could not continue in business. So I had come finally to the place where I had to do what
I had said I would not do.

It was five weeks since the picketing and boycott had
started. During all of this time I had searched my mind over
and over for a means of extricating myself from the situation
which had been thrust upon me without doing irreparable
harm to my business. I was finally forced to the solution that
seemed most likely to do the lesser harm.

No formal announcement was made. I simply told my
barbers that they could begin serving Negro patrons and
instructed one of them to take into his chair a young Negro
employee of the shop and cut his hair. As far as I have been
able to ascertain, my barber shop, at that moment, became the
first one in America serving all white patrons to admit Negroes
as patrons on an equal basis with white people.

I had in no manner communicated with the people of
Davidson College who had brought all this trouble on me. At
the outset of their attack, they had arrogantly demanded that I
sign a written "commitment" to serve Negroes. None of this
was done. Now, I could only wait and see what would happen

under this new set of circumstances which had been brought to bear on me. It was a lonely vigil, and I felt that I knew what the final answer would be. I was cast adrift on a strange sea.

That week's issue of the student newspaper carried the following article:

STUDENT LEADERS CALL OFF BOYCOTT
Johnson Serves Negro Customers

Student leaders of the boycott group called off the boycott of Johnson's Barber Shop this week; the owner, Ralph Johnson, began serving Negro customers May 7.

Johnson declined comment on the action. However, one of his barbers said, "I think it was the right thing to do."

Another barber agreed. "It's something that had to be done, and I'm glad he did it. It takes a lot of pressure off us, the employees, and I think we will profit by it," he said.

The integration of the barber shop followed several weeks of boycotting and a week of picketing by students, although most student activity had already died down when the barber shop was integrated.

The Davidson faculty had also endorsed a student-sponsored resolution calling for integration of the barber shop, a public accommodations ordinance for Davidson, a request for trustee endorsement of the resolution and support for possible establishment of an open barber shop should Johnson refuse to integrate his shop.

Several members of the faculty also had formed an informal committee, headed by Dr. Dan Rhodes of the Bible Department, to seek a compromise with Johnson, including an offer of financial support. Johnson turned down the professors' offers earlier.

Davidson Mayor F. L. Jackson had set up a Mayor's Committee to study a plan for a Davidson public accommodations ordinance. No definite action has been taken by the Town Council. "I can understand how Mr. Johnson feels after 40 Years of running a segregated business," said one of his barbers, "but it was time for something to be done."

Then the following letter came from Professor Raymond Martin, dated May 16, 1968.

Dear Mr. Johnson,

> I would like to commend you on your recent decision to open your barber shop to customers on a non-racial basis. Many of us in the community realize that the difficult situation that was thrust upon you was not of your making, and we admire the open-mindedness and considerable courage that you have shown by changing your policy. My family and I will be proud to patronize your shop, and we shall do everything in our power to bring about complete community acceptance of your new policy.
>
> > Sincerely,
> > Raymond Martin

The letter quoted above was the second one that I received from Professor Raymond Martin. This one was quite different in tone from the first. It was also the only communication that I ever had from anyone at Davidson College that even remotely recognized the fact that I had not created the condition of segregation for which they attacked me. It was also the only expression of any understanding that "the difficult situation that was thrust upon you was not of your own making." It demonstrated, too, that the writer was aware that community acceptance of this policy was necessary to my business.

No one else from the college ever expressed to me any understanding of the existing customs and practices relative to racial separation in barber shops. It was as if they had never heard of it, and that I was apparently totally responsible for its existence in my barber shop. A more than passing strange circumstance for people in the South.

It seemed to me now such a long time since a few weeks ago when I had thought that my situation was improving with the coming of spring. So many things had happened since then to change my life and perspective that the time before seemed remote and unreal, and so did the present.

I was certain that my forced decision to admit Negroes as patrons had not solved my problem. It had only rearranged the elements involved and was an expedient on my part to try to keep intact whatever part of my business I could save from complete and immediate destruction. I hoped that some circumstance in the unknown future would intervene in such a way as to allow me to readjust to the condition most favorable to carrying on the business. I could see no possibility of such a condition arising in the immediate future. But, on the other hand, I had not foreseen the coming of the circumstance which had forced me into my present predicament.

Desegregation of the barber shop had the immediate effect of discontinuing the boycott against me by the people from Davidson College. It also brought in some Negro patrons, but the greater part of my patronage which lay in the town and surrounding area was now my great concern. Some of these people had told me in conversation about the matter that they would continue their patronage in the shop whatever decision I made regarding admitting Negroes.

One thing that stood out boldly in all of this strife was the attitude of the overwhelming majority of the white people of the town and the area from which my patronage was drawn.

They were, nearly all of them, opposed to the integration of the barber shop, but they conceded to me the ownership of the business and the right to make decisions in its management. They were resentful of the pressure that had been brought to bear on me as a result of the attack against me. I knew that many of these people would discontinue their patronage in the barber shop when Negroes were admitted. But they never tried to influence my decision by threats of boycott or other retaliation. Always they respected my right of ownership and management.

This was in direct contrast to the behavior of the college group that did not respect my ownership of the business to the extent of asking my opinion concerning a radical change of policy in the management of my business. When every other device had failed them, they came to me with a scheme which they had the audacity to call "financial aid or assistance." This was not a plan to pay for the great damage they had done to my business nor in any way to make restitution to me. Instead, it was a device to offer a very limited "subsidy," over a short time, in exchange for dictating the business policy in my barber shop.

As of now, it was only the passage of time that would determine what would happen to the barber shop. The students and others from the college began coming in again for haircuts. But a deep rift had come between me and them during the time of their attack and boycott against me. Many of them seemed to consider me an enemy who had somehow gotten in control of a business that they should run.

I, in my turn, had a feeling of outrage at their unwarranted presumptions and the arrogance of their attack on me. It was burning in my whole being that these white people had lynched me and had wantonly destroyed my business.

By early June, when college let out for the summer, it was

apparent that I was caught increasingly in the trend for long hair among young men and the fact that the customers who still had their hair cut were the ones who objected to Negroes in the barber shop and were taking their patronage elsewhere. The Negroes who came did not nearly make up for this loss of patronage, and the mere fact of their presence in the shop drove away more and more of the area business.

Another most disturbing factor that introduced itself with the admission of Negroes was that of discipline. This had never been of any concern whatsoever. The patronage of the shop had always been of that caliber of persons who behaved as ladies and gentlemen. (The shop had a large patronage of ladies who brought their children in for haircuts.) But with the attempt to integrate, some uncouth Negroes came to my shop. That element of the white population had never patronized my business.

For the first time I had to deal with people in different stages of intoxication. Individuals in this condition seemed to feel uncomfortable in this environment, which sometimes led to aggressive behavior. Many just did not understand traditional behavior in such surroundings. I refused service to people who were intoxicated, who spoke loudly, or who came in dirty clothing. This caused resentment toward me because they could see nothing wrong with their behavior, since it was their usual way of life.

Often, the mere fact of these persons having entered the place had its effect on the other patrons. Quite naturally my having to tell them to leave created tense situations that were offensive to all. Now that my place of business was open to everyone, these Negroes came to demonstrate their equality with other people, seeking an acceptance that had not been accorded them in other areas of their lives. In their search after equality and acceptance, they had not made themselves

the equal of others in their deportment. So they were in no
manner acceptable.

Their presence lowered the standards of my place of business and made it less appealing for the patrons who were
accustomed to coming to my barber shop. Further, many of
these undesirables had it fixed in their minds that desegregation had been forced on me, that I had lost all authority over
my business, and that they could flaunt their freedom in my
face and behave as they pleased.

To me, both the college people who had started all of this
and the Negroes who came to take advantage of it were like
plundering marauders who cheerfully and wantonly destroyed
my life's creation.

Many of my white customers felt the mere presence of a
black customer in the shop was enough to cause them to go
elsewhere for barber work. There were some who would
accept Negro patrons in the shop as a way of the changing
times as long as the deportment was not offensive and did not
create tense situations. But even to these last, desegregation in
the barber chair was not their choosing.

Our family's personal life remained stressed.

The highly nervous and fearful state that began for our
mother shortly after the start of the picketing kept my sister
and me on watch over her during many hours of the night.
This meant that all of us were rest-broken at a time when we
needed whatever respite we could get from the conditions that
surrounded us. The picketing and crowds represented extreme
danger to her aged mind, and had fixed itself indelibly in her
consciousness to the extent that she could react to it only with
extreme anxiety for the safety of her children.

When the visual aspect of the attack on me, the picketing,
was removed, she was so conditioned to the fear of violence

that fear stayed in her mind. My sister and I could console her only by being constantly in her presence.

When two months had passed since the inception of her symptoms of distress, and she had not improved, she was hospitalized in Charlotte for evaluation. We expected her separation from us to be a problem; she was past eighty-four years of age at the time, so we reassured her as best we could with promises of frequent visits. She was agreeable to this, and with our daily and nightly visits we were able to keep her fairly contented for the first week.

Then her anxieties became increasingly acute to the point that even with all of our talking to her and our reassurance, it was difficult to persuade her to stay for treatment. The hospital was more than twenty miles from our home, and my sister and I made two trips each day to be with her during visiting hours in an effort to keep her eased.

One morning about 2:00 a.m. the hospital nurses' station called our home to say that she had come into the hall and refused to go back to bed, insisting on going home. We had just left her at 9:00 o'clock that night. At that time she was all right. We had several times walked her up and down the hall before we left. She was at the nurses' station when the call to us was made, and the nurse let us talk to her on the phone.

It was apparent that she was agitated and that she didn't know where she was, nor why she was there, that she was lost in her surroundings. The sound of my voice seemed after a little to connect her with things she understood. I talked to her until I felt certain that she was oriented again, telling her where she was and why. Then my sister and I assured her that we would come in to see her first thing in the morning. She seemed reassured and said she would go back to bed.

The next morning, my sister, who had gone in early to the hospital to see about her, called to say that she thought I should come to the hospital at once, as she had found our mother bound to the bed and unconscious.

Shortly afterwards, I was there, and the sight of that frail old woman lying in a straight-jacket, with her hands tied to the bed rail and still as death in unconsciousness, was almost more than I could bear.

Here was an old lady past eighty years of age who had known every deprivation of a Negro, who had been widowed early in life, who had managed by great sacrifice and hardship to rear her two children, whose body was now diseased and infirm, and who had now been frightened by zealots into such a state of mind that she lay bound here, the picture of death.

When the first emotion of leaden sorrow ebbed from me, I was overcome by a consuming hatred for the ones who had brought this great fear and apprehension into her few remaining years, years in which we hoped to bring some ease and happiness to her. All of the things these fiends had done to me could not equal this in infamy. I was extremely conscious of the all-possessing hate, hate stripped of every other consideration, hate that welled up in my chest and almost stopped my breathing, the kind of hate I had never in my life experienced before.

I knew at that instant that a terrible thing had happened to me. Hate had been stamped hard into every fiber of my being as fear had been driven and fixed into our mother's mind. It was a hate for everyone who had in any manner been a party to the situation that brought this about, whether by act or sentiment. It is difficult to say what act I might have been capable of performing at that moment.

It was well past 1:00 o'clock that day when my mother was sufficiently roused to be put in the car to bring her home again, where her tired and fear-ridden old mind could keep watch over the safety of her children. I was nearing sixty-four years of age and my sister was a few years younger.

The strain of living through the past ten weeks had drained out my energies and dragged my spirits into the lowest level. As summer progressed, I was increasingly beset with problems of discipline regarding some of the Negroes who came into the shop. I had by now begun systematically to deny service to the ones who failed to meet some standards I had devised and fairly rigidly imposed as a condition to their being received as patrons in the shop. Some of them were ordered not to come there again because there was that about their demeanor that disturbed the order and tranquility that I considered necessary to maintain the business. Even so, I was continually harassed by behavior that was unacceptable.

As quietly as possible I struggled with this problem. Too often I had to signal to someone with my hand to come to me, or I went to them, to tell them they would have to leave. Some wanted to protest this, and I had to become insistent. The shop was fraught with apprehension. More and more customers who were accustomed to expecting a relaxing experience in my place of business dropped away as the summer progressed into autumn.

With autumn came the harsh realization that the hoped-for miracle to extricate me from this nightmare of frustration, defeat and ruin, was indeed an empty illusion that I had conjured up out of my despair. Nothing was going to happen to save me.

I had been roughly thrown into the middle of contending forces, and my business put up as a pawn to be destroyed. The people at Davidson College who had catapulted me into this situation now stood safely away. I was certain they would not have dealt with a white man in this manner.

Shortly after the opening of college for the fall term, Hood Norton started accepting Negro patrons in his barber shop. I had no idea what pressures had been brought to bear on him to bring about this decision on his part, but there was a certainty in my mind that some grave influence had exerted itself. I wondered if the same college people had finally acted on what was very evident to everyone else.

Whatever negotiations were carried on to effectuate Hood Norton's change of racial policy in his barber shop were not made known to me, as nothing else pertaining to this was made known to me, nor have I seen any public announcement of it. I was told many times that he was jubilant at the trouble at my door when I was under attack and that he had said he would not integrate his shop "until hell froze over."

There was no communication between Norton and me whatever, since he had for years maintained a bitter enmity towards me that extended so far as not even allowing his barbers to speak or have any association with those of my shop.

The fact of my having admitted Negroes to my barber shop was of tremendous advantage to him, since those white patrons who could not accept this policy could go to his shop and receive their accustomed segregated barber services. This great advantage would not have been lightly abandoned because he had long since sought ways to combat the popularity of my shop and increase the acceptance of his own.

To this day I cannot understand it. Why did the college zealots who were so bent on doing justice to everyone, and who were brilliant in everything else, fail to understand that forcing integration on me, and leaving my competitor to conduct his business with white patrons only, was in itself a grave injustice to me? Surely in their wisdom they could see it placed me in a position where I could lose a large portion of my white patronage to Norton's shop. Oddly, too, some of those persons who were promoting integration for my place of business, even to the extent of parading in the picket line, were customers of the shop they did not attack.

Hood Norton's reasons for his about-face decision to admit Negroes as patrons to his barber shop soon became truly academic. A scant ninety days afterwards, he was dead of a massive stroke that seized him one day and killed him the next. This sudden happening brought to my mind the question whether his recent change in racial policy, and subsequent events relating to this, had been a factor in inducing the cause of his death. I knew him for a strong-willed man, and I had reason to believe that the stress and strain of this sudden change of business policy and its attendant problems could have been difficult indeed for him to endure.

His death confronted us in our little family with a family decision. Would we, or any of us, attend his funeral and burial? He was my mother's brother, but for the most of nearly sixty years there had been enmity between us, since shortly after my father's death when he had taken control of my mother's business. His hostility towards us had continued from that time, with one short exception, until the time of his death.

We felt no loss at his dying, and all of us, my mother, my sister, and I, were mutually agreed that we had no desire to attend last rites for him. We thought he would not have wanted us there. And so a long chapter of bitterness came finally to an end on the January day when he was buried in a country church graveyard thirty miles from his home and life's work.

Later during the spring, when the trustees of Davidson College met on the campus, a few of these men came individually to see me at the barber shop. I had known them thirty to forty years, since their college years at Davidson when they were my customers. Now they came to speak and to "renew old acquaintances."

They stayed around and chatted about many things, but none of them ever initiated a conversation concerning this.

And yet I felt certain they were there because this episode was on their minds. As far as any conversation with me about it was concerned, they treated the whole matter as if it had not happened. Once when I made a pointed reference to it, the only response I received was, "I believe you got caught in the middle on that one." Then silence. The trustees of this rich institution apparently chose to regard my personal loss as a trivial thing and beneath their notice.

My patronage from Davidson College had fallen off sharply during the year since they had attacked me. Many of them in passing cast furtive glances into the barber shop, as if they were guiltily watching its demise. My once proud business was now torn apart by the factions into which it had been divided when Negroes were admitted as patrons. It was no longer attractive in the wide area from which it had formerly drawn a heavy trade. Instead, my barbers were leaving for want of sufficient business.

I knew I was attending the death struggle of a once thriving enterprise. It was sinking into oblivion. The heavy momentum it had gained over nearly half a century of widespread favorable acceptance was falling away, as a wheel slows down and finally comes to a dead stop when the power that moves it is taken away.

As time passed, my difficulties increased. The problem of discipline that had been injected into my business with the admission of Negroes as patrons was ever present, to the extent that I felt I was needed in the barber shop at all times in order to keep at a minimum the possibility of untoward incidents. I had succeeded, partially, in eliminating the local troublemakers who were likely to cause friction. But even as this was being accomplished, others from outlying areas who were strangers to me began coming in. I was afraid of these people, and I was extremely conscious of the danger to me when it became necessary to ask them to leave the shop.

It took three years to unwind and nullify what it had taken me, to this time, a little more than half the century to accomplish. The tremendous appeal and momentum of my business had finally diminished to the extent where I had only one barber left with me. The others had fled the sinking ship that had so recently sailed on a prosperous course. The salable value of my business as a going, prosperous enterprise, once worth a fancy price on the open market, had dwindled away to nothing. It was now an undesirable property, a thing without value. And for me to stay in it was a continuing threat to my safety.

I held on fast as if my holding on and grasping it to me would drive away the monstrous thing that had torn it apart. I was sick in my heart at the senselessness of it all.

I returned from lunch one day to find two strange Negro men confronting each other in anger, one with a knife and threatening to cut the other one. I had walked in unexpectedly on this frightful and disruptive scene. When I asked them to leave, both became surly and hostile to me, and at first refused to leave. When they were finally on the outside and moving away from the building, one turned and made an effort to return but was restrained by others who had joined them. He had meant to come back and settle with me for forcing them to leave.

This raw exhibit made me realize the extreme danger to which I was being exposed. I suddenly knew I had come to the end of the way. My business could not survive incidents such as this, and I had no desire to run a place of business where ugly episodes of behavior occurred. Mine had always been a place where it was safe and pleasant for ladies and children to come. If I could not keep it that way, then I had no further use for it.

The incident related above occurred on Saturday. All of the next day, my mind was in turmoil. I decided, finally, that I must exclude Negroes from patronage in the shop. This was the only way I could begin to find a solution to the problems that were pressing heavily on me.

During that Sunday afternoon, I called on four men for advice and help in the solution of my problem, which had now become unbearable. The first three offered no help at all. The fourth was a long time Davidson businessman. He had some months back been elected mayor of our little town of Davidson. He listened sympathetically to my plan. Mayor Tom Sadler, after some reflection, said softly and kindly that he would do whatever he could to give me protection. I knew from this that he expected trouble.

I went next to talk with my last remaining barber. He knew the problems that beset the business and we talked at length of this. Then he said he was afraid to go on working at the barber shop, if I reversed the present policy and again excluded Negroes from service there. He said he was afraid his young son might be attacked by "some of them" if he worked under that condition.

I had discussed this situation with my mother and sister prior to my calling on the men mentioned above. When I talked with them again about this on Sunday night, my sister suggested that I close the business. This was an idea that had come into my mind many times during and since the attack on me by the college people. But I had refused to deal with it as a distinct possibility. I had preferred to hope that in time the nightmare that engulfed me would go away, and I could again operate my business without strife. Now I was ready to entertain the idea, because I knew no other way out of these hard-pressed circumstances. When I faced up to the fact that my condition could not improve, it was how I imagine a dying man feels when he knows there is no longer hope for him.

All the next day at work I struggled with myself to decide what to do. Would I go on, still trying and clinging to hope, or would I give up and abandon the business and all it had cost and meant to me?

As the 5:30 closing time came nearer, I thought I knew what I would do. Then a strange feeling of elation came over me as I waited for the final few minutes to pass. But I wasn't sure I could utter the words when the moment came. I said nothing of my decision until business was ended for the day and the door closed. Then I told my lone helper that I had decided to close the shop. The spoken words were shocking to both of us, and they were hard to bring from my constricted throat. But they were said and stark emptiness confronted us.

In the next hour we brought to an end our sixteen-year association, an association that had never been marred by an unpleasant word. And when he was gone, I was left alone with my sadness.

It was over. Alone now, in my dead and empty place of business, I was filled to overflowing with tears that washed my face and blinded my eyes. Then the convulsive sobbing came, and I screamed to let out of my body the bitterness and hurt that held me shaking in its grasp. After a long while, when the crying was through and I could see again, I wrote on an index card the following notice and taped it to the glass in the door:

JOHNSON'S BARBER SHOP
CLOSED

Opened March 24, 1921
Closed November 15, 1971

Then I locked the door behind me and went home to stay.

THE END

Today Ralph Johnson is one of Davidson's respected elders. He is one of the last who have lived across a twentieth century of gut-wrenching struggles to prove what many before dared dream but could not realize: "that all men are created not just free...but equal."

Acknowledging bitterness at the injustice of his unwarranted sacrifices, he still enjoys innocent human foibles, especially his own. You'll likely run into him at the town post office eagerly sharing the joys and sorrows of life in our town. He still goes there daily to chat with neighbors...

...neighbors who stand with, against and aside from him.

...neighbors with whose great-grandparents Johnson eked out a life from impossible hardships harkening back to slavery.

...neighbors--grandparents--with whom he bore the brunt of the Great Depression.

...neighbors now parents and their offspring who are in the midst of their own pickets questioning censored privacy, gender marriages, rights to life, neighborhood schools.

...neighbors for whom he hopes the discordant notes and simple harmonies of these chapters will blend into their lives , bringing a deeper appreciation and understanding of the resounding arias of mankind in quest of freedom and justice.

--Taylor Blackwell

WITHDRAWN